MODERN
HISTORY
IN PICTURES

CONTRIBUTORS

R.G. Grant is a writer specializing in military history. He has published more than 20 titles, including DK books *Battle*, *Soldier*, *Flight*, and *History*.

Sally Regan has contributed to several DK titles, including *History* and *World War II*. She is also an award-winning television documentary maker.

Susan Kennedy's writing includes contributions to a number of highly popular history and science titles, including *Take Me Back* (DK).

Richard Overy is a celebrated historian and Professor of History at the University of Exeter in the UK. He specializes in 20th century history.

THE SMITHSONIAN INSTITUTION

David K. Allison is Associate Director of Curatorial Affairs at the National Museum of American History. He served as the Chair of the Division of Information Technology and Communications from 1995 through 2009. His research specialties are military history and information technology.

Established in 1846, the Smithsonian Institution—the world's largest museum and research complex—includes 19 museums and galleries and the National Zoological Park. The total number of objects, works of art, and specimens in the Smithsonian's collection is estimated at 137 million. The Smithsonian is a renowned research center, dedicated to public education, national service, and scholarship in the arts, sciences, and history.

Introduction

The history of the past century is a history of extraordinary contrasts, of incredible achievements and tragic disasters.

The past century was the most violent in history, but it also saw the most rapid progress in medicine, science, welfare, and economic security. It was the century of women's emancipation, but one in which many women lived in poverty or were forced to follow standards of dress and behavior dictated by men. In the greatest paradox of all, nuclear weapons were a triumph of man over nature, but possess the power to wipe out human civilization.

It was also a century of rich discovery. In 1900 the most technologically advanced communities in Europe and North America were using telephones, driving the first cars, and waiting for powered flight. In parts of South America, Africa, and Polynesia, however, isolated tribes still used stone tools.

The 20th century was the most violent in history, but it also saw rapid progress.

Today, cell phones, computers, and mass air travel are widespread, while the tribes that worked in stone live on the poorer fringes of the new world of consumption.

Progress brought new ideologies and new conflict. The German socialist Karl Marx observed that modern industrial capitalism contained a remarkable imperative to spread itself all over the world. Soviet and Chinese leaders attempted to prove Marx wrong and establish global communism. At its peak in the 1960s and 1970s, communism represented perhaps half the world's population. It was seen as so dangerous that, in 1941, Hitler mounted the bloodiest military campaign of all time to destroy the Soviet Union, while after 1945 the USA and its allies fought to prevent its spread. In the end, Marx was proven right. The Soviet bloc collapsed due to economic as well as military and political pressure, while China adopted its own form of aggressive capitalism.

Consumer capitalism perhaps proved so irresistible because it was often linked to liberal politics. Civil rights and modern citizenship went hand-in-hand with rising living standards. Freedom to choose a government is also freedom to choose a job, what to buy, how to be educated. Countries in which these choices were not available saw cycles of dictatorship and repression, profiting the few at the expense of an impoverished majority.

The last decades of the century saw a series of campaigns to overturn such oppressive regimes, most recently in the Middle East. Attempts by outside forces to intervene often caused more harm than good, and it was popular resistance that proved most successful. Among the many heroes of this process, Nelson Mandela stands out as a remarkable example in recognizing that, whatever crimes the apartheid regime may have committed, vengeance and hatred would not build a better South Africa.

The last decades saw a series of campaigns to overturn oppressive regimes, most recently in the Middle East.

There has been no shortage of hatred in the history of the past century. This book contains a great many images of violence, discrimination, and coercion that seem to define the age. But before we write off the last hundred years as a disaster, it is important to recall the long periods of peace, the communities that have seen self-government, security, and economic success, the advances in medicine and agriculture that have saved so many lives, and the growth of mass culture, which has enlivened and enriched our world. The end of the 20th century promised international cooperation to extend political freedom, broaden economic opportunity, and preserve the global environment. If these lessons are learned, the images of the 21st century may tell a brighter story.

Richard Overy,
Professor of History, University of Exeter, UK

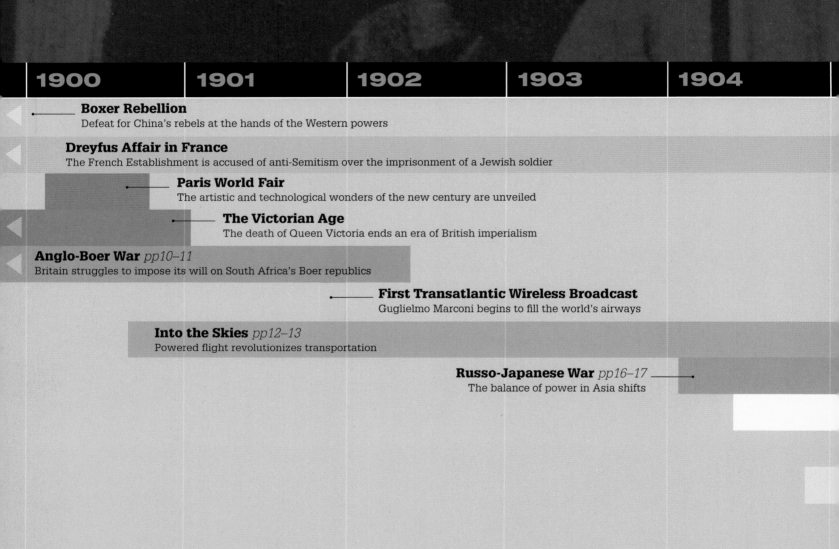

| 1900 | 1901 | 1902 | 1903 | 1904 |

Boxer Rebellion
Defeat for China's rebels at the hands of the Western powers

Dreyfus Affair in France
The French Establishment is accused of anti-Semitism over the imprisonment of a Jewish soldier

Paris World Fair
The artistic and technological wonders of the new century are unveiled

The Victorian Age
The death of Queen Victoria ends an era of British imperialism

Anglo-Boer War *pp10–11*
Britain struggles to impose its will on South Africa's Boer republics

First Transatlantic Wireless Broadcast
Guglielmo Marconi begins to fill the world's airways

Into the Skies *pp12–13*
Powered flight revolutionizes transportation

Russo-Japanese War *pp16–17*
The balance of power in Asia shifts

1900-09

Herero and Namaqua Genocide
Indigenous tribes are exterminated in Germany's African empire

Einstein's Special Theory of Relativity
The movements of the universe are explained

First Russian Revolution *pp18–19*
An empire sways but does not fall

San Francisco Earthquake *pp22–23*
California's golden city is reduced to rubble and ashes

The Road to World War I *pp38–39*
Rivalry among Europe's Great Powers fuels an arms race

Building the Panama Canal *pp20–21*
A vast engineering project links two oceans

Imperial China Falls *pp32–33*
Internal rebellion and foreign interference cripple an empire

Rise of Modern Turkey *pp74–75*
Modernizers strive to reform the Ottoman Empire

Tunguska Event in Siberia
An asteroid or comet brings devastation to Russia's east

Ford Develops Assembly Line Production
New industrial methods are developed in Detroit

Anglo-Boer War
1895–1902

The discovery of gold in southern Africa in the 1870s intensified British colonial ambitions. This lead to tensions with the Boers—farmers of Dutch descent living in Transvaal and the Orange Free State. The result was a bitter colonial war that lasted for three years.

SOUTHERN AFRICA
The Boers migrated north from Cape Colony in the mid-19th century to escape British rule and discover new land. There they founded the independent republics of Transvaal and the Orange Free State. The British territories of Cape Colony and Natal existed in uneasy proximity to the Boer states, and had already gone to war once in 1880–1881.

10/11/1899

OUTBREAK OF WAR On October 11, 1899, Kruger declared war and Boer soldiers, who fought in their everyday farm clothes and slouch hats, crossed into British Natal and Cape Colony. They immediately laid siege to two garrison towns, Ladysmith and Mafeking, and to the diamond town of Kimberley.

> We are **not interested** in the possibilities of **defeat**; they **do not** exist.
>
> QUEEN VICTORIA, 1899

BOER WAR REVOLVER Introduced in 1899, the Webley MK IV was widely used by British officers.

12/15/1899

BLACK WEEK
The railroad bridge over the Tugela River was destroyed by the Boers during the Battle of Colenso in Natal. This was the last in a series of major British defeats that took place in Black Week (December 10–15, 1899), because outdated British military tactics were exploited by their Boer opponents.

05/17/1900

LONDON CELEBRATES
News of the relief of Mafeking, after a siege lasting 217 days, was greeted with wild celebration in England. Robert Baden-Powell, who had led the British defenses, was lauded by the British public. He took advantage of his fame, going on to found the Scouting movement in 1907.

12/18/1900

MOBILE WARFARE
With their conventional army defeated, the Boers changed tactics. They began conducting guerrilla raids, retreating before their opponents could respond. The British used armored trains to transport supplies, and destroyed vast swathes of crops and farms in a bid to starve out the guerrillas.

12/29/1895

JAMESON RAID A British colonial administrator, Leander Starr Jameson, led an armed raid across the border from Rhodesia (modern Zimbabwe) into Transvaal. His ill-conceived plan was to start an uprising among the *uitlanders* (foreigners) working on the Johannesburg gold fields. He would then "restore" calm and take control. The raid was hopelessly botched. After an exchange of fire, Jameson's force of 600 men was captured by the Boers.

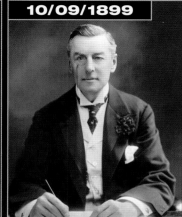

10/09/1899

BRITISH ULTIMATUM In September 1899, the British Colonial Secretary, Joseph Chamberlain, sent an ultimatum to Transvaal's President Kruger, demanding full rights for British residents in Transvaal. Since the Jameson raid, Kruger had built and equipped an army. He issued a counter ultimatum giving the British 48 hours to withdraw their troops from the border. The British greeted it with derision—*The Times* called it "an extravagant farce"—but Kruger wasn't joking.

10/13/1899

UNDER SIEGE The Boers shelled British defenses with French-built Long Tom 100-pounder field guns, of which they had four. The British had little training in the use of modern artillery, and were ill-equipped and unprepared for war. The sieges lasted well into the spring of 1900, and conditions were harsh because food supplies ran desperately low.

11/24/1899

WAR CORRESPONDENT Winston Churchill, then aged 25, was reporting on the Boer War for a London newspaper. Taken prisoner in a Boer ambush on an armored train, he later escaped and took part in the relief of the besieged garrison town of Ladysmith. His well-publicized exploits brought him national fame.

02/27/1900

CHANGE OF FORTUNE The celebrated Boer general Piet Cronjé and 4,000 of his men surrendered to the British at the Battle of Paardeburg on February 27, 1900. Their defeat marked a turning point in the war. Cronjé was sent to the island of St. Helena in the South Atlantic Ocean as a prisoner of war.

03/13/1900

BRITISH OFFENSIVE After relieving the besieged garrisons of Kimberley and Ladysmith, British Field Marshal Lord Roberts led the advance into Orange Free State. He captured Bloemfontein unopposed on March 13, 1900. Oxen trains were used to move armament and supplies across rough terrain.

01/01/1902

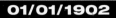

CONCENTRATION CAMPS The British rounded up Boer women, children, and the elderly, placing them in tented concentration camps in order to prevent them from supplying the Boer guerrilla fighters with food. More than 26,000 people died from disease and starvation within these camps.

05/31/1902

PEACE TREATY Both sides had had enough. The 1902 Treaty of Vereeniging placed the Boer Republics under control of the British Empire, but with the promise of eventual self-government. Louis Botha, leader of the Boer guerrilla campaign, became the first Prime Minister of the Union of South Africa in 1910.

Into the Skies

1900–1909

In 1900, few people believed that flight in a heavier-than-air machine would ever be possible, but just three years later, the Wright brothers took to the skies in their flying machine. The race to bring aviation to the world would turn a seeming impossibility into everyday life in a few short years.

07/02/1900

FIRST ZEPPELIN FLIGHT
Count von Zeppelin, a German general and balloon enthusiast, flew the Zeppelin, a lighter-than-air balloon with its own power and steering, at Lake Constance in Switzerland. Airships were a marvel of the time, and provided a carrying capacity far greater than any early airplane, but they were slow and cumbersome. The race was on to create a faster, more reliable alternative.

08/04/1901

12/17/1903

HISTORIC SUCCESS By the end of 1903, the Wright Brothers were ready to test their powered flying machine. Wilbur and Orville tossed a coin to decide who would make the historic attempt. Orville won and took the controls for the first successful powered flight, lasting 12 seconds. There were only five witnesses.

FESTIVAL OF FLIGHT A 1909 poster hailed a "Grand Week of Aviation" at Reims, France, and offered large cash prizes. The award for speed was won by Glenn Curtiss, flying *Reims Racer*.

09/17/1908

FATAL CRASH Orville Wright's plane crashed during a demonstration flight at Fort Myer, Virginia, after a propeller shattered at a height of 75 ft (22 m). His passenger, Army Lieutenant Thomas Selfridge, was killed, becoming the world's first airplane fatality. Orville was badly injured.

07/25/1909

CHANNEL CROSSING
Louis Blériot took 37 minutes to fly 22 miles (35 km) across the English Channel from Calais to Dover. He was competing for a £1,000 prize offered by the London *Daily Mail*, and was flying the world's first successful monoplane, built to his own design.

SMITHSONIAN

MODERN HISTORY IN PICTURES

A VISUAL GUIDE TO THE EVENTS THAT SHAPED OUR WORLD

**LONDON, NEW YORK, MELBOURNE,
MUNICH, AND DELHI**

DORLING KINDERSLEY
Senior Project Editor Daniel Mills
Senior Art Editor Vicky Short
Editors Ruth O'Rourke-Jones, Peter Preston,
Sam Priddy, Laura Wheadon
US Senior Editor Rebecca Warren
US Editor Jill Hamilton
Designers Richard Horsford, Peter Laws
Picture Researcher Sarah Hopper
Cartographer Merritt Cartographic
Jacket Designer Mark Cavanagh
Production Editors Ben Marcus, Rebekah Parsons-King
Production Controller Erika Pepe
Managing Editor Julie Ferris
Managing Art Editor Owen Peyton Jones
Publisher Sarah Larter
Art Director Phil Ormerod
Associate Publishing Director Liz Wheeler
Publishing Director Jonathan Metcalf

DK INDIA
Senior Editor Alka Ranjan
Senior Art Editor Devika Dwarkadas
Editors Rahul Ganguly, Megha Gupta
Art Editors Parul Gambhir, Vaibhav Rastogi
Production Manager Pankaj Sharma
DTP Manager Balwant Singh
Senior DTP Designer Harish Aggarwal
DTP Designer Nand Kishor
Managing Editor Rohan Sinha
Consultant Art Director Shefali Upadhyay

First American Edition, 2012

Published in the United States by DK Publishing,
375 Hudson Street, New York, New York 10014
12 13 14 15 16 10 9 8 7 6 5 4 3 2 1
001–181315–09/12

Published in Great Britain by Dorling Kindersley Limited

A catalog record for this book is available from the
Library of Congress

ISBN: 978-0-7566-9818-8

DK books are available at special discounts when purchased in bulk
for sales promotions, premiums, fund-raising, or educational use.
For details, contact: DK Publishing Special Markets, 375 Hudson
Street, New York, NY 10014 or SpecialSales@dk.com

Printed and bound in Hong Kong by Hung Hing

Discover more at
www.dk.com

Contents

GLIDER EXPERIMENT

Orville and Wilbur Wright, brothers who owned a bicycle workshop in Dayton, Ohio, were fascinated by the idea of flight and began experimenting with gliders built in their workshop. They traveled each summer to the sand dunes of Kitty Hawk in North Carolina to test their designs, attempting both unmanned and piloted flights.

03/23/1903

FLYING MACHINE

The Wright brothers applied for a patent on a powered flying machine they were constructing in their workshop. Based on their earlier success with glider designs, the new machine was made of wood and canvas, and powered by a fuel-injection engine. Cast in aluminum, the engine weighed 79 lb (36 kg) and generated 12 horsepower.

12/08/1903

THAT SINKING FEELING Other pioneers were less successful. *Aerodrome*, a powered airplane designed by Samuel Langley, crashed into the Potomac River on takeoff.

> I confess that in 1901 **I said** to my brother Orville that **man would not fly** for 50 years.
>
> WILBUR WRIGHT,
> NOVEMBER 5, 1908

10/05/1905

WILBUR GOES FARTHER

The brothers spent the next two years improving their plane. Wilbur's flight of 24 miles (38 km) in 1905 was the longest to date. Secretive by nature, they refused to publish details of their designs while pursuing patents for their machine, so news of their success was muted. The US government turned down an offer to buy the plane.

11/12/1906

FRENCH MILESTONE

In front of a large crowd, Brazilian-born aviator Alberto Santos-Dumont took to the skies above Paris, flying his fixed-wing *14-bis* plane a distance of 722 ft (220 m). The Wright brothers' achievements were virtually unknown in Europe, so the Aéro-Club de France proclaimed the flight a world record.

07/04/1908

FLYING PRIZE Glenn Curtiss flew more than 0.6 miles (1 km) in his *June Bug* to win the Scientific American Cup, the first prize offered for flying in the USA. An innovative designer, Curtiss later developed seaplanes.

09/29/1909

NEW YORK DISPLAY

More than 1 million New Yorkers turned out to watch Wilbur Wright fly his *Model A* flyer twice around the Statue of Liberty. A magazine headline described the feat as "A New Kind of Gull in New York Harbor." Aviation had caught the popular imagination and would change transportation forever.

A CENTURY OF

Flight

In the early years of the 20th century, flying was an adventure, making popular heroes of the brave men and women who embarked on pioneering flights. Gradually, improving technology made powered flight practical and reliable. Passenger airliners shrank the globe and military aircraft transformed the nature of warfare. As flying became part of everyday life, it generated new challenges for science, and a whole new frontier of exploration opened up in space.

1900–1930 Wilbur and Orville Wright made the first sustained heavier-than-air flight at Kitty Hawk, North Carolina, in 1903. Experiments with powered lighter-than-air craft, notably promoted by German Count Ferdinand von Zeppelin, were also under way, and for years the winged airplane and the airship developed side by side. By the end of the first decade of the century, the world was in the grip of a flying craze. Crowds flocked to air shows to see intrepid pilots risk their lives in flimsy flying machines, and newspapers offered cash prizes for long-distance air races. Frequent crashes were part of the thrill. At first there appeared to be little practical use for aircraft, but this changed during World War I when they were much in demand for reconnaissance and for bombing the enemy. Tens of thousands of pilots were trained to fly and aircraft began to be mass produced in factories, rather than made by hand in workshops.

INSTRUMENT PANEL Early aircraft had few instruments in the cockpit and those that did exist were often unreliable. This early device has airspeed and altitude gauges.

1930–1945 After the war, progress was rapid. Passenger air services were established between major European cities. Pioneering intercontinental flights by individuals such as Charles Lindbergh, Amelia Earhart, and Amy Johnson blazed the trail for commercial airlines. At first, airships looked set to dominate long-distance travel, providing the first airborne trans-Atlantic passenger services in the 1930s, but they proved too slow and too vulnerable to bad weather. Concerns about their safety came to a head when a fireball engulfed the airship *Hindenburg* in 1937. Winged aircraft, in contrast, grew bigger, safer, faster, and steadily more comfortable. Aircraft began to be constructed out of metal

LONG-HAUL PASSAGE This 1931 poster advertises Zeppelin airship flights between Europe and South America. The crossing took just three days.

1900s

BLÉRIOT MONOPLANE In July 1909, Louis Blériot became the first man to fly a heavier-than-air machine across the English Channel, crossing from Calais to Dover in 37 minutes. His aircraft was made of fabric, wood, and wire.

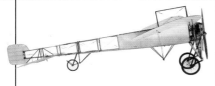

1920s

LONG-DISTANCE PIONEER US pilot Charles Lindbergh enthralled the world in May 1927 when he flew solo non-stop from New York to Paris. He made the 3,600-mile (5,800-km) flight in a single-engine monoplane, the *Spirit of St Louis*.

1930s

AIRCRAFT AT WAR The German Messerschmitt 109 was one of a new generation of fighter aircraft that transformed warfare. An all-metal, single-seat monoplane with a retractable undercarriage, it had a top speed of 350 mph (570 kph).

1940s

HELICOPTERS EVOLVE The first prototype helicopters had been developed in the 1930s by French pioneer Louis Breguet. Igor Sikorsky launched the first mass-produced helicopter, the Sikorsky R4, in 1940.

3½ HRS

Concorde's average travel time from London to New York. The same journey in a Boeing 747 takes more than 7 hours.

instead of wood and canvas, and were equipped with better flight instruments and navigational devices.

1945–1960 During World War II aircraft were a dominant force at sea and on land. The first jet aircraft entered service during the war, as did the first practical helicopters. In the following years, military aviation continued to set the pace, achieving phenomenal speed and altitude records with jet airplanes in the 1950s. Commercial aviation was slower to abandon the propeller, but the arrival of the jet-powered de Havilland Comet in 1952 definitively marked jet air travel as the way of the future.

SPY PLANE A high-altitude military reconnaissance aircraft capable of flying at a speed of more than 2,200 mph (3,600 kph), the Lockheed SR-71 Blackbird was revolutionary when it entered service in 1966.

1960–1970 The Cold War brought a race to be the first to fly beyond Earth's atmosphere. Scientists had experimented with rockets since the early part of the century, but it took the military advances of World War II for these ideas to become reality. The Soviets took an early lead when Yuri Gagarin became the first human being in space in 1961, before US astronaut Neil Armstrong became the first man on the Moon in 1969.

1970– Through the final decades of the century, the volume of passenger air travel multiplied dramatically. Supersonic passenger flights in Concorde, a joint French and British enterprise, were the height of luxury in the 1970s, but soon technological progress

SPACE TRAVEL From 1981 until its retirement in 2011, the Space Shuttle was the backbone of the US manned space program.

began to focus on fuel economy, safety, and size rather than speed. By the end of the 20th century, airlines were carrying billions of passengers every year. Wealthy tourists were taking flights into space, while the USA set its sights on a manned mission to Mars.

The **modern airplane** creates a new geographical dimension... the **world is small** and the world is one.

WENDELL WILLKIE, AMERICAN POLITICIAN, 1943

1950s

FIRST PASSENGER JET
In 1952, the de Havilland Comet became the first commercial jet to take to the skies. Though a groundbreaking technical achievement, it suffered a series of high-profile disasters and was overtaken by rival models.

1950s

JET BOMBER The English Electric Canberra was one of the first post-World War II military jets. With a top speed of 570 mph (920 kph), it could act as a high-altitude reconnaissance aircraft as well as a bomber.

1970s

CONCORDE TAKES FLIGHT
The world's first supersonic passenger aircraft entered service in 1976. Concorde enabled rapid trans-Atlantic flights but rising costs and fears over safety led to the retirement of the fleet in 2003.

2000s

DOUBLE-DECKER AIR TRAVEL
The world's largest ever passenger jet, Airbus A380 entered service in 2007. Capable of carrying up to 853 passengers, it is hoped that the jet represents the future of affordable, efficient air travel.

Russo-Japanese War

1904–1905

As the Chinese Empire went into terminal decline, the rivalry between Japan and Russia over power in the Far East grew into conflict. Japan's decisive victory in the first great war of the 20th century confirmed its emergence both as a modern industrial nation and as a major force in East Asia.

04/11/1904

INTO MANCHURIA
By April, three Japanese divisions had landed in Korea, and the army began to march north. Victory over Russian forces followed in May in a fierce battle at the Yalu River, after which the Japanese crossed into Manchuria. A smaller force then continued to push the Russians back toward Mukden (Shenyang), Manchuria's capital.

05/25/1904

SLOW PROGRESS TO PORT ARTHUR
After victory at the Yalu River, the main Japanese force began landings on the Liaodong Peninsula. Encountering strong Russian defensive positions around Port Arthur, the Japanese dug trenches and launched a series of costly frontal attacks.

12/05/1904

RUSSIAN FLEET DESTROYED
In December, Japanese troops took the strategically vital 203-Meter Hill after a long and costly struggle, with 8,000 Japanese casualties in the final assault alone. From this vantage point their artillery bombarded the trapped Russian fleet, sinking all but one battleship, and leaving several wrecks around the harbor.

04/18/1905

WAR IN EAST ASIA

The war was fought on land in southern Manchuria, in disputed areas of China, and in the seas around Korea and Japan.

KEY

- Japan
- Qing China
- to Russia 1897, to Japan 1905
- area leased to Japan 1895
- → Japanese advances 1904–05
- -- route of Russian Baltic fleet
- ✕ Japanese victory, with date

02/08/1904

JAPANESE ASSAULT LAUNCHED The Japanese army landed in Korea at Chemulpo, assisted by Chinese laborers. At the same time, Japanese ships mounted a surprise attack on the Russian navy at Port Arthur (Lüshun). This naval base on the Liaodong Peninisula, seized by Russia in 1898, threatened Japan's ambitions in Korea.

I am firmly **convinced** that I am the reincarnation of **Horatio Nelson**.

JAPANESE ADMIRAL TOGO HEIHACHIRO, PERSONAL JOURNAL, 1905

JAPANESE PROPAGANDA
A naval officer's hand prepares to grab Port Arthur in this poster by artist Kobayashi Kiyochika.

08/01/1904

THE SIEGE OF PORT ARTHUR By August, the Japanese army had completed their encirclement of Port Arthur on land, while their navy blockaded the harbor. The port's defenses consisted of well-fortified rings of forts, barbed wire, and trenches. The Japanese brought in batteries of heavy siege artillery to pound the Russian positions.

01/02/1905

PORT ARTHUR FALLS Despite inflicting huge casualties on the Japanese during their assault, the Russian will to fight ebbed away after the destruction of the fleet. With the wrecked ships still visible in the harbor, and most of his own garrison of 50,000 lost, Major General Anatoly Stessel surrendered Port Arthur to the Japanese.

02/20/1905

RUSSIAN ARMY DESTROYED AT MUKDEN With Port Arthur taken, the main Japanese army turned north to confront the Russian forces at Mukden. In the last major land battle of the war, fought over a 90-mile (140-km) front, the attacking Japanese gradually encircled the Russian lines. The battle quickly turned into a rout as the Russians abandoned their weapons and supplies.

NEW RUSSIAN FLEET Russia's last hope of victory lay with its Baltic Sea fleet. After a six-month voyage the ships arrived in the South China Sea too late to help Port Arthur. Instead they steamed toward the Russian port of Vladivostok. They sailed at night to avoid detection, but were spotted and intercepted by the Japanese.

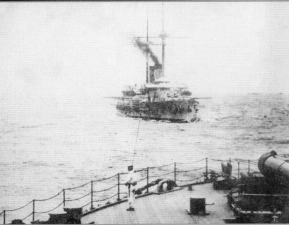

05/28/1905

BATTLE OF TSUSHIMA In the narrow Tsushima Strait, superior Japanese ships destroyed the Russian fleet. Peace talks followed, mediated by US President Theodore Roosevelt, but Russia was humiliated, while Japanese imperial ambition would grow in the coming decades.

First Russian Revolution

1904–1906

For centuries, Russia was an oppressive, autocratic state ruled by the czars. But by the early 1900s change was in the air. Liberal politicians demanded Czar Nicholas II hand over power to an elected parliament. At the same time, socialist movements inspired by political theorist Karl Marx were calling for a workers' rebellion. The uprising that followed would change the face of Russian politics, and sow the seeds of future revolution.

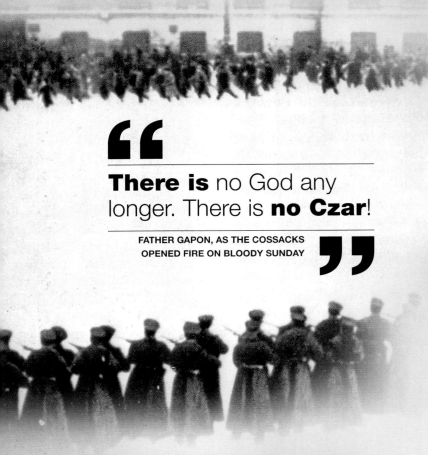

> **There is** no God any longer. There is **no Czar**!

FATHER GAPON, AS THE COSSACKS OPENED FIRE ON BLOODY SUNDAY

12/29/1904

THE FIRST STRIKE
The first stirrings of rebellion came when a protest over the sacking of four men from the Putilov factory in St. Petersburg escalated into a full-scale strike. The strikers called for better pay and working conditions, and for the formation of an elected committee to represent the workers in disputes.

01/22/1905

BLOODY SUNDAY Gapon led the strikers in a peaceful march to present a petition at the Winter Palace, the czar's residence in St. Petersburg. Nervous authorities ordered troops to prevent the crowd from reaching the palace. As the crowd pressed forward, the soldiers opened fire. This Bloody Sunday massacre became a symbol of repression, immortalized in a later film.

02/01/1905

REVOLUTION IN FILM Sergei Einsenstein's silent film *Battleship Potemkin* was made in 1925 to commemorate the 20th anniversary of the mutiny.

06/27/1905

POTEMKIN MUTINY
Unrest in the military came to a head when sailors on the battleship *Potemkin* mutinied over supplies of rotten meat. They took control of the ship and sailed to the Black Sea port of Odessa. The mutiny became another proud symbol of the revolution, and was lionized by Soviet rulers in later years.

10/17/1905

OCTOBER MANIFESTO
As the revolution spread, Count Sergei Witte, an influential politician, joined calls for reform. Urging concessions, he persuaded the Czar to sign the October Manifesto granting freedom of the press and other basic civil rights. Crucially, an elected national parliament (Duma) would be formed.

12/07/1905

MOSCOW REVOLT Dismissing the October Manifesto as a cynical sham, revolutionary groups of Mensheviks and Bolsheviks organized an armed uprising in Moscow. Bombs were manufactured, and barricades, manned by workers and students, were erected in the streets.

12/19/1905

01/07/1905

THE MOVEMENT GROWS By January the situation was still unresolved, and workers in factories across the city joined the strike in sympathy. The protest found a leader in an Orthodox priest named George Gapon. As popular support grew, tens of thousands of workers joined the strike, paralyzing industry in St. Petersburg.

UNREST GROWS As news of the Bloody Sunday killings spread, workers' strikes erupted all across the country. Universities closed down and students joined the protests. Unrest grew throughout the spring and summer, as general strikes and rural uprisings brought the Russian economy grinding to a halt. The socialist Bolshevik and Menshevik parties gathered many supporters from among the protesters.

03/10/1905

WAR WEARINESS
The Czar's unpopularity grew with news that the Russian army had been defeated by the Japanese at Mukden in Manchuria. The Czar was widely held responsible for the war with Japan, which was rapidly turning against Russia. The armed forces were the Czar's last resort in the face of popular revolt, but their morale was at rock bottom.

06/29/1905

ODESSA ON FIRE Strikers in Odessa hoped the sailors would come to their support and flocked to the port. As unrest spread, troops fired on the crowd and parts of the city were set ablaze.

10/13/1905

ST. PETERSBURG SOVIET FORMED
Leon Trotsky, a Marxist revolutionary who had been living in exile, secretly returned to Russia and made his way to St. Petersburg. There he helped organize the first workers' soviet (elected council). Similar soviets were soon established in some 50 cities.

PRESNIA SHELLED
Bitter street fighting lasted more than a week as the army was sent in to retake the city. At one point six of the city's railroad stations were in rebel hands. Then the army brought in artillery to shell the factory district of Presnia, the main stronghold of the workers, and the resistance was crushed. Large areas of Moscow were left in ruins.

09/19/1906

SUPREME AUTOCRAT
Liberal hopes were dashed when the Czar issued the Fundamental Laws, a new constitution confirming his right to dismiss the Duma and retain an absolute veto over legislation. The Czar remained absolute ruler, and thousands were imprisoned or executed for their part in the rebellion.

09/19/1906

ON TRIAL Trotsky and other leaders of the St. Petersburg soviet were put on trial and deported to Siberia, a harsh, isolated region in Russia's far north. Trotsky managed to escape in 1907 and spent the next decade in exile.

1907

Building the Panama Canal

Stretching more than 50 miles (80 km), the Panama Canal remains one of the largest engineering projects ever attempted. It is never less than 40 ft (12 m) deep, and is 300 ft (90 m) wide at its narrowest point. More than 5.3 billion cubic ft (150 million cubic m) of rubble was removed in its construction. Before it was built, ships traveling between the Atlantic and Pacific Oceans were forced to undertake a long and dangerous diversion around Cape Horn, the southern tip of South America. The new route would provide vital trade links to the American West Coast and to the countries of the Pacific. French engineers had begun to construct a crossing in the late 19th century, before the US Government took over the project in 1904. Over the next 10 years, the USA poured tens of millions of dollars into the Canal, which was completed in 1914. It remains a vital artery of global trade, and a wonder of modern engineering.

San Francisco Earthquake

1906

At 5:13 a.m. on the morning of April 18, the city of San Francisco was struck by a massive earthquake, measuring between 7.9 and 8.25 on the Richter scale. The violent shock, which shook the city for 48 seconds, was felt from Oregon in the north to Los Angeles in the south, and as far inland as central Nevada. As the tremors subsided, the wealthy city of San Francisco—the largest on the West Coast and the ninth largest in the USA—lay in ruins, with much of its population homeless and desperate.

> **Men** worked like **fiends** to combat the **laughing**, roaring, onrushing **fire demon**.
>
> SAN FRANCISCO NEWSPAPER, APRIL 18, 1906

04/18/1906

PALL OF SMOKE As fires burned across the city, General Funston, commander of armed forces in the area, took charge of rescue operations. Nob Hill, the wealthiest part of the city, was particularly badly hit, while Chinatown was almost entirely destroyed.

04/18/1906

ESCAPING THE FIRES Rescuers fought desperately against the fires, which burned for three days. At least 25,000 houses were destroyed, many of them dynamited to prevent the spread of the flames. Survivors salvaged whatever they could from their homes. Thousands fled across San Francisco Bay.

04/18/1906

WARNING TO LOOTERS Mayor Schmitz posted notices around the city warning that looters would be shot on sight. He also imposed a nighttime curfew until street lighting could be restored, and warned of the prevailing danger of further fires from broken chimneys and leaking pipes.

PROCLAMATION BY THE MAYOR

The Federal Troops, the members of the Regular Police Force and all Special Police Officers have been authorized by me to KILL any and all persons found engaged in Looting or in the Commission of Any Other Crime.

I have directed all the Gas and Electric Lighting Co.'s not to turn on Gas or Electricity until I order them to do so. You may therefore expect the city to remain in darkness for an indefinite time.

I request all citizens to remain at home from darkness until daylight every night until order is restored.

I WARN all Citizens of the danger of fire from Damaged or Destroyed Chimneys, Broken or Leaking Gas Pipes or Fixtures, or any like cause.

E. E. SCHMITZ, Mayor

Dated, April 18, 1906.

04/18/1906

TENT CITIES As the initial panic subsided, the army quickly erected military-style camps in city parks and squares to house the city's homeless population of around 250,000 people. Makeshift tents were erected in parks and on beaches. It would be months, in some cases years, before many of the displaced returned to their rebuilt homes.

04/21/1906

ASSESSING THE DAMAGE Whole areas of the city were leveled by the quake, and other neighborhoods were gutted by fire. Estimates of the damage ran to more than $200 million. Officials gave the number of dead as 375, in an effort to prevent panic, but the actual figure was probably closer to 3,000.

04/18/1906

EARTHQUAKE STRIKES Citizens of San Francisco were awakened in terror by the first tremors. The city was both a center of culture and finance, and one of the largest industrial ports on the Pacific coast, with a large working-class and immigrant population. The earthquake struck both rich and poor.

04/18/1906

CITY IN FLAMES Ruptured gas supplies caused fires that swept through the city. Firefighters were hampered by the lack of water as pipes were torn open.

04/23/1906

CLEANUP BEGINS Work started immediately on clearing away the damage. Gangs of workers removed piles of rubble, all that remained of buildings in the area around Montgomery Street.

04/23/1906

REBUILDING THE CITY Architects submitted grandiose schemes for rebuilding, but in the end the original street grid was retained. Work was completed quickly, but much of California's development had moved south, toward Los Angeles. San Francisco rose as a new city, but its future trajectory had been irrevocably altered.

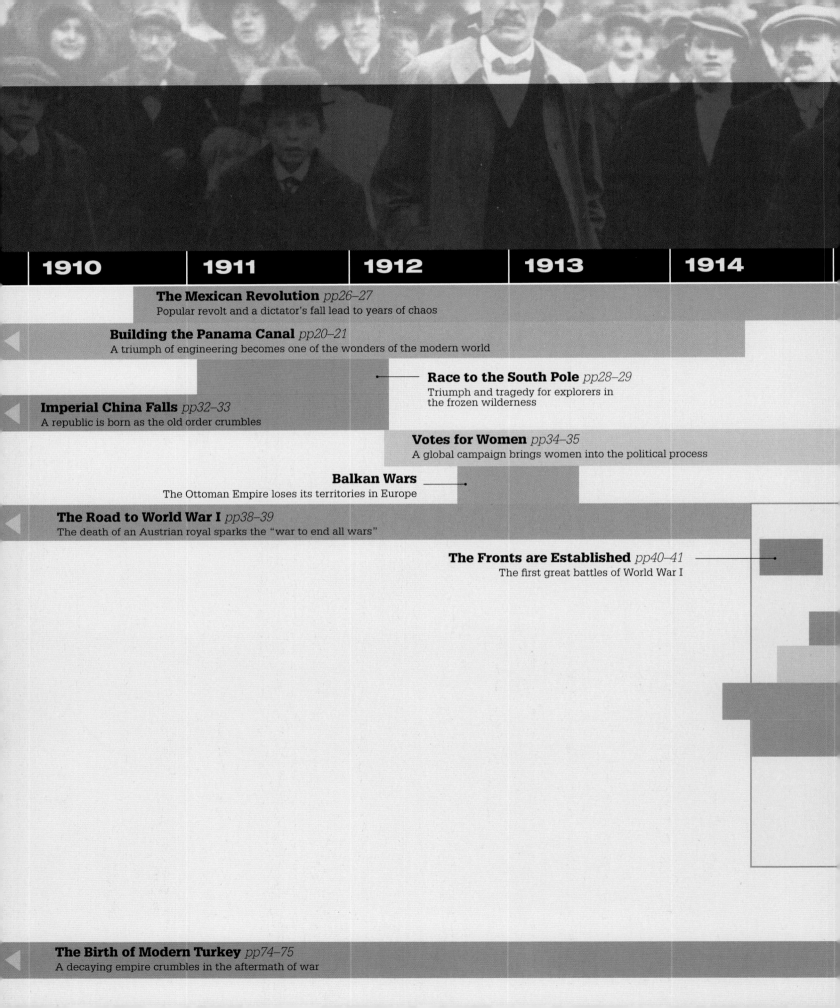

WORLD WAR I

Aircraft Go to War *pp44–45*
The art of war gains a new dimension

Gallipoli Campaign *pp46–47*
The Ottoman Empire holds off invading forces

The Somme *pp48–49*
A volunteer army learns a harsh lesson in a deadly battle

Ireland's Easter Rising *pp50–51*
Republicans see a chance to realize their dream

Arab Revolt *pp52–53*
The desert tribes rise up

The Battle of Verdun *pp54–55*
France is bled dry in a battle of attrition

Revolution in Russia *pp56–57*
The Bolsheviks take Russia out of the war and into the unknown

The War Ends *pp58–59*
The guns fall silent as the slaughter of World War I ends

Spanish Flu Epidemic *pp60–61*
A new tragedy casts its shadow across the globe

The Rise of Stalin *pp70–71*
A ruthless dictator comes to dominate the new USSR

The Mexican Revolution

1910–1920

President Porfirio Diaz ruled Mexico with an iron fist for more than 30 years. In 1910 he was approaching 80, and hopes were high that he would retire. Instead he ran again for president, declaring victory in a fraudulent election. This time, however, the frustration of the people boiled over into a mass revolution against corruption in government. The rebellion developed into a civil war that would create unlikely heroes, spark treacherous rivalries, and give rise to decades of political instability and violence.

07/08/1910
STOLEN ELECTION
Diaz's main rival was Francisco Madero, a wealthy lawyer. He campaigned vigorously against the President and, on the eve of the election, seemed certain to win. Instead, Diaz had him thrown into jail and announced his own landslide victory. Few believed his claim, and opposition mounted.

06/07/1911

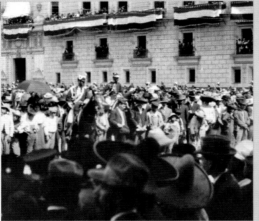

HERO'S RETURN
Madero entered Mexico City in triumph. He was elected President, but things did not go well. He had promised land reform to his peasant allies, and his failure to deliver led to further unrest. On February 19, 1913 army general Victoriano Huerta overthrew Madero and claimed the Presidency.

02/26/1913
THE WAR IS RENEWED
To Villa and Zapata, Huerta's military rule was no better than Diaz's dictatorship, and they renewed their guerrilla war. Lawyer Venustiano Carranza and wealthy farmer Alvaro Obregón were also opposed to the regime and raised their own Constitutional Army to join the battle. Villa, Zapata, Carranza, and Obregón—the so-called Big Four—formed an uneasy alliance.

04/21/1914

US INVOLVEMENT
Mexico's most powerful neighbor, the United States, kept a close eye on the conflict. A diplomatic dispute with Huerta led US President Woodrow Wilson to impose a ban on arms imports to Mexico. American marines occupied the port of Veracruz to enforce the ban, depriving Huerta of essential supplies.

06/24/1914
BATTLE OF ZACATECAS
Pancho Villa, the bandit turned state governor of Chihuahua, used everything from train robbery to forced loans to equip his formidable army, the Division of the North. In June 1914 he attacked the heavily defended city of Zacatecas and inflicted a crushing defeat on Huerta's forces. Huerta resigned and fled the country, and Villa's fame and popularity spread.

04/15/1915

ALLIES NO MORE
With Huerta defeated, the Big Four started to fall apart. Obregón and Carranza came from wealthy backgrounds, and were suspicious of Villa and Zapata, who called for better rights for peasants. Before long violence erupted again, as Obregón defeated Villa's cavalry at the Battle of Celaya.

03/15/1916
SHOW OF FORCE
In desperation, Villa's forces mounted a raid for supplies across the American border. US General Pershing was sent at the head of an American expeditionary force to capture Villa. Despite the introduction of new technology, the military airplane, he was unable to bring back the guerrilla.

10/06/1910

CALL TO REVOLUTION
Madero escaped from jail and was smuggled across the border to Texas. There he declared the election null and void, issuing a call to the Mexican people to rise up in armed revolution at 6 pm on November 20, a day the Mexican people still celebrate as Revolution Day.

02/14/1911

UNLIKELY ALLIES
In need of an army, Madero joined forces with Pancho Villa, a former bandit. They also recruited Emiliano Zapata, a campaigner for peasants' rights, who raised a guerrilla army in the south. Together they defeated Diaz, and the President was forced to resign on May 25.

PEASANT CAMPAIGN
This Zapata poster reads "The land should belong to those who work it."

> "
> It is better to **die on your feet** than to **live on your knees**.
>
> EMILIANO ZAPATA, 1913
> "

07/11/1917

A NEW PRESIDENT Peace seemed closer when Carranza was elected president under the new constitution. However, Zapata's rebels continued to fight, defying Carranza's attempts to stamp them out. Zapata was finally killed in an ambush on April 10, 1919, but a year later Obregón ousted Carranza, claiming he had betrayed the constitution. Carranza was assassinated while trying to flee the country.

12/01/1920

A FRESH START
With Carranza and Zapata dead and Villa in retirement, Obregón was the last of the Big Four left. He was elected president in 1920. Obregón, who had lost his right arm fighting against Villa, proved a popular leader. While violence and instability continued in some areas, his election marked the end of the Mexican Revolution.

Race to the South Pole

1911–1912

Between 1892 and 1922, 16 major expeditions were launched to Antarctica. This "Heroic Age of Antarctic Exploration" saw men from around the world battle extreme cold and hostile conditions with only basic equipment. By 1910, the geology and meteorology of the continent had been widely explored, but no expedition had made it farther south than 88°23S—still more than 100 miles (160 km) from the South Pole. Two men, British explorer Robert Scott and Norwegian Roald Amundsen, were each determined to break that record and reach the Pole in 1912, sparking a desperate race that would end in victory for one, and tragic failure for the other.

AMUNDSEN'S FLAG
This Norwegian flag was retrieved from the South Pole by a later expedition.

04/03/1911

WAITING FOR SPRING
With their base camps set up, both expeditions sat out the intense cold and bitter storms of the Antarctic winter. From April until October, the teams overhauled their equipment and checked their supplies, while overcoming boredom with lectures on geology from the scientists and soccer games on the ice.

12/14/1911

AMUNDSEN WINS THE RACE Roald Amundsen and his four companions, with 16 surviving dogs, planted the Norwegian flag at the South Pole. Their journey across the ice had taken just 55 days. They left letters for both Scott and the Norwegian king, Haakon VII, before setting out on their successful return journey. They would be welcomed as heroes on their return.

01/04/1912

03/10/1912

ROBERT SCOTT

A captain in the British Royal Navy, Scott had previously led the 1901–1904 Discovery Expedition to explore Antarctic conditions.

ROALD AMUNDSEN

Norwegian Amundsen was an experienced Polar explorer, who had already achieved fame for his Arctic discoveries.

01/19/1911

A CHILLY ARRIVAL
Both parties reached their starting points in January 1911, during the Antarctic summer. Roald Amundsen and his crew in their ship *Fram* set up base camp in the Bay of Whales, while Scott's expedition, having arrived in the *Terra Nova*, set up their camp on Ross Island, some 120 miles (200 km) to the west, on the far side of the Ross Ice Shelf.

11/01/1911

THE JOURNEYS BEGIN
On October 19, Amundsen and four companions set out with four sleds, each pulled by a team of 13 husky dogs. When the dogs became exhausted, they were shot and their meat used for food. Supply depots on route had already been set up. Scott's journey began on November 1, but immediately encountered difficulties. Scott relied on mechanical sleds, which quickly failed, and pack ponies, which died within days from cold and exhaustion.

Victory awaits him who has everything in order—**luck**, people call it.

ROALD AMUNDSEN, IN
THE SOUTH POLE, 1912

SCOTT BATTLES ON
Unaware that he had already lost the race to Amundsen, Scott struggled on, his party reducing in size as support teams returned to base. By January 4, a team of five was left to make the final march to the Pole. Hampered by their thick woolen clothing, many of his men suffered frostbite and exposure.

01/17/1912

A BITTER ARRIVAL
Robert Scott and his four companions reached the South Pole only to discover that Amundsen had beaten them by 35 days. Exhausted and demoralized, they spent the next two days resting, after which they began the long trek back to their base camp on Ross Island.

02/17/1912

THE RETURN At first the party made good progress, covering 300 miles (500 km) of the 800 miles (1,300 km) back to Ross Island in three weeks. But the long, grueling descent of the Beardmore Glacier was still to come. The glacier caused the first casualty of the expedition on February 17, as Edgar Evans died after a fall. The remaining members of the team struggled on in appalling conditions.

THE LAST DAYS The four explorers reached the foot of the glacier, but still faced a 400-mile (670-km) trek across the Ross Ice Shelf. Titus Oates, barely able to walk, voluntarily left the party and walked to his death on March 16, and on March 19 Robert Scott, Edward Wilson, and Henry Bowers were hit by a blizzard and forced to halt. With no supplies and unable to leave their tent, the three men succumbed to cold, hunger, and exhaustion, and died.

SCOTT'S SUNDIAL Scott carried a range of devices to monitor weather and aid navigation.

A CENTURY OF
Agriculture

In the 20th century, new technologies and scientific advances combined to bring about a revolution in agriculture. Beginning in the developed world, crop yields increased beyond farmers' wildest dreams, while vast areas of previously barren land were brought under the plow. New equipment and new farming methods spread around the globe, and by the end of the century the sudden increase in food production had fueled a global population boom.

1900–1930 Seismic changes in farming began with the development of tractors and combine harvesters. Machines took over the work of men and animals at a fraction of the cost and at a much greater speed and scale. New, industrially produced chemical fertilizers replaced manure and guano, hugely increasing land fertility. At the same time,

THE NEW STANDARD In 1917, the Ford Motor Company of Detroit introduced the Fordson, the world's first mass-produced tractor.

improved transportation links and the development of refrigeration and container shipping made it much easier to transport goods to markets over long distances, to support ever-growing cities. Large-scale monoculture—in which one crop

925

The number in millions of hungry people in the world in 2010 according to the United Nations Food and Agriculture Organization.

was grown over a vast area—became the dominant system of farming in the developed world.

1930–1950 The Great Depression brought hardship to millions of farmers. In the USA and Canada, the problems were exacerbated by drought and dust storms, which tore off fertile topsoil and rendered vast swathes of farmland useless. Intensive monoculture,

MOBILIZED FOR FOOD
Limits on overseas food supplies during World War II encouraged intensive farming. Women's Land Armies filled the labor shortage as men fought abroad.

which had damaged the deep root systems that held the soil in place, was blamed for the severity of the disaster. World War II brought further upheaval as global trade was disrupted. Many countries

1900s

HORSE-DRAWN PLOW
Before 1900, agriculture was small-scale and labor intensive. Farmers depended on animals for much of the heavy work.

1910s

CHEMICAL PIONEER
In 1910, German chemist Fritz Haber discovered a way to synthesize ammonia. His work allowed fertilizer to be produced cheaply on an industrial scale.

1920s

FORDSON TRACTOR
The birth of the gasoline-driven engine spurred industry to mass-produce general purpose tractors that allowed ordinary farmers to mechanize their work.

1940s

IMPROVED PESTICIDES
Crop dusting (spraying crops with pesticides) began in the 1920s, but from 1940 more sophisticated pesticides and better delivery methods saw yields increase.

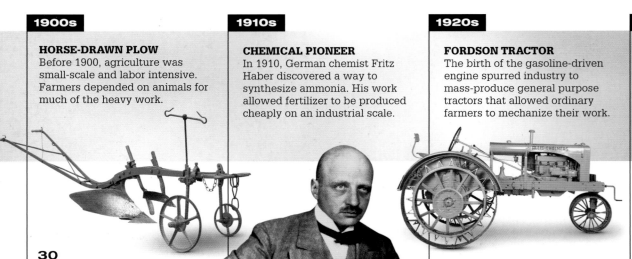

MODERN FARM HORSE
Highly mechanized farm machinery like this Case IH Magnum series tractor has dramatically increased yields and profit.

CONTROVERSIAL METHODS
Intensive farming of chickens produces eggs on an industrial scale, but raises concerns about animal welfare.

experienced food shortages, hastening the spread of intensive farming techniques.

1950–1970 A new prosperity spread through the West, bringing innovations such as supermarkets and home refrigerators. Increasingly sophisticated selective breeding and hybridization created stronger, more productive crops.

The 1960s saw agricultural revolution as campaigners such as scientist Norman Borlaug sought to spread these technologies to the wider world, greatly increasing food production in Africa and Asia. However, while intensive farming practices increased output, scientists became increasingly aware of the cost to the natural world. Monoculture led to the destruction of traditional farmland and wilderness areas. Pesticides such as DDT were found to have

unexpected consequences, poisoning birds and mammals. A growing environmental movement called for responsible agriculture, seeking to feed the world without sacrificing animal welfare or natural ecosystems.

1970– New scientific developments brought genetically modified crops, in which DNA had been manipulated to improve yields. At the other end of the spectrum, a growing organic movement rejected chemical

fertilizers and pesticides to grow more "natural" produce. By the early 21st century, scientific management of food production had made basic nutrition cheaper and safer than ever before, but millions still lacked sufficient food. The challenge became balancing the needs of the hungry with sustainable food production, a problem that continues to provoke debate.

> **"**
> The first **essential** component of social justice is **adequate food for all mankind**.
> **"**
> AGRICULTURAL ACTIVIST NORMAN BORLAUG, 1970

1950s

CONSUMER BOOM
Improved living standards made appliances like refrigerators readily available, altering consumer habits.

1960s

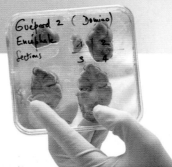

大力支援农业

COLLECTIVIZED FARMING
Experiments with state-run, quota-based farming caused widespread famine in China.

1980s

CONTAMINATED FOOD
Contamination scares in the 1980s led to increased regulation in farming. Cattle tissue was tested in the wake of the BSE crisis.

1990s

GENETIC MODIFICATION
Genetically modified foods may come to define farming in the 21st century, but concerns remain about their safety.

Imperial China Falls

1898–1912

As the 19th century drew to a close, Imperial China, ruled by the Qing Dynasty, was in sharp decline. Popular resentment against the foreigners who controlled China's overseas trade, and against the increasing number of Christian missionaries, came to a head in a violent rebellion led by the so-called Boxers. Thousands of rioters rampaged through the countryside before marching on to Beijing. Although their rebellion failed, it hastened the demise of imperial rule.

03/01/1898

PEASANT UNREST Across northern China, groups of discontented peasants joined forces. They formed a secret society known as the League of Righteous and Harmonious Fists. The Boxers, as they came to be known, saw foreign influence as a threat to their traditional way of life and wanted to end imperial rule.

06/14/1900

UNDER SIEGE Urged on by her conservative advisors, Empress Cixi declared war on all the Western powers, for their exploitation of China. Boxers and Imperial Army soldiers united to lay siege to the crowded Legation Quarter. A force of 400 European marines, boasting just one small cannon, managed to keep the attackers at bay.

07/14/1900

08/15/1900

VIOLENT CONSEQUENCES In the aftermath of the failed Boxer Rebellion, Beijing was thoroughly looted. The occupying forces, which consisted of Japanese, Russian, British, French, American, German, Austrian, and Italian soldiers, summarily executed hundreds of suspected Boxers.

09/07/1901

11/15/1908

THE NEW EMPEROR On her deathbed, Cixi chose two-year-old Puyi to succeed his uncle, the Guangxi Emperor, who had died under suspicious circumstances the day before. Puyi, seen here with his father Zaifeng and baby brother, was taken to live in the Forbidden City, where his father served as his regent.

09/21/1898

DUPLICITY The Boxers, sworn to rid China of foreigners, began massacring Christian missionaries. They were backed by Qing Empress Cixi, who had taken power after usurping her nephew, the reformist Guangxu Emperor. Cixi was eager to divert the rage of the Boxers away from the imperial family.

06/20/1900

RIOTING SPREADS The rebellion spread from the countryside to the main cities. Hundreds of Boxers went on the rampage in Beijing, burning and looting churches and attacking Christians. Many missionaries and converts fled for safety to the Legation Quarter where the Western embassies were housed.

BATTLE OF TIANJIN The Eight-Nation Alliance army, a large force representing the nations trapped in the Legation, was sent to lift the siege and protect Western interests. As thousands of armed Alliance troops headed toward the Legation, they captured the Boxer-held city of Tianjin, rescuing about 2,000 foreigners trapped in the city.

08/14/1900

RELIEF OF BEIJING The international force stormed Beijing, reducing the Qianmen Gate of the Inner City to ruins. Empress Cixi escaped from the imperial palace disguised as a peasant and fled to the ancient capital of Xi'an.

> … **drive away the devils**…
> Pull up the **railroad lines**!
> Smash the **great steamships**!
>
> BOXER REVOLUTIONARY POSTER,
> JUNE 1900

PUNITIVE TERMS Under the agreement of the Boxer Protocol, foreign nations received favorable commercial terms and were allowed to station their troops in Beijing. China was also forced to pay a crippling 450 million taels of silver (approximately $6.6 billion today). Cixi, permitted to remain Empress, began to make overdue reforms, but the rebellion had permanently weakened the Qing Dynasty.

10/10/1911

WUCHANG UPRISING Supporting a new wave of revolutionaries, army officers staged a coup in Wuchang, Hubei province, and took over the city. The Qing court was slow to act, and by November most provinces in the south had joined the revolution. Nationalist Sun Yat-sen returned from exile to head a new Chinese republic in the city of Nanjing.

03/10/1912

CHINESE REPUBLIC Sun Yat-sen agreed to hand over power to the military strongman Yuan Shikai, head of the New Army. Yuan brought about the abdication of Puyi and was inaugurated as first president of the Republic of China. This marked the end of 4,000 years of imperial rule and the birth of modern China.

Votes for Women

1912–1921

By 1912 women had been campaigning for the vote for more than half a century, but only a few countries had agreed to their demands. Women's suffrage movements, angered by the broken promises of male politicians, became increasingly militant. By the end of the decade, the movement had spread beyond Western borders and had caught the imagination of women in Asia.

03/04/1912

SHOP WINDOWS BROKEN Campaigners in Britain, known as the suffragettes, became infamous for their forceful protests. On one day of violence they smashed shop windows across London's West End and attacked government buildings. Many were arrested and jailed.

06/04/1913

TRAGEDY AT EPSOM In Britain, suffragette Emily Davison died after throwing herself in front of the King's horse at the Epsom Derby. Thousands joined her funeral procession.

01/28/1914

WOMEN'S PARLIAMENT Canadian social activist Nellie McClung staged a mock women's parliament in a theater in Winnipeg, Manitoba. Debating whether to give men the vote, it satirized male politicians and their attitudes to women. In 1916 Manitoba became the first Canadian province to grant women the vote.

WOMEN'S INTERNATIONAL DAY This 1914 German poster exhorts women to go out to support women's right to vote.

01/10/1917

WOMEN WORKERS During World War I, women across Europe and the USA filled many vital jobs left vacant by men fighting at the front. They took up work in factories and coal mines, or on trams and buses. Attitudes changed, and when the war ended many countries were ready to give voting rights to women.

08/18/1920

SUCCESS AT LAST American campaigner Alice Paul and her supporters celebrated the news that Tennessee had ratified the 19th Amendment, which prohibits any US citizen to be denied the right to vote based on sex. It was the 36th and deciding US state that tilted the balance in favour of women's suffrage.

06/06/1921

MOVEMENT SPREADS TO JAPAN In 1921 the Japanese parliament overruled Article 5 of the Police Security Act and granted women the right to attend political meetings. This led to a surge in the number of women's groups, who campaigned for the right to vote. It took until 1945 for their demands to be met.

SUFFRAGETTE COLORS A jeweled pendant in the colors chosen by Emmeline Pankhurst for the suffragettes— purple for dignity, white for purity, and green for hope.

05/06/1912

MARCHING IN STEP The suffrage march through New York City was an annual event. Women could vote in only a few US states and not at all in national elections.

01/02/1913

RADICAL ACTION Alice Paul and Lucy Burns formed the Feminist Congressional Union in the USA to call for a Constitutional Amendment to bring about full female suffrage. Influenced by the British suffragettes movement, they advocated civil disobedience and picketed the White House to publicize their cause.

03/03/1913

WASHINGTON PARADE Feminist lawyer Inez Milholland led a huge suffrage parade held in Washington, DC on the day before President Woodrow Wilson's inauguration. Half a million people came to watch and 200 people were injured. A brainchild of Alice Paul, the parade deepened support for women's rights.

04/26/1914

FRENCH CAMPAIGN Lawyer Maria Vérone was president of the French League for Women's Rights. The French women's suffrage movement was largely middle-class and city-based. Although it seemed poised for success, female suffrage was delayed until 1945 because of deep-rooted conservatism in France's male population.

05/22/1914

LEADER ARRESTED WSPU leader Emmeline Pankhurst was arrested outside Buckingham Palace, one of many such arrests in the British suffragette's fiery career. At the outbreak of World War I, she suspended the suffragette campaign and turned her energies to the war effort.

> ## I am a **law breaker** because I want to be a **law maker**.

AMERICAN SOCIAL ACTIVIST ANNE COBDEN SANDERSON SPEAKING IN COURT, OCTOBER 1906

1913

Ford's Factory Revolution

The world of industry had been revolutionized in the 19th century by the introduction of the factory. However, complex products such as machines were still produced in workshops, by teams of mechanics working on a single unit at a time. Industrialist and automobile manufacturer Henry Ford changed all this. His idea was simple. Rather than mechanics moving from one unit to the next, the units themselves would move along a track, stopping at each station for workers to perform a specific task. At a stroke, the rate of manufacture could be greatly increased, and the price of individual units slashed. The moving assembly line made his iconic Model T automobile the first car to be widely affordable, not a luxury item. Ford's innovation would go on to bring not just the automobile but a huge range of consumer goods to the mass market, opening the door to modern consumer culture.

The Road to World War I

1906–1914

Europe at the turn of the 20th century was a complex network of alliances and counter-alliances. The precarious balance of power was upset by the assassination of the Austrian Archduke Franz Ferdinand, sparking a war that would spread across the world.

02/09/1906

ARMS RACE As the European powers jostled for position, they raced to build the largest and most modern weaponry. Heavily armed with huge guns and powered by steam turbines, Britain's *HMS Dreadnought* was the world's first modern battleship. The Germans responded by spending vast sums of money on their own fleet. As Europe militarized, war seemed inevitable.

BOSNIAN CRISIS

The situation in the Balkans was summed up in a French cartoon. Emperor Franz-Joseph of Austria-Hungary is shown snatching Bosnia away from the Ottoman Sultan, while the King of Bulgaria declares his independence. The neighboring state of Serbia had already formed an alliance with Russia.

08/10/1913

OTTOMAN COLLAPSE
Conflict erupted in the Balkans in 1912 when, driven by a wave of Slav nationalism, the Balkan states attacked the Ottoman Empire. The Empire lost almost all its territories in the region. After the conflict ended in 1913, Ottoman prisoners were marched through the streets of the Serbian capital.

07/28/1914

DECLARATION OF WAR Bolstered by promises from its allies, Austria-Hungary declared war on Serbia. The next day artillery shells bombarded Belgrade. As expected, Russia mobilized its troops in defense of Serbia and, on August 1, Germany declared war on Russia.

EAGLE EMPIRE
This spiked helmet is adorned with an imperial eagle, symbol of the German Empire.

08/01/1914

WAR SPREADS France mobilized in support of Russia. Germany then declared war on France, invading Belgium to reach the French border. Britain declared war on Germany. Italy left the Triple Alliance and the Ottomans joined Germany and Austria-Hungary as the Central Powers.

> **“**
> The **lamps are going out** all over **Europe**. We will not see them lit again in our **lifetime**.
> **”**
>
> SIR EDWARD GREY, BRITISH FOREIGN SECRETARY,
> AUGUST 3, 1914

08/31/1907

TWO CAMPS Europe was dominated by vast imperial powers, which competed for economic and colonial gain. Germany, Austria-Hungary, and Italy were joined in the Triple Alliance, forming a buffer between Britain and France in the west, and Russia to the east. With the signing of the Anglo-Russian Entente in 1907, Britain, France, and Russia made up an opposing alliance, the Triple Entente. Smaller, independent states, such as Belgium, sought protection in treaties with their larger neighbors.

THE POWDER KEG

Austria-Hungary was keen to gain control of Bosnia-Herzegovina in the Balkans but the Ottoman Empire (Turkey) also laid claim to the region. As the empires competed, many Balkan states called for independence.

KEY
- The Kingdom of Hungary
- The Austrian Empire
- Bosnia–Herzegovina
- Border of Austria–Hungary

06/28/1914

THE SPARK IS LIT
With Austria-Hungary and Russia looking to profit from the situation in the Balkans, tension mounted. Heir to the throne of Austria-Hungary, Archduke Franz Ferdinand, was visiting the Bosnian capital Sarajevo when he and his wife were shot dead. The killer was Gavrilo Princip, a 19-year-old Bosnian-Serb nationalist. Austria demanded that Serbia hand over Princip and his accomplices.

07/23/1914

THE DOMINOS FALL Austria-Hungary accused the Serbian government of supporting the assassins and served an ultimatum threatening military action if they were not brought to justice. Frantic diplomatic activity ensued. Germany pledged to support Austria in military action against Serbia. Russia had promised to back the Serbs. With members of the Triple Entente and the Triple Alliance involved, the crisis was poised to engulf all of Europe.

08/17/1914

TROOPS LAND Across Europe, poised armies began to move. The British Expeditionary Force (BEF) landed in France in mid-August 1914. Like troops on all sides, the soldiers of the BEF believed that the war would soon be over. They would prove to be tragically mistaken.

The Fronts are Established

1914

When the Germans went to war in August 1914, their plan was to defeat France before turning east to fight Russia. They defeated the Russians at Tannenberg in East Prussia, but were repulsed in France at the Marne.

08/04/1914

READY FOR WAR
By August 1914 many European countries had millions of soldiers ready for war—a mix of professional soldiers, conscripts, and trained civilian reservists. These vast armies were moved to the front with impressive speed and efficiency. Most people expected the war to be won or lost by Christmas.

08/23/1914

THE BATTLE OF TANNENBERG
The Russians mobilized faster than expected and advanced across the German border into East Prussia. The Germans deployed primitive aircraft to observe the Russians' movements. Commanded by General Paul von Hindenburg and his chief of staff, Erich Ludendorff, the German army outmaneuvered the Russians at Tannenberg in a stunning victory.

08/30/1914

> **A soldier** who can no longer advance… **must be killed** where he stands **rather than draw back**.
>
> FRENCH GENERAL JOSEPH JOFFRE, SEPTEMBER 5, 1914

09/05/1914

TAXIS TO THE FRONT
From September 5, General Joseph Gallieni, commanding the French garrison in Paris, struck at the exposed flank of the German armies passing east of the city toward the Marne. During the fight, Gallieni commandeered taxis and buses to rush reserves from Paris to the front. The cabs became famous as the "taxis of the Marne."

09/12/1914

FIGHTING AT YPRES
The fight developed into a race to the sea. A series of battles were fought closer and closer to the northern coast, ending in a savage encounter at Ypres in western Belgium, where the two sides fought to a standstill. The Allies lost more than 300,000 men in the first four months of the war.

12/25/1914

CHRISTMAS TRUCE By the end of 1914, the opposing armies on the Western front had dug into lines of trenches. Soldiers faced one another across a narrow strip of "no man's land." At Christmas some declared a spontaneous truce, climbing out of the trenches to exchange gifts and play soccer. But the truce quickly ended and the war continued, with no victory in sight for either side.

08/04/1914

BELGIUM INVADED
The Germans invaded neutral Belgium, intending to march swiftly on to France, but the small Belgian army put up a stiff fight. At the city of Liège, the Germans had to deploy massive siege guns to batter down fortifications. Frustrated by Belgian resistance, German troops killed many civilians and burned down the university library at Louvain.

08/09/1914

FRENCH AND BRITISH LOSSES French troops attacked along France's border with Germany. Wearing bright uniforms, they made easy targets for German machine guns and suffered massive casualties. The British Expeditionary Force (BEF), which crossed the Channel to aid France, found itself in the path of the German advance through Belgium. After a pitched battle at Mons, the British fell back.

RUSSIAN SETBACKS
More than 90,000 Russian soldiers surrendered at Tannenberg and were captured. The Russian commander General Alexander Samsonov committed suicide. In Germany, Hindenburg and Ludendorff were hailed as national heroes. However, even after another defeat at the Battle of the Masurian Lakes, Russia fought on.

09/01/1914

ALLIES RETREAT
On the Western Front, the Germans advanced through Belgium into France. The French and British armies fell back to the Marne River, east of Paris, by early September. But the long march exhausted and disorganized the German forces. The French commander, General Joseph Joffre, prepared a counterattack.

09/05/1914

BRITISH AT THE MARNE The BEF turned to counterattack alongside Joffre's French armies. The Germans, shaken by Gallieni's attack on their flank, reversed direction and withdrew, abandoning all hope of a quick victory in the West.

FRENCH CLUB Primitive weapons were improvised for use in raids on opposing trenches, when enemy troops might be clubbed or stabbed at close quarters.

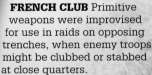

1914

Trench Warfare

The early days of World War I saw horrendous casualties on both sides, as outdated military tactics encountered the unprecedented killing power of mechanized weaponry. Infantry and cavalry units charging over open ground were easy prey for machine guns and artillery. A new arms race began, this time a defensive one. Trenches developed from a simple line of cover, such as this outpost where German troops are sleeping, into extensive underground complexes where fighting men lived and died. Conditions were miserable—the trenches filled with mud, ice, and rats, and shells, snipers, and gas attacks could bring death at any moment. By the end of the war, new weapons such as tanks, and new tactics such as the creeping artillery barrage had evolved to break through defensive lines. The face of warfare had changed forever, but at the cost of the lives of a generation of young men.

Aircraft Go to War

1911–1918

The first use of aircraft in war was in 1911, when Italian airmen dropped bombs on Turkish troops in Libya. At the start of World War I in August 1914, combatant countries had only a few hundred aircraft among them. By the war's end, tens of thousands of aircraft were in action.

11/01/1911

PRIMITIVE AIRCRAFT Until the beginning of World War I, military aircraft were flimsy, accident-prone machines, with a top speed of around 60 mph (100 kph). One such aircraft was the Rumpler Taube, recognizable by its swept-back, birdlike wings.

09/08/1915

ZEPPELIN AIR RAID In 1915 the Germans began air raids on British cities using Zeppelin and Schütte-Lanze airships. These huge, lighter-than-air machines carried a heavier bombload than the airplanes of the era and caused substantial damage. On September 8, 1915, 22 civilians were killed in an air raid on London.

THIS IS A PIECE OF GENUINE **ZEPPELIN WIRE,** FROM THE FIRST ZEPPELIN BROUGHT DOWN AT CUFFLEY IN ESSEX SEPT. 3RD. 1916.

Given by H.M. War Office exclusively to the British Red Cross Society.

ZEPPELIN WIRE Wire from a crashed German airship was used to make brooches to raise funds for the British Red Cross.

3/31/1916

08/01/1917

THE FLYING CIRCUS By 1917 aircraft with machine guns were engaging in aerial combat over the Western Front. Germany's most successful fighter squadron was Jasta 11. The squadron formed part of the "Flying Circus" air wing, so called for the bright colors in which its aircraft were painted.

> **Fight on** and **fly on** to the last drop of **blood** and… to the last **beat of the heart**.
>
> **GERMAN AIR ACE MANFRED VON RICHTHOFEN, DRINKING A TOAST TO FELLOW PILOTS, 1917**

SEEING THE ENEMY Initially aircraft served as eyes in the sky. From 1915 onward, slow-moving aircraft equipped with heavy cameras flew up and down the Western Front taking photos of enemy trenches. The early days of the war also saw the beginnings of naval aviation, with air raids launched from basic aircraft carriers.

EARLY BOMBERS At first, techniques for aerial bombing were basic, with grenades dropped by hand from the side of the aircraft. As the war went on, more sophisticated bomber aircraft evolved with automatic release mechanisms and aiming devices. The effectiveness of bombing was limited by the small weight that aircraft at the time could carry. However, some larger bombers were built, with two or four engines, to carry out raids on enemy cities.

AIRSHIP SHOT DOWN As British air defenses improved, slow-moving airships proved vulnerable to fighter planes and ground fire. This German Zeppelin L15 was among those shot down by antiaircraft guns over the Thames estuary.

WARTIME LESSON British schoolchildren were taught how to respond to bombing, with an emphasis on "pluck." A blackout (ban on lighting) was enforced and civilians took refuge in Underground stations during heavy raids. In all, 1,414 people were killed in raids by German aircraft on Britain during World War I.

If the Zeppelins come, Keep indoors. Put lights out and keep quiet. British means Pluck

ALLIES IN THE AIR Before the USA entered the war in 1917, hundreds of American pilots fought for France as volunteers. Their most famous squadron was the Lafayette Escadrille, which earned a high reputation during the Battle of Verdun in 1916. In 1917 they were integrated into the US Army Air Service.

THE BLUE MAX Fighter "aces"— pilots who shot down many enemy aircraft— became popular heroes, celebrated as "knights of the air." In Germany, aces were awarded the coveted *Pour le Mérite* military decoration, commonly known as the Blue Max.

THE RED BARON A former cavalry officer, Baron von Richthofen was one of the outstanding German fighter aces of World War I. He commanded the Flying Circus air wing in 1917, and his red-painted fighter earned him the nickname "Red Baron." He is credited with shooting down 80 enemy airplanes.

A SOLDIER LAID TO REST Baron von Richthofen was shot down over Allied lines in April 1918. He was buried by his enemies with full military honors.

Gallipoli Campaign

1914–1916

Turkey entered World War I as an ally of Germany in October 1914. Seeking an alternative to the stalemate on the Western Front, British First Lord of the Admiralty Winston Churchill proposed an attack on the Turks. Instead of an easy victory, landings at Gallipoli on April 25, 1915 proved to be a costly military disaster and a brutal initiation for troops from Australia and New Zealand.

03/18/1915

ATTEMPT TO BREACH THE DARDANELLES
British and French warships tried to steam through the Dardanelles strait into the Sea of Marmara and bombard the Turkish capital of Constantinople. Attacked by shore guns, they sailed into an uncleared minefield. Three battleships were sunk and the operation failed.

04/25/1915

INFANTRY HEAD FOR GALLIPOLI The Allies turned the Aegean island of Lemnos into their advanced base for the invasion. It was there that troops embarked to be carried to the Gallipoli peninsula. Hamilton had decided to carry out landings at several places where he believed Turkish resistance would be weakest.

04/25/1915

BRITISH ADVANCES
Most British troops went ashore at Cape Helles on the southern tip of Gallipoli. They suffered heavy casualties from Turkish fire during the landings and were then slow to advance inland. This gave the Turks time to form an impregnable defensive line across the peninsula to the north of the landing site.

04/25/1915

RENEWING THE CHARGE Shortly after the landings, the fighting at Gallipoli settled into the stalemate of trench warfare. When troops charged at enemy trenches with bayonets, many were cut down by machine guns.

05/26/1915

CHURCHILL SACKED By late May 1915 it was obvious that the Gallipoli campaign was in serious difficulty. Winston Churchill, the British politician who had most actively promoted the operation, was forced out of the government. But Britain was unwilling to abandon Gallipoli. On August 6 fresh troops poured in at Suvla Bay on the Aegean coast in an attempt to reignite the campaign.

TURKISH GRENADE
At Gallipoli, troops often fought at close quarters, hurling grenades, like this Turkish model, into enemy trenches.

08/04/1915

IMPROVISED WEAPONS
The Suvla Bay landing and renewed offensives elsewhere at Gallipoli failed to break the stalemate. Troops were trapped in filthy trenches in the heat of summer, suffering heavy losses to disease as well as in combat. Supplies were inadequate, and soldiers made improvised bombs out of empty jam cans.

08/06/1915

TURKISH PRISONERS
In August Australian troops won control of Turkish trenches at Lone Pine after heroic fighting, earning seven Australians the Victoria Cross medal. Many Turkish soldiers were taken prisoner, but the Allies were still unable to achieve a decisive breakthrough.

03/22/1915

BAPTISM BY FIRE

The governments of Australia and New Zealand supported Britain at the outbreak of World War I, and men flocked to volunteer for overseas service. Combined as Anzac (Australian and New Zealand Army Corps), their first deployment in the war would be the assault on Gallipoli.

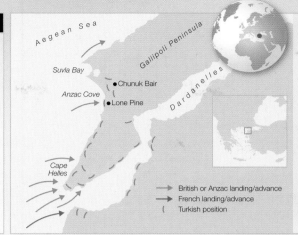

British or Anzac landing/advance
French landing/advance
Turkish position

LAND INVASION PLANNED

The Allies decided to land troops to capture the shores of the Dardanelles, to allow the navy to pass through. British General Sir Ian Hamilton was appointed to command the invasion, planning simultaneous landings at several points. Lacking accurate knowledge of the conditions they would face, the assault was a leap in the dark.

04/25/1915

LANDING AT ANZAC COVE The Anzac force landed farther north on the Aegean coast of the peninsula, at a site that became known as Anzac Cove. Steep cliffs were defended by Turkish forces. The Anzac troops were unable to break out of their previous beachhead and were pinned down with their backs to the sea.

> Damn **the Dardanelles**— they will be **our grave**.
>
> ADMIRAL LORD JOHN FISHER, IN A LETTER TO CHURCHILL, APRIL 5, 1915

08/07/1915

DEFIANT HERO

Heading the resolute Turkish defense at Gallipoli was Mustafa Kemal. He led the initial resistance to the landings and then inspired his men with a fanatical spirit during the long period of fighting. The reputation he gained at Gallipoli helped Kemal become Turkey's national leader after World War I.

01/09/1916

ALLIED FORCES LEAVE GALLIPOLI The Allied troops were finally evacuated from Gallipoli in January 1916. Carried out without significant losses, the withdrawal was the best executed part of the entire operation.

The Somme

1916

The first day of the Battle of the Somme brought carnage on an unprecedented scale. Tens of thousands of soldiers, many of them entering combat for the first time, were cut down by machine guns as they assaulted German trenches. The battle continued for five months at a staggering cost in lives, a brutal introduction to the horrors of mechanized warfare.

08/04/1914

KITCHENER'S ARMIES At the outbreak of World War I, Britain's army was relatively small, and made up of professional soldiers. Lord Horatio Kitchener, Secretary of State for War, put out a call across the country for volunteers to join up for the duration of the war. They would form Britain's first mass citizen armies.

12/18/1915

05/30/1916

SOLDIERS AT THE FRONT The war in France had reached stalemate, with both sides dug into fortified trenches. British commander Douglas Haig planned to use the new army to punch through the deadlock.

06/23/1916

ARTILLERY BARRAGE Haig ordered a massive artillery bombardment as a prelude to the infantry assault. More than 2,000 guns pounded the German line for eight days. Hague believed that the German defences would be crushed and his soldiers would simply walk into the enemy trenches. He was tragically mistaken.

07/01/1916

WOUNDED MEN More than 35,000 British and Commonwealth soldiers were wounded on the first day of the Somme. Many lay stranded for days in no man's land, hiding in shell holes or hooked on the German barbed wire. The lucky ones were brought back by stretcher parties under cover of darkness.

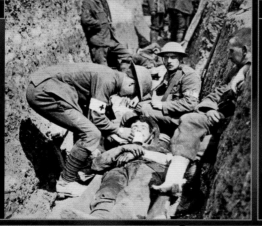

07/28/1916

FIGHTING CONTINUES The British and their French allies continued the offensive over the following months. Both sides employed poison gas in their attempts to breach the enemy fortifications, adding to the terror of life on the Western Front.

09/15/1916

FIRST USE OF TANKS It was during the Battle of the Somme that tanks first entered warfare. The British deployed 32 slow-moving, unreliable Mark I tanks to lead an attack at Flers-Courcelette on September 15.

11/18/1916

TRENCHES TAKEN By the time the Somme offensive was called off in November, British and French soldiers were occupying former German trenches. But their small territorial gains had come at the cost of half a million casualties. The Germans had suffered similar losses in ill-judged counter-attacks.

QUEUING TO ENLIST

Hundreds of thousands of British men rushed to sign up for the army—initially far more than could be equipped with weapons or uniforms. Recruitment and training continued through 1915. Many of the volunteers joined up with colleagues from their local town, workplace, or even sports club. These groups of friends were known as the "pals' battalions".

04/28/1916

WOMEN AT WORK

The rapidly expanding army required a vast amount of equipment, and British factories began to produce guns, bullets, and shells on a massive scale. As men left to join the fighting, women took over many traditionally male jobs. Almost a million women were employed in British arms factories by the war's end.

07/01/1916

OVER THE TOP

At 7:30 am on July 1, 1916, heavily laden British infantry climbed out of their trenches to begin the assault. The Germans, had been protected from artillery fire by deep dug-outs and emerged to man their machine-guns. They mowed down the advancing troops in their thousands. Almost 20,000 were killed in a single day.

> " The **nation** must be prepared to see **heavy casualty** lists. "
>
> GENERAL DOUGLAS HAIG, JUNE 1916

FIELD TELEPHONE

Telephone lines were the sole link between commanders and troops.

Ireland's Easter Rising

1914–1922

Ireland was on the verge of being granted partial self-government, or Home Rule, by Britain when the outbreak of World War I in August 1914 caused the measure to be postponed. At Easter 1916, a minority of Irish Republicans staged an armed uprising in Dublin. The rising was suppressed, but propelled southern Ireland on the road to full independence from Britain.

04/25/1914
ARMED VOLUNTEERS
Home Rule was welcomed by Irish Catholics but opposed by Irish Protestants, who feared Catholic domination. Protestants formed the Ulster Volunteer Force (UVF) to resist Home Rule, and armed themselves with illegally imported weapons. Catholics formed their own paramilitary force, the Irish Volunteers.

08/01/1915
CALLS FOR REVOLT
A minority of Irish Catholics instead saw the war as a chance to revolt against British rule. Patrick Pearse, a leader of the Irish Volunteers and of the secret Irish Republican Brotherhood, led preparations for an uprising, supported by James Connolly's small Citizen Army.

04/21/1916
OVERSEAS HELP
Roger Casement, a former British diplomat devoted to the cause of Irish nationalism, tried to organize German support for an uprising in Ireland. Germany, eager to disrupt the British war effort, sent the rebels a weapons shipment by sea, but the British intercepted it. Casement was arrested and hanged.

04/24/1916
EXCHANGE OF FIRE British troops engaged in fierce gun battles with the rebels, suffering heavy casualties. More than 500 soldiers were killed or wounded. The army brought in artillery to shell rebel positions that were resistant to infantry assault.

04/29/1916
SURRENDER On April 29, with their headquarters at the General Post Office in flames, the rebels surrendered. Fifteen leaders of the uprising, including Pearse and Connolly, were executed by firing squad after trial by a military court. Éamon de Valera (who would later become the first head of the Irish Free State following independence) was spared.

04/30/1916

DUBLIN AFTER THE BATTLE Much of central Dublin was wrecked in the fighting—buildings were battered by shelling and gutted by fire. There were more than 2,000 civilian casualties.

BULLET CRUCIFIX
This brass crucifix was made from rifle bullets fired during the Easter Rising by a British soldier.

05/02/1916

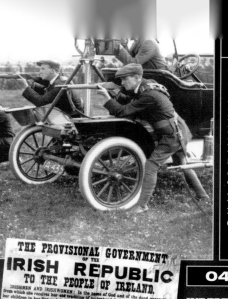

08/04/1914

WAR WITH GERMANY
The outbreak of war in August 1914 averted a probable armed conflict between Catholic and Protestant Irish. Men of both denominations were swept up in the initial enthusiasm for the war. The Home Rule bill became law, but its implementation was deferred during the war.

09/01/1914

LEAVING FOR FRANCE
The Protestant Ulster Volunteers were incorporated directly into the British Army as the 36th Ulster Division. Many of the Catholic Irish Volunteers also joined up, forming the 16th Irish Division. Both divisions marched off to fight and die in trench warfare in France.

04/24/1916

INDEPENDENCE PROCLAMATION
On Easter Monday 1916, Patrick Pearse read a proclamation of Irish independence at Dublin General Post Office. Armed rebels seized key buildings across the city.

04/24/1916

STREET FIGHTING
Most Irish Volunteers did not join the rising, but about 1,600 rebels manned barricades and fortified buildings as British troops were sent in to retake Dublin.

> ## "Ireland, through us, **summons her children** to her flag and strikes for her **freedom**. "
>
> PATRICK PEARSE, PROCLAMATION OF THE PROVISIONAL GOVERNMENT, APRIL 24, 1916

REBEL PRISONERS
Almost 1,500 rebels were sent to internment camps. Most were released in 1916, returning to lead the growing agitation for Irish independence. By December 1918, the Republican Sinn Féin party was able to win most of the southern Irish seats in a UK general election, and set up its own parliament in Dublin.

06/01/1922

IRISH MARTYRS
The rebels executed after the Easter Rising were remembered as martyrs for the Irish cause, their graves the object of annual ceremonies of commemoration. By the time this wreath was laid on Pearse's grave in June 1922, southern Ireland was on its way to becoming independent as the Irish Free State.

Arab Revolt

1914–1919

In 1914 Turkey ruled most of the Arab lands of the Middle East. When the Turks joined World War I on the German side, the British encouraged the Arabs to rise in armed rebellion, promising them independence after the war—a promise that was only partially kept.

FAISAL IBN HUSSEIN

A member of the Hashemite clan, traditional leaders of the Arabian Hejaz, Prince Faisal was the leader of the revolt.

T. E. LAWRENCE

A British intelligence officer, Lawrence joined Faisal in 1916 and became his closest ally in the war against the Turks.

ARMY UNIFORM The Turkish infantry wore khaki-colored uniforms. The brown jacket and black leather belt were similar in style to German uniforms, but the brown kalabash hat gave them a distinctive Turkish touch.

12/03/1917

HEJAZ RAILWAY UNDER ATTACK Trained by Lawrence in guerrilla warfare, Faisal's Arab fighters carried out a campaign of sabotage and hit-and-run attack. Running between Damascus and Medina, the Hejaz Railway was a tempting target. Trains were ambushed and sections of the line repeatedly blown up.

10/01/1917

ARAB CAVALRY ON THE MOVE With Aqaba as their base, Faisal's camel-mounted forces, by now known as the Northern Army, began long-distance raids as far north as Syria, and supported the British army that was advancing from Egypt.

PROCLAMATION OF REVOLT On June 27, 1916, Hussein bin Ali, Sharif of Mecca and Prince Faisal's father, issued a formal proclamation announcing the start of the Arab revolt. He promised to free the Arabs "from the rule of strangers" and to uphold the Muslim faith.

12/15/1916

FAISAL'S MILITARY ADVISOR A former archaeologist and Middle East expert, Lawrence fitted in with the Arabian tribesmen he fought alongside, adopting traditional Arab dress and customs. He provided Prince Faisal with military advice and liaised between the Arabs and the British. After helping defend the rebel-held port of Yenbo in December 1916, he gained the complete trust of rebel commanders.

07/06/1917

AQABA TAKEN Arab fighters captured the port of Aqaba in July 1917 in a bold desert offensive. The port allowed the Arabs to receive supplies of money and weapons shipped in from British-controlled Egypt. Faisal shifted his headquarters to Aqaba and it became his base of operations for the remainder of the war.

> " ... **Arab-speaking** peoples [must] be recognized as **independent sovereign** peoples...
>
> **FAISAL IBN HUSSEIN, LEADER OF THE ARAB REVOLT, JANUARY 1919** "

11/02/1917

TURKS IN SYRIA The Turkish army was defeated in a major battle against British and Commonwealth forces at Gaza in November 1917, but the Turks were determined to hold on to Palestine and Syria. The Turkish army paraded through the streets of the Syrian capital, Damascus.

12/30/1917

JERUSALEM FALLS TO THE BRITISH In December 1917, British General Edmund Allenby led his army into Jerusalem. The capture of the holy city was a great symbolic victory for Britain, but it opened the door to future disputes. Britain had promised the Jews a homeland in Palestine, contradicting promises they had made to the Arabs.

10/03/1918

THE WAR ENDS In October 1918 Damascus fell to Faisal's fighters and Australian cavalry operating under Allenby's command. Turkey surrendered soon after, ending the war in the Middle East. The following year, Faisal set up an independent Arab government in Damascus, proclaiming himself King of Syria.

01/18/1919

PEACE CONFERENCE Faisal attended a peace conference in Paris, hoping to confirm his independent Arab state. Instead, the British and French split the Middle East between them, Britain taking Palestine and Jordan, and France Syria and Lebanon. The British later compensated Faisal by making him King of Iraq.

CHANGING BORDERS World War I ended Ottoman dominance in the Middle East. After the war, Britain and France took control of large areas of the region, under the mandate of the newly formed League of Nations, despite Arab protests.

OTTOMAN EMPIRE

SYRIA

Mediterranean Sea

• Damascus

MESOPOTAMIA

PALESTINE
Jerusalem •

Aqaba •

ARABIA

EGYPT

Red Sea

Ottoman Empire 1914
— Hejaz Railway

• Medina

The Battle of Verdun

1916

By 1916 the war in France had reached a stalemate, as German troops faced French and British forces in static lines of trenches. German General Erich von Falkenhayn planned a major offensive against the French, choosing the fortress city of Verdun, near the northeastern edge of France, as his target. Almost 700,000 men lost their lives in the battle of attrition that followed.

01/20/1916

GERMANS PREPARE FOR OFFENSIVE
In January 1916 around 1,200 German heavy guns and vast quantities of shells were moved to the front near Verdun. The French front line in this sector consisted of shallow trenches thinly manned by infantry. Delayed by bad weather, the German offensive opened on February 21.

> "
> The forces of **France will bleed** to death…
> "
>
> GERMAN CHIEF OF STAFF ERICH VON FALKENHAYN, SPEAKING TO KAISER WILLIAM II, DECEMBER 25, 1915

02/24/1916

THE FRENCH FIGHT BACK
The French high command rejected the option of a withdrawal from Verdun and instead decided to hold on at all costs. General Philippe Pétain kept his troops on the defensive. They remained behind city walls and bombarded the attackers with artillery fire. The German advance was halted. At the same time, French reinforcements were rushed to the battlefield.

02/25/1916

06/03/1916

STUBBORN FRENCH DEFENSE From March onward, the French endured repeated attacks. After prolonged fighting, the Mort Homme ridge on the northwestern edge of Verdun fell to the Germans in late May. To the northeast, Fort Vaux, which had survived for months under heavy bombardment, was finally taken by German troops on June 7.

07/06/1916

DEFENSES FORTIFIED
France increased its output of artillery shells to meet the growing demands of the fighting at Verdun, but through the month of June it appeared the Germans might nonetheless force a French retreat. In July the British launched an offensive at the Somme, and Germany was forced to transfer troops from Verdun. The Germans no longer had the strength to achieve a decisive breakthrough.

10/21/1916

FRENCH RECOVER TERRITORY In the last stage of the Battle of Verdun, the initiative passed to the French. Commanded by the newly appointed General Robert Nivelle, French troops carried out a series of dogged attacks that regained most of the ground they had lost. Even hurling rocks became a valid way of fighting at close quarters.

02/24/1916

INITIAL GERMAN SUCCESS The Germans hammered French trenches with a massive artillery bombardment, after which German infantry swept unstoppably forward. Crossing the trench line they quickly took Fort Douaumont, the largest of a ring of fortresses protecting Verdun, with barely a shot fired.

MOVING SUPPLIES ON THE VOIE SACRÉE Supply was a major problem for the French army at Verdun. A single road connected the battlefield to the rear areas. Every soldier, every gun, and every load of munitions had to travel along this narrow route, which became known as the Voie Sacrée (the Sacred Road). French trucks plied the road incessantly, one passing on average every 14 seconds. The strain on drivers and vehicles was intense.

02/25/1916

DOGGED FIGHTING French casualties were heavy in the repeated pattern of attack and counterattack. To maintain morale, Pétain instituted a system of troop rotation, so that usually no soldier fought at the front for more than eight days.

08/27/1916

GERMAN CHANGE OF COMMAND General Falkenhayn was sacked as Germany's senior commander. Although his attack had caused the French heavy casualties, it had been at a high cost to his own troops. Field Marshal Paul von Hindenburg replaced Falkenhayn and quickly cancelled all further attempts to take Verdun.

FRENCH MACHINE GUN The gas-operated French Hotchkiss MLE 1914 machine gun was typical of weapons used by both sides at Verdun. Its rapid rate of fire caused heavy casualties among troops advancing over open ground.

12/19/1916

A COSTLY BATTLE The fighting at Verdun caused devastation on an incredible scale. In addition to those killed, more than 400,000 men were wounded, many hideously injured by poison gas or high explosives. The following year, there were widespread mutinies in the French army to protest the unbearable losses.

Revolution in Russia

1917–1922

For centuries the czars had ruled as absolute monarchs of the Russian Empire, but revolution was in the air. The revolt of 1905 had forced Czar Nicholas II to make some concessions to parliamentary rule, but power and wealth remained in the hands of the elite. When workers and soldiers joined a massive strike in St. Petersburg, the monarchy crumbled, sparking a bloody struggle that would give rise to the world's first communist state.

03/08/1917

CZAR OVERTHROWN Workers in St. Petersburg called a huge strike to protest against food shortages. Soldiers ordered to arrest the protesters instead chose to join them. The rebels formed the Petrograd Soviet (St. Petersburg Council) and, as their power grew, the Czar was persuaded to abdicate.

07/16/1917

PROTESTORS SHOT IN PETROGRAD Protests against the Provisional Government in July 1917 were suppressed when soldiers fired into a crowd in Petrograd. The Bolsheviks were blamed for the disturbances and Lenin fled the country once again to avoid arrest.

> **Bread, peace,** and **land**!

BOLSHEVIK SLOGAN
1917

09/01/1917

ARMING THE RED GUARD The Petrograd Soviet remained a rival to the Provisional Government's power base. Their position was strengthened when Kerensky, fearing a coup by the Russian army, allowed them to take up arms. The coup was averted, but the newly formed Red Guard were now a military force.

12/16/1917

04/16/1917

LENIN RETURNS

The socialist Bolshevik movement had long advocated revolution in Russia. Their exiled leader, Vladimir Lenin, hurried back, aided by Germany. The Russian parliament proclaimed a Provisional Government to replace the Czar, but Lenin called for nothing short of full socialist revolution.

07/01/1917

FAILED OFFENSIVE

Alexander Kerensky emerged as the leading figure in the Provisional Government. In 1917 he renewed Russia's involvement in World War I, sending troops to Galicia. The military offensive failed and exhausted soldiers mutinied, forming elected committees, or soviets.

09/25/1917

TROTSKY PREPARES A TAKEOVER

Following the failed coup, the Bolsheviks gained a majority in the Petrograd Soviet. With Lenin fled to Finland, his ally Leon Trotsky took control of the socialist movement. He quickly set about organizing the armed overthrow of Kerensky's Provisional Government.

11/07/1917

LENIN SEIZES POWER

Lenin returned to Russia in October, and on November 7 soldiers, sailors, and Red Guards loyal to the Petrograd Soviet seized control of St. Petersburg and drove out the Provisional Government. Lenin declared himself leader of a new all-Bolshevik government of "people's commissars."

RUSSIAN CIVIL WAR

After taking power in Petrograd, the Bolsheviks set out to extend their authority over the rest of the Russian empire. The ensuing civil war between the Bolshevik Red Army and anti-Bolshevik "White" forces lasted more than three years, causing mass death and widespread destruction in Russian territories.

01/05/1918

DEMOCRACY DENIED

In January 1918, a democratically elected Constituent Assembly met in Petrograd, only a minority of whom were Bolsheviks. Determined to maintain his one-party government, Lenin had the Assembly dispersed at bayonet point, dashing hopes of a democratic Russia.

07/16/1918

CZAR AND HIS FAMILY MURDERED

By summer 1918, former Czar Nicholas II was a prisoner of the Bolsheviks. On July 16, Nicholas, his wife, and their five children were shot dead in the cellar of a house in Ekaterinburg, central Russia. A family doctor and three servants were also murdered.

08/01/1919

FOREIGN TROOPS IN RUSSIA

From summer 1918 foreign powers including American forces intervened in Russia, supporting the czarist White forces in the Civil War. The foreign troops did little fighting, however, and could not prevent the eventual defeat of the Whites by the Bolshevik Red Army.

12/30/1922

FOUNDING OF THE SOVIET UNION

By 1922, the Bolsheviks, renamed Communists, had established their rule over most of the former Russian empire. At the end of 1922, the Communists founded the Union of Soviet Socialist Republics, or Soviet Union, which Lenin led as a single-party state.

RED ARMY BADGE

The Bolsheviks adopted the red star and the hammer and sickle as their insignia.

The War Ends

1917–1919

After a series of mighty battles in 1917–1918, Germany collapsed in military defeat and political upheaval. The victorious powers redrew the map of Europe at the Paris Peace Conference of 1919, but failed to establish a durable peace.

04/06/1917

USA JOINS THE WAR Provoked by German U-boat (submarine) attacks on American merchant ships, the USA declared war on Germany on April 6, 1917. The first troops of the American Expeditionary Force, nicknamed the "doughboys," were dispatched to France that summer, but they did not enter combat until 1918.

06/01/1918

US MARINES AT BELLEAU WOOD The American General John Pershing threw his troops into action to help the Allies stop the advancing Germans. In early June 1918, at Belleau Wood in France, the US Marines fought so fiercely that the Germans dubbed them "devil dogs." Under Pershing, the US troops launched an offensive at St. Mihiel in northeastern France in September. By the war's end there were 1.4 million US combat troops in Europe.

07/01/1918

PRISONERS OF WAR Demoralized at the prospect of defeat, more than 300,000 German soldiers surrendered in the final months of the war, and were imprisoned in camps in France.

10/02/1918

ALLIED VICTORY From August to November 1918, the Allies carried out a series of successful attacks, known as the Hundred Days' Offensive. Using tanks and aircraft, as well as improved infantry and artillery tactics, they broke through the defenses of the German Hindenburg Line. British soldiers seized the St. Quentin Canal, one of a series of holes punched in the German defenses.

11/08/1918

SAILORS' MUTINY In a series of incidents, German sailors mutinied, refusing orders to sail on a final death-or-glory mission against the British fleet. The mutiny at the port of Kiel triggered uprisings in cities across the country. The German ruler Kaiser Wilhelm II fled into exile. On November 9 Germany became a republic.

11/10/1918

ARMISTICE SIGNED On the night of November 10, German political and military representatives signed an armistice, agreeing to end the fighting on terms laid down by the Allies. The signing took place in a railroad car in the Forest of Compiègne in eastern France. The fighting was to stop at 11 am on November 11.

10/12/1917

THE PASSCHENDAELE STALEMATE British and Commonwealth troops launched a series of offensives in Flanders, culminating in the notorious Battle of Passchendaele. Fighting in atrocious conditions, with the battlefield a sea of mud, they gained only a few miles of ground at a fearful cost in dead and wounded.

03/21/1918

GERMANS ATTACK In spring 1918 the Germans massed their forces on the Western Front for a major onslaught, which was their last hope to win the war. They launched the Spring Offensive, also known as *Kaisersschlacht,* on March 21. A major breakthrough, it drove the Allies back toward Paris but failed to achieve final victory.

> **"**
> We have **won the war**. Now we must **win the peace**.
>
> GEORGES CLEMENCEAU, FRENCH PRIME MINISTER, NOVEMBER 11, 1918
> **"**

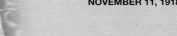

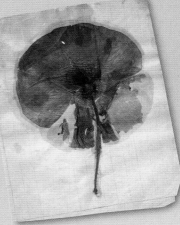

HAUNTING MEMORIAL This pressed Flanders poppy was sent by British Private Jack Mudd to his wife before he died at Passchendaele. The Flanders poppy became a symbol of remembrance for those killed in the war.

11/11/1918

ALLIED FORCES REJOICE The news of the armistice was greeted with wild and boisterous celebrations all across the victorious Allied nations. Soldiers on leave took the lead, relieved that they would not now be sent to die at the front. The war is thought to have cost 10 million lives, and the total of dead and wounded is estimated at 37 million.

06/28/1919

GERMANS SIGN THE VERSAILLES TREATY As onlookers struggled for a view of the event, German representatives signed a peace treaty in the Hall of Mirrors at Versailles, France. Most Germans resented the terms imposed on their country, especially the demand for reparations payments and the "war guilt" clause blaming the conflict on German aggression.

1919

Spanish Flu Pandemic

On March 4, 1918 a soldier called Albert Gitchell reported sick on a US Army base in Kansas. Within a week, hundreds more had fallen ill with Spanish Flu, in what would become the most deadly natural disaster of the 20th century. Across the world, vast numbers of troops were returning from the battlefields of World War I, and the speed and scale of mass transit spread the disease with terrible swiftness. Victims experienced extreme fatigue and fever, as well as a wracking cough that caused bleeding inside the lungs. Mortality rates were staggering as war-shattered economies struggled to cope, and to families devastated by years of bitter fighting this new loss of life was heart-rending. Exact figures may never be known, but is it thought that, by the end of 1919, 500 million people across the world had been infected, and as many as 100 million of those (approximately 6 percent of the world's population) had died.

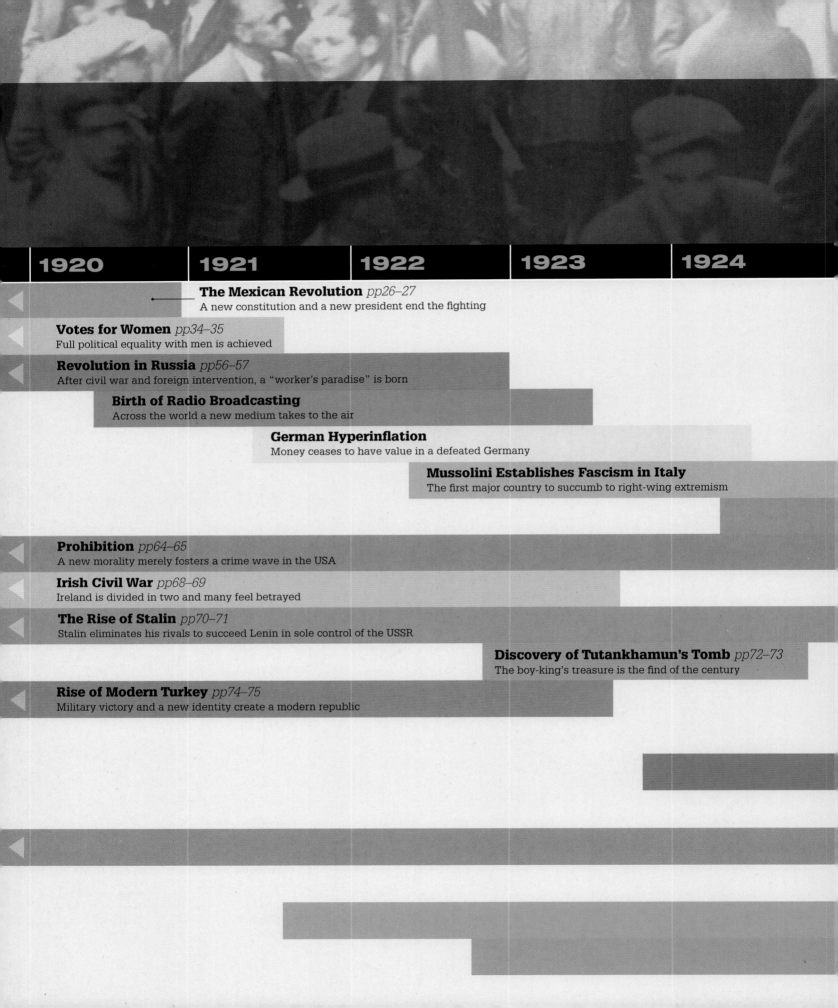

1920 **1921** **1922** **1923** **1924**

The Mexican Revolution *pp26–27*
A new constitution and a new president end the fighting

Votes for Women *pp34–35*
Full political equality with men is achieved

Revolution in Russia *pp56–57*
After civil war and foreign intervention, a "worker's paradise" is born

Birth of Radio Broadcasting
Across the world a new medium takes to the air

German Hyperinflation
Money ceases to have value in a defeated Germany

Mussolini Establishes Fascism in Italy
The first major country to succumb to right-wing extremism

Prohibition *pp64–65*
A new morality merely fosters a crime wave in the USA

Irish Civil War *pp68–69*
Ireland is divided in two and many feel betrayed

The Rise of Stalin *pp70–71*
Stalin eliminates his rivals to succeed Lenin in sole control of the USSR

Discovery of Tutankhamun's Tomb *pp72–73*
The boy-king's treasure is the find of the century

Rise of Modern Turkey *pp74–75*
Military victory and a new identity create a modern republic

1920-29

Search for Permanent Peace
Plans and treaties strive for a lasting settlement of Europe's affairs

The Great Depression *pp78–79*
Stock markets rocket up and then crash down with calamitous global consequences

Rise of the Nazis *pp86–87*
Dark forces gather in Germany's fragile democracy as economic disaster looms

Lindbergh Crosses the Atlantic
A glamorous new hero for the century of flight

Gandhi Resists British Rule *pp82–83*
Nonviolence and the fight for India's freedom

Talkies Revolutionize Cinema
The brief era of silence is killed by technology

China at War *pp88–89*
Ambitious and hungry, Japan seeks an empire in China

Mussolini Invades Ethiopia *pp92–93*
One of Africa's last independent states succumbs to a new Roman Empire

Prohibition

1919–1933

In 1919 the USA attempted to ban alcohol in a bid to reduce crime and immoral behavior. However, the "noble experiment," as it came to be known, was a huge failure. The law was widely violated and alcohol remained readily available through new clubs frequented by gangsters and bootleggers.

05/12/1919

BIDDING FOR THE BAN As industrial urban areas expanded, American society began to change. Alcoholism was on the rise, and the Prohibition movement grew as an effort to combat the social ills of excessive drinking. One of the more extreme advocates was preacher Billy Sunday, whose spicy sermons attracted both support and ridicule.

03/16/1921

THE SPEAKEASY IS BORN The public soon became weary of Prohibition. Speakeasies, or illegal drinking dens, sprang up in most communities and did a roaring trade. Many were not even that secret, because bribing the police was commonplace. Some 30,000 speakeasies were opened in New York City alone during the Prohibition era.

04/25/1923

ENFORCING THE LAW Federal Prohibition agents regularly raided speakeasies, arresting both owners and patrons. But corrupt cops often warned speakeasy operators of coming raids, and as one joint was closed down, another would soon spring up in its place.

06/06/1925

BREWED AT HOME As the ban came into effect, suppliers of illicit alcohol came up with substitutes. Moonshine, or home-brewed alcohol, could be made from wood scraps and plants. Corn whisky and "bathtub" gin led to a rise in alcohol-related deaths. The authorities struggled to contain the spread of home brewing, with little success.

11/13/1925

DISGUISED ARM OF THE LAW Enforcing the law became almost impossible. New York agents Izzy Einstein and Moe Smith relied on disguises during their raids, once posing as man and wife. Their record of 4,392 arrests and 5 million bottles of liquor confiscated attests to their dedication. They also refused to be bribed.

02/26/1926

THE JAZZ AGE Although the Roaring Twenties began on a dry note, people were determined to have fun. The speakeasies needed music to play to their patrons, and most of the jazz players of the age found ready employment. The nightclub scene exploded, gender roles shifted, and jazz music became intoxicating.

EARLY JAZZ RECORD Louis Armstrong, with his rasping voice and relaxed style, pointed toward a new, and distinctly American, jazz tradition.

02/14/1929

GANG WAR Secret bars were supplied with alcohol by gangs of bootleggers and criminal syndicates, who often resorted to open warfare. Alphonse "Scarface Al" Capone of Chicago was the most notorious gangster. He famously murdered seven rivals in what became known as the St. Valentine's Day Massacre.

10/28/1919

THE BAN BEGINS
Billy Sunday and his fellow campaigners got their way with the passing of the Volstead Act, despite opposition from President Wilson. The Act prohibited the manufacture, trade, and supply of any drink with an alcohol content greater than 0.5 percent. The battle for booze had begun.

02/01/1921

DOWN THE DRAIN
Initially law agents pursued enforcement with zeal, leaving no stone unturned in banishing booze from homes and bars. Many barrels of liquor ended up being poured into sewers.

"
Prohibition has made **nothing but trouble**.

INFAMOUS GANGSTER
AL CAPONE "

01/26/1926

CONCEALING LIQUOR
Many flouted the law by carrying illegal liquor flasks, inventing ingenious methods of smuggling booze. The term "bootlegging" referred to the practice of hiding bottles of liquor inside boots. Women could hide flasks strapped to their legs, hidden under skirts or overcoats.

BOOZING IN SECRET
During Prohibition, hard liquor gained favor because it packed more alcohol into a small quantity of liquid. This set of bottle and shot glasses is cleverly hidden in a kettlebell.

10/31/1931

TURN OF THE TIDE America sank into the Great Depression in the 1930s. People looked for relief and came to resent the ill-advised Prohibition. Revolt was in the air. Several large cities staged "We Want Beer" marches, pushing for repeal.

04/01/1933

END OF PROHIBITION
Prohibition came to a halt in 1933. Considered a failed social experiment, it was difficult to enforce and provided gangsters with revenue. Franklin D. Roosevelt campaigned for the Presidency promising to legalize alcohol. He was swept into the White House, along with several cases of legal beer.

A CENTURY OF

Art

The enormous social, cultural, and economic changes of the 20th century transformed artistic expression. In 1900, Paris was the art capital of the world. The French Impressionists prioritized light and movement over traditional academic formalism. Their work was seen as revolutionary, but it was only the first in a series of sea changes in the theory and practice of art. By the end of the century, art was no longer restricted to traditional forms, creating startling new modes of expression.

"THE CITY RISES" (1910) Umberto Boccioni's painting reflects the Italian Futurists' obsession with speed, the urban landscape, and modernity.

1900–1915 The first great challenge to the Impressionists was mounted by Cubism, pioneered by Pablo Picasso and Georges Braque. This radical style of painting ignored all previous traditions of perspective by showing the subject from several viewpoints at the same time. Cubism would inspire many other movements,

25,000

The approximate number of artworks produced by Picasso in his lifetime, including 13,500 paintings, ceramics, prints, and sculptures.

including Futurism and Surrealism. It also led the way to the pure abstraction of Kazimir Malevich and Pieter Mondrian, whose works depicted feelings rather than objects. At about the same time, Henri Matisse and André Derain (known as the Fauves or "wild beasts") were applying bold colors to their paintings. Color, they believed, should express the artist's feelings about a subject, rather than simply describe it. Their work had a major influence on the Expressionists in Germany, such as Wassily Kandinsky and Paul Klee.

"WOODEN CENTAUR" (1955) Pablo Picasso's Cubist works made him one of the most influential artists of the 20th century.

1915–1945 Reacting against the horrors of World War I, a group of writers and artists known as the Dadaists set out

1910s

ANTI-ART MOVEMENT In 1917, Marcel Duchamp submitted a porcelain urinal entitled "Fountain" to an exhibition as an example of "ready-made" art. It was a slap in the face to traditional art.

1930s

SURREALIST DREAMSCAPE Spanish surrealist Salvador Dalí explored Freudian ideas of the unconsious mind through painting, sculpture, photography, and film. He was a flamboyant self-publicist, famed for his grandiose behavior.

1940s

ACTION PAINTING Jackson Pollock believed that a painting had a life of its own that emerged through the process of creation. He created his paintings by throwing paint onto the canvas.

STREET ART Keith Haring's "Red Dog" series was inspired by the New York street culture of the 1980s.

to shock and provoke. Their anti-art, consisting of collages, montages, and kinetic (moving) sculptures, would prove highly influential later in the century. Surrealism, which emerged in the 1920s, was in part a rejection of Dadaism's negativity. It aimed to liberate the artist's imagination by tapping into the unconscious mind to discover a superior reality ("sur-reality").

1945–1960 In the Soviet Union art was dominated by socialist realism—officially approved pieces that glorified the worker. By contrast, abstract expressionism came to dominate Western modern art after 1945, emerging in New York among a group of painters that included Jackson Pollock and Mark Rothko. This emotionally intense, anarchic style aimed to capture emotional processes through the action of painting. In the late 1950s, a counter movement developed in the form of Pop Art, which played with iconic images from mass media, such as film stars and advertisement logos, to blur the boundaries between high art and popular culture.

1960– From the 1960s, conceptual art came to the fore. Artists considered themselves free to work in whatever form or material they wished—the concept of their work taking precedence over aesthetic considerations. Art works incorporating animal corpses, excrement, or blood were designed to provoke a visceral reaction from the viewer. At the same time, artists such as Francis Bacon and Lucian Freud continued to work in paint and canvas. By the end of the 20th century the notion of art had expanded to include everything from digital experiments to street graffiti, producing an unprecedented variety of forms and messages.

> # There is **no abstract art**. You must start with something. Afterward you can **remove** all traces of **reality**.
>
> PABLO PICASSO, 1934

"SURROUNDED ISLANDS" (1983)
For this installation, artists Christo and Jeanne-Claude surrounded 11 islands off Florida with floating pink fabric.

1950s

FIGURATIVE SCULPTURE The elongated bronze figures produced by Swiss surrealist Alberto Giacometti in the 1950s expressed the loneliness and alienation of human experience.

1960s

POP ART Andy Warhol's screenprinted works became icons of Pop Art, which used images from popular culture and advertising (such as soup cans and comic books) as the basis for works of art.

1970s

PERFORMANCE ART Influenced by conceptual art, Gilbert and George, who met as art students, declared themselves to be "living sculptures." Their matching tweed suits were part of the performance.

Irish Civil War

1919–1923

In 1919, Sinn Féin, the Irish nationalist party, declared an Irish Republic independent from British rule. A bitter war of independence followed, waged between Irish Republican Army (IRA) guerrillas and the hated "Black and Tans," a British auxiliary force. The war ended in July 1921, but within months, Irishmen would be fighting Irishmen in a bloody civil war that tore Ireland apart.

01/21/1919

ATLANTIC OCEAN

Londonderry • • NORTHERN IRELAND

Belfast •

• Galway   Dublin •

IRISH FREE STATE

Cork •

Celtic Sea

Northern Ireland
Irish Free State

IRELAND DIVIDED

Irish Republicans, led by Sinn Féin, issued a declaration demanding independence for all of Ireland. However, Irish Unionists living in the six largely Protestant counties in the north of Ireland sought to maintain union with Britain. War broke out between the IRA and British forces and their supporters.

12/06/1921

FREE STATE FOUNDED

The Anglo-Irish Treaty was agreed following the truce. An Irish Free State was established as a self-governing territory within the British Empire. Sinn Féin leaders Arthur Griffiths and Michael Collins led the Irish negotiators. However, for some Republicans, the treaty did not go far enough.

02/12/1922

TREATY ATTACKED

De Valera was one high-profile opponent. In a series of speeches he branded the treaty a betrayal of independence. He highlighted elements that seemed to support continuing British rule, such as the clause that obliged members of the Irish Dáil (parliament) to take an oath of allegiance to the British Crown.

06/28/1922

CIVIL WAR BEGINS

Bowing to British pressure to expel the IRA garrison, Collins ordered the bombardment of the Four Courts. The response was electric. For eight days street battles raged in Dublin before the Free State army gained control. Fighting then spread to the south and west of Ireland.

08/28/1922

"

I tell you this—early this morning I signed **my death warrant**.

IRISH POLITICIAN MICHAEL COLLINS ON THE ANGLO–IRISH TREATY, 1921

"

MEMORIAL BUST
This memorial to Michael Collins stands in Merrion Square, Dublin, Ireland.

MICHAEL COLLINS 1890–1922

05/24/1923

IRA DUMPS ARMS

Returning to guerrilla tactics, the anti-treaty IRA sabotaged railroads and burned the homes of Free State sympathizers. The Free State responded with military courts and summary executions. However, anti-treaty forces failed to find broad popular support, and by spring the campaign had fizzled out.

10/14/1920

BATTLE WITH THE BRITISH The IRA used guerrilla tactics, assaulting the British with bomb attacks and assassinations. The British and their supporters responded with brutality. The Black and Tans became infamous for their reprisal attacks on civilians.

07/09/1921

CEASEFIRE AGREED At last, exhausted by the bloody struggle, both sides agreed a peace. Crowds gathered in Dublin as Éamon de Valera, President of the Irish Republic, and Sinn Féin leader Arthur Griffith arrived to sign a truce with the British government.

04/14/1922

FOUR COURTS OCCUPIED Anti-treaty Republicans began to threaten a return to violence. A splinter group of 200 IRA militants, led by Rory O'Connor, occupied the Four Courts, the building in the center of Dublin that housed Ireland's law courts.

FUNERAL OF MICHAEL COLLINS As the violence rekindled, Michael Collins was killed by anti-treaty Republican forces in an ambush in County Cork. More than 500,000 people attended his funeral. Arthur Griffiths had died of a brain hemorrhage just 10 days before. The fragile Free State found itself without its two most prominent leaders.

08/15/1923

DE VALERA JAILED The civil war left deep scars. Almost 5,000 people had died, twice as many as were killed fighting the British. Éamon de Valera was arrested, along with thousands of other anti-treaty campaigners. Sinn Féin's dream of a fully independent Ireland would not be realized until 1937.

The Rise of Stalin

1917–1939

Joseph Stalin began life as Josif Dzhugashvili, a cobbler's son from Georgia. By the mid-1920s he had risen to become one of the most powerful men in the world, the leader of the Soviet Union. His rapid rise to power was based on masterful propaganda and a ruthless will to silence his political rivals by any means necessary. For many ordinary Russians his rule was a disaster. His economic policies led to widespread famine, and his paranoid political whims saw millions killed, imprisoned, and exiled. Nonetheless, his clever manipulation of public opinion left him a hero in the popular imagination, and his cult of personality endured for decades.

1924

LENIN'S FUNERAL
Lenin's death sparked mass public mourning across the USSR. In the power struggles that followed, Stalin suppressed the Last Testament and began to gather allies in his quest for power. His main rival was Leon Trotsky, who had led the Red Army in the civil war. Stalin had a plan to discredit him.

1927

TROTSKY'S FALL
Stalin's expert political machinations pushed Trotsky and his allies to the margins of the Communist Party. In 1927, Trotsky was expelled from the Party and later forced into exile. His family were killed or imprisoned, and he was eventually assassinated in Mexico City by a Soviet agent.

1929

MARCH TO THE FIELDS
Huge collective farms were established. The land was taken from kulaks, land-owning peasants, more than 5 million of whom were deported or sent to labor camps.

> "
> ### Ideas are more powerful than guns.
>
> **JOSEPH STALIN**
> 1942
> "

1917

PARTY MAN Stalin's revolutionary activities saw him exiled four times to Siberia by the czarist government. As editor of *Pravda*, the Communist Party paper, he supported Lenin in the October Revolution. Lenin appointed him General Secretary of the Communist Party as a reward, a post Stalin never relinquished.

1922

STALIN AND LENIN During Lenin's last illness Stalin was a frequent visitor to his country dacha. Lenin began to fear Stalin was using his position as General Secretary to build up a personal power base. In his Last Testament he proposed that Stalin should be replaced.

1928

FIVE-YEAR PLAN Now in sole charge, Stalin launched the Five-Year Plan, a campaign to boost Soviet industry. Factory workers were given ambitious daily targets for production. Those who failed to reach the required output were publicly criticized and humiliated.

WAR OF WORDS The slogan on this propaganda poster reads "The victory of the Five-Year Plan is a blow against capitalism."

1932

MANMADE FAMINE Collectivized agriculture proved a tragic failure. Grain grown on the collectives went to fill government quotas, leaving none to feed the peasant workforce. Productivity declined, and Ukraine, the main grain-growing region of the USSR, was hit by a devastating famine that led to millions of deaths.

1935

HERO OF LABOR Stalin pressed on with his plan. Success stories were lionized by his propaganda machine. Miner Alexei Stakhanov was said to have dug out a record 102 tons of coal in just under six hours, 14 times his quota. He became a hero, and fellow workers were urged to imitate his efforts.

1938

THE GREAT PURGE Ever fearful of dissent, Stalin mounted a campaign to destroy his political enemies, real and imagined. Suspected dissidents were rounded up and tortured. Some of the victims were forced to proclaim their guilt at show trials in Moscow. As many as 700,000 people were killed.

1939

OUT OF THE PICTURE Those who fell out of favor were not only killed but removed from history. Nikolai Yezhov was a head of the secret police renowned for his brutal interrogation methods. When he fell from favor, Stalin ordered him erased from official photographs, to destroy all record of their friendship.

Discovery of Tutankhamun's Tomb

1922–1924

At the turn of the century, many archaeologists believed that the Valley of the Kings, ancient Egypt's royal burial ground, held no more secrets. However, British archaeologist Howard Carter was on a lifelong mission to find the tomb of a young pharaoh named Tutankhamun. He was convinced that it lay somewhere beneath thousands of years of limestone rubble.

> With **trembling** hands, I made a tiny breach… **gold**—**everywhere** the glint of **gold**.

HOWARD CARTER DESCRIBES OPENING THE TOMB, NOVEMBER 26, 1922

11/23/1922

CARNARVON VISITS THE SITE Carnarvon immediately traveled to Egypt with his daughter, Lady Evelyn Herbert. The sealed doorway was opened. It revealed a passage leading to another sealed door marked with the royal impressions of Tutankhamun. With Carnarvon at his side, Carter started to break through this second door.

11/30/1922

TOURISTS THRONG THE SITE Once the press got wind of the discovery, tourists flocked to the site, keen to catch a glimpse of what had been found. Carter's men had to painstakingly carry the treasures out of the tomb on stretchers, under the eager gaze of photographers and reporters.

01/09/1923

STRIKING A DEAL Media attention soon began to interrupt the work. Carnarvon struck an exclusive deal with *The Times*, much to the disgust of other journalists. However, this provided more funds, enabling Carter to put together a formidable team of museum specialists and set up a field laboratory in the empty tomb of Seti II nearby. They continued investigating the newly discovered tomb.

02/17/1923

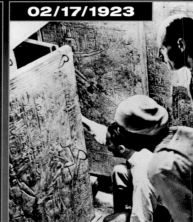

02/19/1923

RICHES UNCOVERED The burial chamber held an astonishing array of treasures. A time capsule of ancient Egyptian art, it contained golden shrines, jewelry, statues, and clothing.

04/05/1923

CURSE OF THE MUMMY Just seven weeks after the opening of the burial chamber, Carnarvon died of blood poisoning. This fueled rumors of an old "mummy's curse"—anyone disturbing a pharaoh's tomb would be punished. However, these rumors were probably a means to deter grave robbers seeking the treasures.

FUNERAL MASK Tutankhamun's magnificent funeral mask, discovered inside the sarcophagus, was made of two layers of beaten gold, inlaid with semiprecious stones. The mask weighs 22 lb (10 kg).

HOWARD CARTER

British archaeologist Howard Carter had been searching for Tutankhamun's tomb since 1914, but had so far met with little success.

11/04/1922

EXCAVATION WORK After seven unproductive years in the Valley of the Kings, Carter's benefactor Lord Carnarvon was threatening to pull out. Given just one more season to find the boy-king's tomb, Carter's luck changed when his team stumbled on some workmen's huts at the base of the tomb of Rameses VI. Excavation revealed a flight of 16 steps leading to a walled-up doorway. The door was stamped with the seal of the royal necropolis.

11/27/1922

ANTEROOM DISCOVERED As the hole in the second door became larger, Carter was able to peer inside. Holding up a small candle, he was stunned to see an anteroom packed with treasures. Gold furniture, broken chariots, and beautiful objects littered the floor. One of four rooms in the antechamber, it was the discovery of the century.

CARTER OPENS THE BURIAL CHAMBER It took Carter and his team more than 10 weeks to carefully clear and catalog the finds from two of the rooms. However, any attempt to open the final room, which Carter believed was the king's burial chamber, had to wait for permission from the Egyptian authorities. In February 1923 Carter and Carnarvon, accompanied by state officials, opened the sealed doorway and found the sarcophagus of Tutankhamun.

11/03/1924

MUMMY REVEALED
It took Carter more than a year to open and document the two outer layers of the sarcophagus. When he finally opened the third coffin, he found the mummy of Tutankhamun, covered with amulets and jewels. The mummy was pried loose, measured, and photographed, then rewrapped and laid to rest in its outer coffin.

Rise of Modern Turkey

1908–1923

In 1908 the Ottoman Empire included all of modern Turkey (Anatolia), most of the Middle East, and the southern Balkans. Dominated by Turks, its population also included Arabs, Greeks, Armenians, Kurds, Jews, and other ethnic minorities. However, this once powerful empire—an Islamic caliphate ruled by an autocratic Sultan—was in decline. A new movement wanted to bring Turkey into the modern world. At its head was the Committee of Union and Progress (CUP), a group of well-educated military officers known as the Young Turks.

08/03/1914

GERMAN ALLY The Ottoman Empire received military advice and aid from Germany. As Minister of War, Enver Pasha decided to ally with the Germans when World War I broke out in 1914.

02/25/1915

ARMENIANS MASSACRED The war raised ethnic tensions within the empire. Following a pro-Russian uprising in the city of Van, the government ordered the deportation of the entire Armenian population in eastern Anatolia. One million people were driven from their homes and up to 800,000 perished.

01/07/1917

IN THE THICK OF WAR As the war progressed, the Ottomans fought on several fronts—against Russia in the Caucasus, on the Balkan and Eastern Fronts in Europe, at Gallipoli, and in Sinai and Mesopotamia. They proved harder to defeat than the Allies had expected.

11/13/1918

ISTANBUL OCCUPIED The Ottoman capital, Istanbul, was bombed by British planes during the war. Following the Ottoman surrender, a British fleet sailed into Istanbul and occupied the city, dealing a severe blow to Turkish pride.

01/18/1919

PARTITIONING THE EMPIRE At peace talks in Paris, the Allies discussed the division of the Ottoman Empire. The Middle East would be divided between France and Britain, Greece would have the Aegean coastline, and Armenians their own state. The Turks, they thought, were too broken to resist.

05/19/1919

WAR OF INDEPENDENCE The hero of Gallipoli, Mustafa Kemal (on the right, talking to an advisor) was determined to retain an independent Turkish state. In May 1919 his forces landed at Samsun on the Black Sea and began organizing national resistance. By 1920 he had set up a parliament at Ankara that called upon Turks to reject the Allies' treaty.

08/26/1922

GREEK ASSAULT Kemal's first challenge was an invasion by Greek forces, who were welcomed by the ethnic Greek population of Smyrna (modern Izmir). After striking deep into Anatolia, the invaders were defeated by Kemal's army and forced to flee to the coast.

09/13/1922

SMYRNA BURNS Four days after the Turkish army took control of Smyrna, the port city was destroyed by fire. Greeks and Armenians trying to flee were trapped on the waterfront, as Allied ships stood by observing strict neutrality. Thousands died. Controversy still remains over who started the fire.

07/03/1908

YOUNG TURKS REVOLT

The revolt, led by two Young Turk officers, Enver Pasha and Niyazi Bey, began when an army regiment stationed in Macedonia rebelled and fled to the hills. Niyazi Bey headed a march to Istanbul to demand constitutional change. Protests spread and Sultan Abdulhamid agreed to democratic reform.

04/28/1909

SULTAN OVERTHROWN

Abdulhamid's reforms failed to satisfy the rebels. He was deposed and replaced by his brother Mehmet V. The Young Turks of the CUP took charge of the empire and introduced fundamental changes to reduce the power of the Sultan.

10/08/1912

BALKAN WARS The people of the Balkans saw the rebellion as their chance for independence. The Turks fought back, employing irregular troops such as these Albanians, but lost almost all of their Balkan territory.

10/26/1918

END OF THE WAR

At last, Ottoman soldiers in Syria were defeated by an alliance between the British and the Arabs. The war in the Middle East ended four days later with the signing of an armistice at Mudros. The Ottomans had lost more than 700,000 men in the conflict. Their empire was in ruins.

> ## No inch of the motherland may be abandoned...
>
> **MUSTAFA KEMAL ATATÜRK, IN AN ORDER TO THE TURKISH ARMY, AUGUST 26, 1921**

07/24/1923

TURKS CELEBRATE

The unexpected ferocity of the Turkish defense forced the Greeks into retreat. On November 1, 1922 Kemal's supporters celebrated victory. Signed on July 24, 1923, the Treaty of Lausanne established the frontiers of the modern Turkish state—a republic, with Kemal as president.

FAREWELL TO THE FEZ
Mustafa Kemal outlawed the traditional Ottoman fez as part of his modernizing reforms. He introduced Latin script and traveled the country teaching the new alphabet.

German Financial Crisis

In the aftermath of World War I, the new German goverment, the Weimar Republic, struggled to rebuild its economy. The victorious Allied powers demanded reparations in cash and material, and Germany was also burdened with a vast war debt. International confidence in the German currency, the mark, collapsed in 1922, causing runaway hyperinflation. By November 1923 a loaf of bread cost billions of marks. Banknotes became worthless just weeks after they were printed, good only for notepaper, kindling, or children's kites. The government paid off its debt with worthless notes, and in late 1923 a new currency was launched. Germans who had bank accounts or cash assets were ruined, but production and employment soon reached new heights. The years from 1924–1929, known as the Roaring Twenties, were an era of economic and cultural flourishing in Germany, until the Wall Street Crash in 1929 brought chaos across the Western world. The economic and political turmoil that followed would provide a platform for the rise of Hitler.

The Great Depression

1929–1941

North America recovered relatively briskly from the recession that followed World War I. While Europe struggled in the 1920s, American factories switched to producing consumer goods and the economy showed consistent growth. However, when ordinary Americans began investing heavily in the New York stock market in a desire to get rich quickly, the boom rapidly turned to bust.

10/29/1929

WALL STREET CRASH
After months of fevered speculation, share prices began to decline and the financial bubble burst on October 29. Panic hit Wall Street as more than 16 million shares were sold in a single day and distressed investors flooded the streets. Banks were forced to close, bankrupting millions overnight.

11/08/1930

MASS UNEMPLOYMENT
Following the Wall Street collapse and subsequent bank failures, businesses across the USA started laying off workers. Unemployed people took to the streets in New York, wearing banners stating their professions, and offering to work for a dollar a week. By 1933, 25 percent of American workers were unemployed.

01/29/1932

PROTEST MARCHES
Record levels of joblessness fueled public anger in many parts of the world. Frustrated workers organized regular protest marches, in London and other major cities. People lost faith in democratic governments, leading to the rise of extremist groups, such as the Nazis in Germany.

05/18/1933

NEW DEAL AT WORK The construction of a huge dam by the Tennessee Valley Authority (TVA) was one of many programs set up under Roosevelt's New Deal package of reforms. More than $6 billion was spent on large-scale public works to help revive economic activity across the country.

THE GRAPES OF WRATH
John Steinbeck's Pulitzer-prize winning novel described the tribulations of migrants, driven from farms in Oklahoma.

03/12/1930

GLOBAL DEPRESSION

Following the Wall Street Crash of 1929, American investments dried up and imports reached record lows. This led to a decade of severe economic depression, which was felt across the world. People lost their jobs and savings, which culminated in a housing crisis because many could no longer afford their mortgages. In Canada, homeless workers shared rooms to afford the rent.

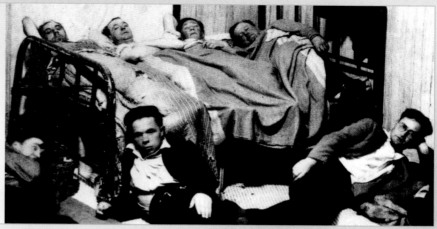

07/07/1932

HOOVERVILLES

Large shantytowns emerged across the USA to house the homeless, numbering more than 2 million by 1932. They were mockingly named "Hoovervilles" after President Hoover, who was widely blamed for his failure to solve the crisis. One of the largest was built on the Great Lawn of New York's Central Park, then an empty reservoir.

03/04/1933

FDR BECOMES PRESIDENT

Franklin D. Roosevelt, the popular governor of New York, replaced Hoover as president following elections in 1932. His campaign was based on the promise of a "new deal for the American people." He later introduced informal radio chats to build his rapport with the nation.

05/09/1934

DUST BOWL

Violent dust storms hit the Great Plains of the USA in the early 1930s, worsening the problems of the Depression. Successive years of drought exposed the light soils of the region to damaging wind erosion. The storms removed large amounts of fertile topsoil and buried fields and houses in a sea of dust.

04/14/1935

HEADING WEST

Thousands of farmers migrated from the devastation of the dust bowl to find seasonal work in California. Because so many of them came from Oklahoma, they were known as "Okies." Whole families traveled the roads, carrying only what possessions they could fit into their cars.

THE GRAPES of WRATH
John Steinbeck

04/17/1941

WARTIME RECOVERY

The Depression ended earlier in some parts of the world than others. Entry into World War II following Pearl Harbor turned around the US economy, as industry expanded rapidly to supply the war effort. Factories supplying vehicles and munitions created thousands of jobs across the industrialized world.

> The only thing we have to **fear** is **fear itself**.

US PRESIDENT ROOSEVELT'S INAUGURATION SPEECH, MARCH 3, 1933

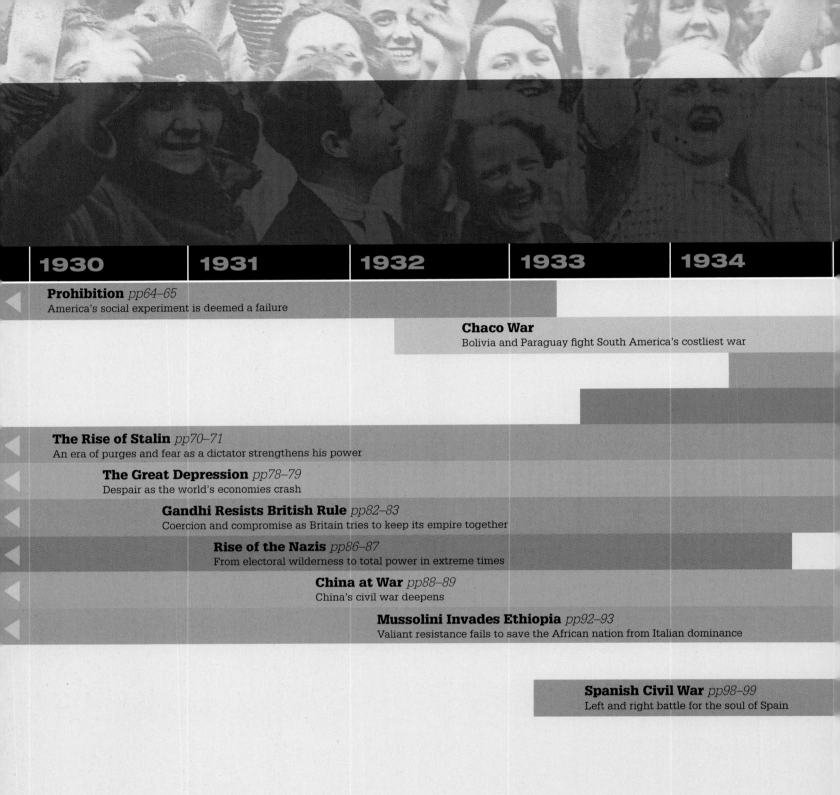

1930 1931 1932 1933 1934

Prohibition *pp64–65*
America's social experiment is deemed a failure

Chaco War
Bolivia and Paraguay fight South America's costliest war

The Rise of Stalin *pp70–71*
An era of purges and fear as a dictator strengthens his power

The Great Depression *pp78–79*
Despair as the world's economies crash

Gandhi Resists British Rule *pp82–83*
Coercion and compromise as Britain tries to keep its empire together

Rise of the Nazis *pp86–87*
From electoral wilderness to total power in extreme times

China at War *pp88–89*
China's civil war deepens

Mussolini Invades Ethiopia *pp92–93*
Valiant resistance fails to save the African nation from Italian dominance

Spanish Civil War *pp98–99*
Left and right battle for the soul of Spain

1930-39

Mao's Long March
China's communists struggle to survive

Roosevelt's New Deal
Radical policies and government intervention in the USA

Abdication Crisis *pp96–97*
A king chooses between duty and love

Independence for India and Pakistan *pp136–37*
With Britain distracted, Indians turn up the heat

The Road to World War II *pp102–03*
Germany is restless and confident, while a petrified Europe stares into the abyss

From Blitzkrieg to Resistance *pp104–05*
Germany's lightning war begins the subjugation of a continent

War in the Atlantic *pp110–11*
Britain's navy prepares to defend the homeland

The Holocaust *pp128–29*
Institutionalized Anti-Semitism writes the
darkest chapter in Europe's history

The Iron Curtain Descends *pp132–33*
The USSR comes to dominate Eastern Europe

WORLD WAR II

Gandhi Resists British Rule

1917–1937

Mohandas Karamchand Gandhi was a small, softly spoken man who defied the might of the British Empire. His policy of nonviolent resistance attracted millions of followers, making him a hero not just to the Indian people but to civil rights campaigners across the world.

04/20/1917

SATYAGRAHA BEGINS
Gandhi spent 21 years as a barrister in South Africa before returning to India in 1915. His experiences abroad shaped his political ideas. On his return, Gandhi launched the *satyagraha* (noncooperation) campaign from Champaran in Bihar. He protested alongside landless peasants who were fighting for better conditions on British-run indigo plantations, gaining the name Mahatma ("Great Soul").

03/27/1930

THE SALT MARCH
In order to protect high salt taxes, British laws made it illegal to make or collect salt. In a famous act of nonviolent protest, Gandhi marched 240 miles (388 km) to the sea, where he collected a handful of salt. Huge crowds joined him on his 24-day journey to the coastal village of Dandi in Gujarat.

04/06/1930

SALT LAW BROKEN
Gandhi's act of defiance encouraged thousands of others to break the law. Women joined in the protests by boiling bowls of seawater on the streets to make illicit salt. A number of protests took place outside the Bombay headquarters of the Indian National Congress (INC), a party at the forefront of the independence movement.

09/14/1931

04/07/1934

CHAMPION OF THE POOR
Back home, Gandhi launched the All-India Village Industries Association to promote rural development. He encouraged the use of the spinning wheel for making *khadi* cloth.
Gandhi also campaigned ceaselessly on behalf of the Untouchables, the lowest caste of Indian society, whom he fondly referred to as the Harijan ("Children of God").

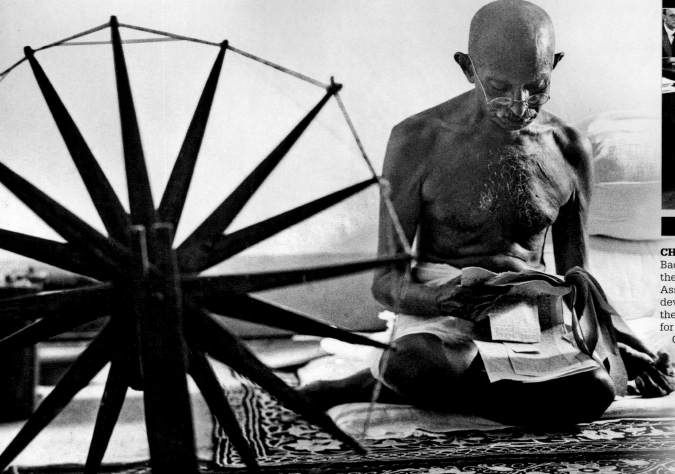

07/31/1922

BOYCOTTING IMPORTED TEXTILES

Cheap imports were destroying traditional Indian industries. In a bid to emphasize the idea of self-reliance, Gandhi set a pile of foreign cloth on fire. This symbolic protest against imports was widely imitated by his followers. He called upon Indians to make and wear *khadi* (home-woven cloth).

MAN OF FEW POSSESSIONS

Gandhi modeled his life on ascetic principles, owning very few possessions. His white robe, simple sandals, and round glasses became icons of the Indian independence struggle.

05/05/1930

GANDHI IS ARRESTED

As he set out on another salt march, Gandhi was arrested and imprisoned. News of his arrest sparked protests, and a long procession made its way through the streets in Bombay to demonstrate against the British rulers. The mass renewal of *satyagraha* led to the arrests of tens of thousands of his followers.

LONDON TALKS

After his release, Gandhi attended the Round Table Conference in London on behalf of the INC, the party he guided and represented. The talks, held to discuss *swaraj* (Indian self-rule), failed to produce an agreement between Hindus, Muslims, and the British, and left Gandhi disillusioned, but determined to continue his campaign.

09/23/1931

MEETING LANCASHIRE MILL WORKERS

While in Britain, Gandhi visited cotton mills in Lancashire, which were affected by the Indian boycott of imported cloth. He discussed the plight of Indians with the mill workers. While his simple attire attracted a good deal of press attention, UK politician Winston Churchill scornfully dismissed him as a "half-naked fakir."

02/02/1937

PROVINCIAL ELECTIONS

The Government of India Act (1935) granted Indian provinces the right to run their own affairs. The largely Hindu INC dominated the first elections in 1937, leaving Muslim groups fearful of being sidelined. Gandhi, who had left the INC, pleaded with Muslim and Congress leaders to reconcile their differences. His peaceful efforts to gain independence for India would continue unabated.

> "
> For me [**nonviolence**] is both a **means and** an **end**.
>
> **GANDHI, IN A LETTER TO A SUPPORTER, JUNE 26, 1933**

1930

Soccer's First World Cup

The International Federation of Football Associations (FIFA) had sought to arrange a global tournament since 1904. It was not until 1930 that the dream came true. In July, after months of preparation, 13 sides arrived in Montevideo, Uruguay: seven teams from South America, four from Europe, with Mexico and the USA completing the roster. The tournament was a rousing success, with 18 matches played in 18 days. The final was held in a specially constructed stadium. An estimated 93,000 people crammed into the stands to watch the hosts, Uruguay, face off against their neighbors, Argentina. It was the visitors who had the better first half, leading 2–1 at half time, but a rousing speech from the Uruguayan captain inspired the hosts to fight back. A last-minute goal from one-armed striker Hector Castro brought Uruguay a 4–2 victory. The World Cup was firmly established as one of the world's most popular sporting events.

Rise of the Nazis

1923–1934

In 1921, Adolf Hitler, a former soldier, became leader of the extremist Nazi Party. An inspired speaker and ruthless political operator, he transformed this small party into the leading voice of German nationalism. Aided by the worsening economic situation, Hitler took power and established a single-party dictatorship in 1933.

11/08/1923

BEER HALL PUTSCH Hitler first achieved nationwide fame in November 1923, when he led his National Socialist German Workers' (Nazi) Party in an attempted seizure of power. Launched from a beer hall in Munich, this "putsch," or coup, was easily suppressed by the army and police.

08/20/1927

FIRST NUREMBERG RALLY The Nazis held a series of propaganda rallies. At the time, they were a small party, attracting less than 3 percent of the vote in national elections. Mass unemployment, combined with their effective campaign to stir up popular fear of communism, rapidly increased their following.

03/13/1932

HINDENBURG DEFEATS HITLER In 1932, war hero Paul von Hindenburg stood for re-election as German president. Hitler, by then one of Germany's most popular politicians, ran against him. Despite a spectacular campaign that was organized by his propaganda chief Joseph Goebbels, Hitler was defeated.

03/22/1933

CONCENTRATION CAMP OPENS The Nazi police rounded up thousands of communists, socialists, and trade unionists. Germany's first concentration camp was established at Dachau, where these prisoners were used as slave labor.

05/10/1933

> Whoever can **conquer the street** will one day **conquer the state**.

JOSEPH GOEBBELS, NAZI PARTY PROPAGANDA CHIEF, 1931

06/29/1934

NIGHT OF THE LONG KNIVES The SA, led by Ernst Röhm, were loathed by the German army, who regarded them as rivals. Hitler needed the army's support and in June 1934 he had Röhm and other SA leaders murdered, along with other political opponents. These killings came to be known as the Night of the Long Knives.

02/21/1924

HITLER IN PRISON Arrested after the Munich putsch, Hitler was tried for treason. He exploited his trial to make widely reported speeches, publicizing his political ideas. Found guilty, he was sentenced to five years in prison, of which he served less than nine months. While in Landsberg prison he lived in comfort and worked on his political memoir, *Mein Kampf (My Struggle)*.

MEIN KAMPF Published in 1925–1926, Hitler's book expressed his hatred of Judaism and communism, and his belief in the need to win *Lebensraum,* or living space, for the German people by establishing an empire in the east.

03/16/1932

STREET-FIGHTING IN BERLIN Although Hitler took part in elections, he despised democracy and believed in the triumph of force. During the early 1930s, his Nazi paramilitaries, the Stormtroopers (SA), intimidated opponents and fought battles with communists on the streets of German cities. Police strove in vain to contain the rising tide of violence.

01/30/1933

HITLER BECOMES GERMAN CHANCELLOR By 1930, the Nazis had gained a noticeable presence in the German parliament. Following a backstairs political deal, Hitler became head of a German coalition government in January 1933. Ignoring his coalition partners, he placed his followers in key positions of power.

02/27/1933

THE REICHSTAG DESTROYED BY FIRE In February 1933, a fire broke out in the Reichstag—the German parliament. Hitler used this as a pretext for assuming exceptional emergency powers. In March, the parliament in effect voted its own abolition, and by the summer the Nazis were the only legal political party in Germany.

BOOK BURNING CAMPAIGN In the spring and summer of 1933, as Hitler consolidated his hold on power, pro-Nazi students organized ceremonies in which thousands of books by Jewish and left-wing authors were publicly burned. The book burning expressed the Nazis' determination to eradicate all supposedly "un-German" elements in the national culture.

08/02/1934

DEATH OF THE PRESIDENT The aged President Hindenburg died in 1934. After leading the elaborate public mourning, Hitler proclaimed himself *Führer,* or leader, of the Third Reich—Nazi Germany. The officers of the German army swore a solemn oath to serve him with unconditional loyalty.

China at War

1921–1941

After its last emperor, Puyi, abdicated in 1912, China fell apart. A three-way conflict between the Chinese Nationalist Party (the Kuomintang), the Chinese Communist Party (CPC), and the Japanese pushed China into bloody civil strife, and into the larger conflict of World War II.

FIELD OF CONFLICT Throughout the 1920s, communist and Kuomintang forces allied against the warlords of northern China. However, at the end of the campaign, communist forces were scattered across the country, at the mercy of their former allies. Japan sought to take advantage of this internal conflict to expand its power base.

- Japanese territory
- Japanese sphere of influence at start of war
- Japanese sphere of influence by end of war
- → Route of the Long March

09/09/1926

WARLORDS ARE DEFEATED Between 1926 and 1928, Chiang Kai-shek crushed the regional warlords through skillful political maneuvering and a series of bold military campaigns. The Kuomintang won control of the country, and Chinese who were caught fighting for the wrong side could expect no mercy.

04/12/1927

MASSACRE OF COMMUNISTS In 1927 Chiang Kai-shek turned against his communist allies. Kuomintang forces massacred communist activists in Shanghai and brutally suppressed a communist uprising in Canton. Driven from the cities, the communists took refuge in remote rural areas.

01/29/1932

FIGHTING IN SHANGHAI In January 1932 Japanese forces carried out land, sea, and air attacks on the port city of Shanghai in northern China. They were responding to alleged Chinese attacks on Japanese-controlled areas of the city. A peace deal brokered in March allowed Japanese troops to remain in the city.

10/16/1934

CHINA'S CIVIL WAR Meanwhile, Chiang Kai-shek continued to campaign against the communists. In fall 1934 communist forces in Jiangxi province, led by Mao Zedong, embarked on a Long March northward to evade capture. They reached Shaanxi province after a perilous journey of 8,000 miles (12,500 km).

LONG MARCH STAMP This stamp honors the Long March as a heroic achievement.

12/13/1937

MAO ZEDONG

A founder member of the Chinese Communist Party, Mao Zedong became its leader in the 1930s.

CHIANG KAI-SHEK

Leader of the Kuomintang from 1925, Chiang Kai-shek was a ruthless military commander.

07/23/1921

RISE OF COMMUNISM
In 1919 Chinese students protested the transfer of the Shandong province in China to Japan, following World War I. This caused an upsurge of political radicalism, known as the May Fourth Movement. In 1921 radicals inspired by anti-imperialist ideals held the first congress of the Chinese Communist Party (CPC).

KUOMINTANG POSTER This 1927 propaganda poster acclaims Chiang Kai-shek's Northern Expedition, a campaign in which the Kuomintang army won control of Beijing.

09/19/1931

JAPANESE INVADE MANCHURIA Japan controlled a railroad in the Chinese province of Manchuria. In September 1931, falsely accusing the Chinese of attacking the railroad at Mukden, Japanese troops invaded and occupied Manchuria. Japan turned the province into the state of Manchukuo, and installed Puyi as its puppet ruler. From here the Japanese sought control of the whole of northern China.

> The **slaughter** of civilians is appalling… **rape** and **brutality**… beyond belief.

US SURGEON ROBERT O. WILSON WORKING AT THE NANJING HOSPITAL, DECEMBER 1937

07/07/1937

SINO-JAPANESE WAR
A full-scale war started between China and Japan in 1937. After clashes near Beijing in July, sustained fighting broke out in Shanghai, and Japanese aircraft bombed the city. Kuomintang troops fought street by street until a Japanese invasion force, landed by sea, threatened them with encirclement. Chiang Kai-shek abandoned Shanghai in November.

RAPE OF NANJING
In December 1937 Japanese forces captured the Kuomintang capital, Nanjing. There followed an orgy of violence that shocked the world. Japanese soldiers raped and murdered tens of thousands of Chinese women and young girls. Prisoners of war were used for bayonet practice or buried alive. The massacres continued for six weeks.

05/23/1939

CHINESE CONTINUE RESISTANCE Despite the scale of their suffering and destruction, the Chinese continued to resist Japan. The Kuomintang and the communists suspended their civil war to fight the invaders from bases deep in the Chinese interior.

12/08/1941

CHINA JOINS THE ALLIES The USA became a supporter of the Kuomintang in its war against Japanese aggression. Chiang Kai-shek was recognized as one of the Allied leaders when the USA went to war with Japan in December 1941. The war in China became a part of the wider conflict of World War II.

A CENTURY OF
Architecture

The quickening pace of industrialization and urbanization opened up new challenges and horizons for architects. Changing societies demanded new types of buildings, such as apartment and office buildings, cinemas, and airports. At the same time, new building materials allowed innovative architectural styles. Buildings grew upward. By the 1950s, modernism was the prevailing style, but the last two decades of the century saw startling innovations.

1900–1910 At the turn of the century, the predominant architectural style was Art Nouveau, which took its inspiration from nature. It was characterized by plantlike curves and ornamentation in glass and iron. Buildings ranged in style from the organic forms of Antoni Gaudí's villas in Barcelona to Charles Rennie Mackintosh's towerlike Glasgow School of Art. Modern industrial techniques were used to bring art and beauty to the urban environment, with decoration given a new importance.

1910–1920 The modernist movement was born as a growing number of architects came to hold the contrary view that buildings should be sparse and simple, and that visual interest should come from the structure itself. Prominent modernist architects included Frank Lloyd Wright, Mies van der Rohe, and Walter Gropius.

PARIS EXPOSITION IN 1900
Hector Guimard's famous iron-and-glass entrances to the Paris Metro were made for this exhibition, a celebration of Art Nouveau.

Modernist buildings were typically flat-roofed, supported on metal or concrete pillars, with horizontal rows of windows.

REACHING FOR THE SKY In the 1930s, New Yorkers were gripped by the race to build the tallest skyscraper. Construction workers could be seen poised high above the streets of Manhattan.

1920–1940 The Art Deco style became hugely popular in the 1920s. An eclectic blend of influences, from Cubism to Ancient Egypt, it embodied the aspirations of the machine age, combining glamour with functionality. Art Deco was

CASA MILA Begun in 1906 and completed four years later, Antoni Gaudí's townhouse does not contain a single straight line. The undulating balconies look like a series of waves.

FIAT LINGOTTO FACTORY Matté Trucco's design for the Fiat automobile company in Turin, Italy, was an attempt to visualize a new, futuristic style of living.

FALLINGWATER Frank Lloyd Wright's modernist masterpiece of 1934 embodied his belief that architecture should be in harmony with nature.

SEAGRAM BUILDING Mies van der Rohe designed this steel-framed bronze and glass skyscraper as the corporate headquarters of the Seagram Company in New York.

1,141

Buildings designed by Frank Lloyd Wright during his 70-year career; 532 were completed and 409 still stand.

most famously displayed in the stainless-steel spire of the Chrysler Building in New York.

1940–1970 Modernist architecture spread as Europe's shattered cities were rebuilt following World War II. Many architects adopted the brutalist style of French modernist Le Corbusier, which was characterized by walls and staircases of gray poured concrete. Architects increasingly saw themselves as planners of the urban landscape,

influencing and improving the way people lived in society. Brazilian Oscar Niemeyer was given the opportunity to design an entire capital city—Brasilia. By the 1960s, functional steel and glass corporate skyscrapers had come to dominate the skylines of downtown business centers around the globe, from Toronto to Hong Kong.

1970– The development of high-tech architecture in the 1970s broke all the architectural norms. Buildings were turned inside-out, with the inner structure and service systems placed on the outside. A famous example was the

INFLUENTIAL ARCHITECT Le Corbusier proposed that high-rise residential blocks, seen most prominently in his Unité d'Habitation in Marseilles, were the architecture of the future.

Pompidou Center in Paris. In the 1980s, an influential group of American architects abandoned the modernist concept of functionalism, bringing decoration and individuality back into the built environment. The movement quickly became known as postmodernism. New materials and technologies, especially computer design software,

GREEN ARCHITECTURE Energy conservation was a pressing concern by the end of the century. The Sun Dial building in Dezhou, China, is the world's largest solar-powered building.

brought an explosion of innovation to architecture. In the 21st century, architecture seems to defy gravity, with soaring curves and fragile-looking structures that dominate futuristic skylines.

Space and **light** and **order**. Those are the **things** that **men need** just as much as they need bread or a place to sleep.

FRENCH ARCHITECT LE CORBUSIER, 1923

1960s

ASSEMBLY HALL Le Corbusier's assembly hall, part of his designs for Chandigarh, the new capital of Punjab, India, made stark use of raw concrete, sculpted into sweeping curves.

1970s

SYDNEY OPERA HOUSE The concrete shells on the roof of Jørn Utzon's iconic building mimic the shape of sails on Sydney Harbor. The design pushed the limits of technology at the time.

1980s

LLOYD'S BUILDING The water pipes, elevators, and electrical conduits are on the outside of Richard Rogers' high-tech building in London. It was initially likened to an oil refinery.

1990s

PETRONAS TOWERS At 1,483 ft (452 m), this building in Malaysia was the world's tallest from 1998 to 2004.

Mussolini Invades Ethiopia

1922–1936

Benito Mussolini formed the Fascist movement in Italy after World War I. Muscling his way to power, he embarked on a quest for military glory and empire. In 1935–1936 his forces conquered the independent African state of Ethiopia, driving out that country's ruler, Haile Selassie.

This act of aggression alienated Mussolini from Britain and France, driving him into a fatal alliance with Nazi Germany. Italy ruled Ethiopia until 1941, when British troops defeated the Italians in East Africa and returned Haile Selassie to his throne.

11/02/1930

EMPEROR RISES
In Ethiopia—the only fully independent African country at the time—Ras Tafari was crowned emperor. He adopted the name Haile Selassie and embarked on political reforms, giving Ethiopia its first written constitution. He also sought to modernize both the army and the economy.

02/23/1935

MASSING FOR THE ATTACK Mussolini sent thousands of troops and aircraft to Eritrea and Somaliland in East Africa. These colonies shared borders with Ethiopia, and provided a military base for the Italian invasion.

04/14/1935

STRESA FRONT
Threatened by the rise of the Nazis, Britain and France were eager to preserve good relations with Italy. At Stresa in Italy, British and French leaders made a pact with Mussolini to oppose Nazi ambitions in Europe. Mussolini assumed that in return they would accept his takeover of Ethiopia.

12/25/1935

POORLY ARMED WARRIORS Haile Selassie assembled a large army to defend the country, but few were trained to use modern equipment. Most were tribal warriors, carrying spears and shields, yet they successfully resisted the Italian advance.

04/26/1936

ITALIAN VICTORY
In early 1936, under a new commander, Marshal Pietro Badoglio, the Italians imposed a series of defeats upon the Ethiopians. By May, the Italian forces had captured the Ethiopian capital Addis Ababa. Haile Selassie went into exile, while Mussolini celebrated his victory in Rome.

04/26/1936

BRUTE FORCE
The Italian victory depended on superior weaponry, including chemical agents. Poison gas was dropped from aircraft, inflicting terrible injuries on unprepared Ethiopians. The brutality of the war helped turn public opinion in Britain and France against the Italian leader.

06/30/1936

AN EMOTIONAL PLEA
Haile Selassie addressed the League of Nations in an emotional plea for help. The speech won him widespread sympathy, but no effective support. Instituted to preserve peace by collective action against aggression, the League responded to the Italian invasion with economic sanctions that had little impact.

10/22/1922

FASCISTS MARCH Mussolini threatened to march on Rome with his Fascist "blackshirts." Intimidated, Italy's King Victor Emmanuel appointed Mussolini the prime minister. The march turned into a victory celebration.

12/24/1925

RISE OF THE DICTATOR Suppressing opposition, Mussolini adopted dictatorial powers, proclaiming himself *Il Duce*, leader of the Fascist party and the regime. He wanted to make Italy "great, respected, and feared," and declared his goal to build an empire in Africa and around the Mediterranean.

10/03/1935

THE INVASION BEGINS With ground troops supported by more than 500 aircraft, Italy launched a full-scale invasion of Ethiopia from Eritrea and Somaliland. However, their motorized forces made slow progress across mountainous terrain with few usable roads.

10/25/1936

THE AXIS IS BORN Public opinion forced the British and French governments to oppose Italy's invasion of Ethiopia. Offended, Mussolini abandoned the Stresa Front and sought an alliance with Nazi Germany. In October 1936 Hitler and Mussolini signed an agreement creating the "Rome–Berlin Axis." The Axis alliance and the failure of the League of Nations to resist aggression set Europe on the path to World War II.

> "It is **international morality** that is **at stake**.

ETHIOPIAN EMPEROR HAILE SELASSIE, IN AN APPEAL TO THE LEAGUE OF NATIONS, JUNE 1936

1936

Hitler's Army of Fanatics

The annual Nazi Party rally at the city of Nuremberg was the centerpiece of Hitler's propaganda machine. Thousands of Hitler's most loyal supporters attended, and at their core stood the uniform ranks of the SS (*Schutzstaffel*), the Nazis' feared paramilitary security force. Hitler used these mass rallies to strengthen his image as the savior of Germany, defending his people from an international conspiracy of Jews and communists. The Führer could be an inspired public speaker, and his frenzied rhetoric whipped his supporters into fury against the enemies of the Reich. The rallies were used as the basis of propaganda films to spread Hitler's message as widely as possible. The fanaticism they inspired became an essential part of the Nazis' political strategy, and the SS developed into a fearsome tool of repression as unofficial state enforcers, brutally subduing resistance in Germany, and later across occupied nations.

Abdication Crisis

1936–1937

When Edward VIII ascended the British throne, he seemed to have everything—good looks, an easy charm, and popularity. The nation eagerly awaited news of his marriage, but his love affair with a divorced woman plunged Britain and its empire into a constitutional crisis, which ended in his abdication.

01/28/1936

11/18/1936

A POPULAR KING Affable and good-looking, Edward won the affection of the British working class. While visiting South Wales, he assured a group of unemployed miners, "I am going to help you. Something will be done for you." Gestures like this cemented his popularity among the people.

12/02/1936

MOUNTING CRISIS Both the Church and the Prime Minister opposed the King's affair. The Archbishop of Canterbury made it clear that, as Supreme Head of the Church of England, Edward could not marry a divorced woman. Baldwin bluntly told the King he had three choices—give up Mrs. Simpson; marry her against the advice of his ministers, who would immediately resign; or abdicate.

12/03/1936

THE KING AND MRS. SIMPSON EVENING STANDARD

12/11/1936

PUBLIC PROTEST Edward's announcement plunged the nation into crisis. The public was divided on the issue: the upper and middle classes tended to agree with the government, while the working class thought the King had been unfairly treated.

HANDS OFF OUR KING ABDICATION MEANS REVOLUTION

INSTRUMENT OF ABDICATION

I, Edward the Eighth, of Great Britain, Ireland, and the British Dominions beyond the Seas, King, Emperor of India, do hereby declare My irrevocable determination to renounce the Throne for Myself and for My descendants, and My desire that effect should be given to this Instrument of Abdication immediately.

In token whereof I have hereunto set My hand this tenth day of December, nineteen hundred and thirty six, in the presence of the witnesses whose signatures are subscribed.

SIGNED AT FORT BELVEDERE IN THE PRESENCE OF

THE INSTRUMENT OF ABDICATION Witnessed by his three brothers, Edward signed the Instrument of Abdication on December 10, 1936.

DEATH OF A KING

Thousands attended the funeral procession of George V. His reign was known for its moral conservatism. A remote figure, George V had never been close to his eldest son, who now became Edward VIII. Aged 41, the new king was unmarried and had a reputation as a playboy. His affair with Mrs. Wallis Simpson, a twice-married American socialite, had begun a few years before.

08/01/1936

THE NOT-SO-SECRET AFFAIR

The couple were snapped together on a holiday in the Mediterranean. The pictures were splashed across the American and European press but kept out of the British newspapers. Although Prime Minister Stanley Baldwin and other Establishment figures knew all about the affair, the public was kept in the dark.

FRONT PAGE NEWS

Aware that the story could no longer be hushed up, the British press broke its self-imposed embargo and published news of the affair—the first the public had heard of it. Once it was out in the open, the news dominated headlines. The papers printed daily accounts of the frenzied discussions and juicy titbits. Facing mounting pressure, Edward was forced to make a decision.

12/11/1936

ABDICATION SPEECH

On December 11, a day after signing the Instrument of Abdication, Edward announced to the nation his decision to step down. He declared that he could never bear the responsibility of a king "without the support of the woman I love." It was the first time in history that a British monarch had voluntarily given up the throne. Edward had reigned for just 327 days and had not yet been crowned.

05/12/1937

NEW KING CROWNED

Edward's brother Albert succeeded him as George VI. Shy, diffident, and loyal to his brother, he was hampered by a stammer. After his coronation, he greeted the crowd from the balcony of Buckingham Palace with his mother, his wife, and his daughters—the future Elizabeth II and Princess Margaret.

> ❝ Hark the herald angels sing, **Mrs. Simpson's nabbed** our **king**.
>
> PLAYGROUND VERSION
> OF A CHRISTMAS CAROL,
> DECEMBER 1936 ❞

06/03/1937

EDWARD MARRIES WALLIS

Made Duke of Windsor on his abdication, Edward went into exile. He and Wallis were married at the Chateau de Candé in France in June 1937. Following their marriage, she became the Duchess of Windsor but was refused the title of Her Royal Highness, a decision that the Duke bitterly resented.

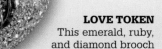

LOVE TOKEN

This emerald, ruby, and diamond brooch was commissioned by the Duke for the couple's 20th wedding anniversary.

Spanish Civil War

1933–1939

In February 1936 a left-wing Popular Front government was elected in Spain. Right-wing Nationalist army generals launched a military uprising in response. They were resisted by left-wing Republican groups and Catalan and Basque nationalists, setting the scene for a bloody civil war that would scar Spain for decades.

10/29/1933

RISE OF FASCISM Aristocratic lawyer José Antonio Primo de Rivera founded the Falangists, a right-wing nationalist movement, in imitation of the Italian Fascists.

REPUBLICAN PROPAGANDA POSTER
This poster calls for all pro-government groups in Spain, including anarchists, communists, socialists, and moderate Republicans, to unite against the Nationalist rebels. Hastily armed workers' militias succeeded in keeping control of major cities, including Barcelona and Madrid.

07/27/1936

REINFORCEMENTS FLOWN IN At the start of the rebellion, German and Italian aircraft flew Franco's Army of Africa from Spanish Morocco into southern Spain. These professional soldiers, hardened in colonial wars, advanced northward through Spain. They became infamous for their terrorist tactics.

09/27/1936

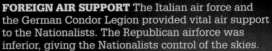

11/01/1936

FOREIGN AIR SUPPORT The Italian air force and the German Condor Legion provided vital air support to the Nationalists. The Republican airforce was inferior, giving the Nationalists control of the skies.

11/08/1936

05/01/1937

REPUBLICAN DIVISIONS Fighting broke out within Republican forces in their stronghold of Barcelona, as moderate Republicans clashed with radical anarchist supporters. Political discord between democrats, communists, and anarchists would continue to hamper the Republican war effort over coming years.

12/24/1937

REPUBLICANS RETREAT Through 1937 and 1938, grueling fighting began to favor the Nationalist side, and the areas of Spain under Republican control gradually shrank. The Republicans were defeated at the battle of Teruel, and after a final desperate offensive on the Ebro ended in defeat in November 1938, the Republic was doomed.

04/01/1939

12/02/1934

SOCIALIST UPRISING On the other side of the political spectrum, Spanish anarchists and socialists launched failed left-wing revolts. Their anti-Catholic revolutionary ideas frightened Spanish conservatives.

07/17/1936

NATIONALIST REBELLION Following the election of a left-wing government in 1936, the Nationalists mounted a coup. General Francisco Franco emerged as leader of the rebels. Franco was a career army officer who, like many of his colleagues, believed rebellion against the Republican government was justified as the only alternative to a left-wing revolution.

SIEGE OF THE ALCAZAR In Toledo, pro-government forces besieged Nationalist soldiers inside the fortress of the Alcazar. Incompetently conducted by poorly armed, undisciplined, untrained militiamen, the siege failed. The defenders held out until the Alcazar was relieved, in late September 1936, by the arrival of Franco's Army of Africa. Both sides knew the value of the press, and the Nationalists were quick to exploit the propaganda value of this unlikely victory.

> **Fire enveloped** the whole city. Screams of **lamentation** were heard everywhere and the people, **filled with terror**, knelt, lifting their hands to heaven...
>
> FATHER ALBERTO ONAINDIA, DESCRIBING GUERNICA, APRIL 26, 1937

SIEGE OF MADRID In November 1936 Franco's troops fought their way into the outskirts of Madrid. Their advance was halted partly through the arrival of foreign volunteers, the International Brigades, to aid the Republic. Repulsed after house-to-house fighting, the Nationalists established a siege of the city that lasted until 1939.

04/26/1937

GUERNICA BOMBED On the afternoon of April 26, 1937 aircraft of the German Condor Legion, abetted by the Italians, bombed the historic Basque town of Guernica. The town was crowded for market day and the population had no defense or shelter. The destruction and heavy loss of life shocked the world.

NATIONALIST VICTORY PARADES The broken Republicans gave up the fight and the Nationalists staged military parades in major cities to celebrate their victory. Franco took power as dictator, remaining ruler until his death in 1975. For those who had fought on the Republican side, defeat was a catastrophe. Hundreds of thousands were imprisoned, executed, or driven into permanent exile. Authoritarian nationalism had triumphed in Spain.

1937

Hindenburg Disaster

The Hindenburg was the largest airship ever built, an engineering triumph of its day. At 800 ft (245 m) long, and held aloft by 7.1 million cubic ft (200,000 cubic m) of hydrogen gas, it was designed to carry 72 passengers across the Atlantic in conditions of luxury. On May 6, 1937, while attempting a routine docking procedure at the Lakehurst Air Station in New Jersey, it burst into flames. Thirty-five of the 97 people on board were killed, along with one member of the ground crew. The tragedy was recorded by cameras, newsreel, and a live eyewitness radio report. It quickly became headline news on both sides of the Atlantic, making it one of the first disasters of the broadcast age. The enduring power of the incident owes much to the novelty at the time of air travel and mass media, but the story itself is timeless: the power of nature, or simple accident, to bring down the mightiest of human creations.

The Road to World War II

1935-1939

When Adolf Hitler came to power in 1933, his goal was to make Germany the dominant power in Europe, and he fully expected to fight to achieve this aim. He began a program of German rearmament, in defiance of the Treaty of Versailles, which limited German military and industrial output after World War I. The horrors of trench warfare were still fresh in the memories of the British and French public, and both countries were desperate to avoid another conflict. A cat-and-mouse game began, with Hitler determined to push forward his plan for German advancement, while his neighbors looked on nervously.

HITLER YOUTH DAGGER
The paramilitary Hitler Youth movement trained millions of young Germans in the principles of Naziism. Their equipment included this ceremonial dagger, whose blade was engraved with the words "blood and honor."

03/12/1938

AUSTRIA WELCOMES HITLER Exploiting a political crisis engineered by the Austrian Nazi Party, Hitler sent troops into Austria in March 1938, bringing Austria into the German Reich. This "Anschluss" (union) was welcomed by the majority of Austrians. Provincial leaders of Austria pledged allegiance to Hitler at a ceremony in Vienna in April 1938.

09/28/1938

PREPARING FOR WAR In mid-September the Czech army crushed a German uprising in the Sudetenland, raising fears of German retaliation. Since Russia and France were committed to defend Czechoslovakia, a European war appeared inevitable. Air raid shelters were dug in parks as Britain prepared for war.

03/15/1939

CONSCRIPTION IN BRITAIN Following the occupation of Prague, Hitler began to threaten the disputed free city of Danzig in Poland. Although still hoping for peace, the British and French were frantically re-arming. In April, for the first time in its history, Britain introduced conscription during peacetime.

05/01/1939

08/23/1939
NAZIS SIGN A PACT WITH STALIN In April 1939 Britain and France pledged to go to war in defense of Poland, if it was attacked. Despite their dislike of Soviet dictator Joseph Stalin, the British and French explored the possibility of an alliance with the Soviet Union. Instead, on August 23, the Soviets signed a surprise pact with Nazi Germany, secretly agreeing to divide Poland between them.

The Treaty of Versailles had given the Allies control over major centers of German industry in the Rhineland. Hitler was determined to win them back to supply his war machine. He was also keen to bring Austria and the Czech-controlled Sudetenland, both German-speaking areas, into his Reich.

■ Germany 1933
■ Area of German expansion
March 1935–March 1939

03/08/1936

GERMAN TROOPS ENTER RHINELAND

In March 1936 Hitler ordered German troops to march into the Rhineland, an area of Germany declared a demilitarized zone under the Versailles Treaty. Britain and France failed to mount a military response to this flagrant breach of treaty obligations, handing the Führer a painless victory.

07/05/1938

NAZI REVOLT IN CZECHOSLOVAKIA

Acting on secret orders from Hitler, local Nazi leader Konrad Henlein urged revolt among the German minority in Czechoslovakia. He demanded that the Sudetenland, an area with a predominantly German population, should separate from Czechoslovakia and form closer ties with Germany.

09/01/1938

APPEASING HITLER

With Germany threatening to go to war over the Sudetenland, British Prime Minister Neville Chamberlain flew twice to meet Hitler in a bid to defuse the crisis. He hoped that peace could be established by appeasement—satisfying Hitler's demands.

GERMAN TROOPS OCCUPY PRAGUE

At the eleventh hour, in a conference at Munich, the Czechs were forced to hand Hitler the Sudetenland. Chamberlain believed that this would "guarantee peace," but Hitler planned further expansion. Fatally weakened by losing the Sudetenland, the Czechs put up no resistance when the Germans marched into Prague in March 1939.

09/01/1939

GERMANY INVADES POLAND

On September 1, 1939 German forces launched a full-scale invasion of Poland. Britain and France made frantic preparations to support the Poles and, on September 3, 1939, seeing no alternative, they declared war on Germany.

> When **starting** and waging a **war** it is **not right** that matters, **but victory**.

ADOLF HITLER, AUGUST 22, 1939

From Blitzkrieg to Resistance

1939–1944

Between 1939 and 1941, Nazi Germany conquered a vast area of Europe in Blitzkrieg ("lightning war") campaigns, using tanks, motorized infantry, and bomber aircraft. Over time, Nazi brutality spurred support for resistance movements in occupied countries, posing a major challenge to German forces.

NAZI EXPANSION
Hitler's ambitious expansion plan began with a swift invasion of Scandinavia. His armies then turned their attention to the Low Countries, conquering Belgium and the Netherlands, before closing in on France.

➡ German advance

04/09/1940

HITLER STRIKES NORTH The Germans occupied Denmark in a lightning campaign lasting six hours, and soon afterward invaded Norway. British and French forces were sent to help the Norwegians, but by June Germany had control of the country.

05/10/1940

ROTTERDAM DESTROYED
On May 10, 1940 the Germans launched their long-awaited offensive in Western Europe. German forces advanced through the Netherlands, Belgium, and France. The Dutch were forced to surrender and the port city of Rotterdam was devastated by German bombers on May 14.

05/10/1940

BREAKTHROUGH IN THE ARDENNES While British and French armies advanced into Belgium to meet the German attacks, a powerful force of German tanks and motorized infantry struck into France through the Ardennes region. Punching a hole in the French defenses, the tanks set their course for the Channel coast.

05/20/1940

THE ALLIES IN RETREAT By end of May, German tanks had raced across northern France to reach the Channel ports of Boulogne and Calais. The Allied forces in Belgium were cut off from the rear. While the Belgian army surrendered, the British and French fell back to the port of Dunkirk in northern France.

05/27/1940

EVACUATION FROM DUNKIRK Between May 27 and June 4, 220,000 British and 120,000 French and Belgian troops were evacuated from the port and beaches of Dunkirk. The operation was carried out by Royal Navy warships, aided by a flotilla of civilian vessels, under almost constant air attack. Many men waded out to sea to reach the boats.

06/14/1940

PARIS OCCUPIED German troops entered Paris on June 14. Three days later the French surrendered. German forces occupied most of France, but the southeast was left under the control of Marshal Philippe Pétain's government based at Vichy. While the Vichy regime collaborated with the Nazis, General Charles de Gaulle set up a Free French headquarters in London and called for continued resistance.

07/06/1940

BRITAIN'S SECRET WAR Led by Prime Minister Winston Churchill, Britain continued the fight against Hitler. In July 1940 Britain set up the Special Operations Executive (SOE) to promote espionage, sabotage, and subversion in German-occupied countries. The SOE sent spies to Europe, supported local resistance networks, and supplied arms to guerrilla groups and saboteurs.

08/30/1944

FRENCH RESISTANCE About 200,000 people were active in the French resistance. They provided military intelligence to the Allies, aided the escape of prisoners of war, and carried out guerrilla warfare. During the Normandy landings in June 1944, they inhibited the movement of German troops by blowing up railroads and bridges.

09/01/1939

POLAND OVERRUN
The German conquest of Poland took only four weeks. Although Britain and France declared war on Germany, they did nothing to help the Poles. The Soviet Union joined Germany in the onslaught from September 17, and after Poland was defeated the Germans and the Soviets divided the country between them.

05/13/1940

BLITZKRIEG BOMBERS
The German air force (the Luftwaffe) was trained to operate alongside the ground offensive. Bombers provided close air support for advancing tanks, disrupted communications by destroying roads and bridges, and shattering enemy airfields and military supplies. German fighter planes outclassed their British and French opponents.

> Our **strength** lies in our **speed** and our **brutality**.
>
> ADOLF HITLER, AUGUST 22, 1939

GERMAN INCENDIARY BOMB
Luftwaffe bombers were armed with high explosive and incendiary bombs. This combination caused maximum destruction when dropped on urban areas.

10/02/1944

PRICE OF DISSENT
Resistance movements arose in many occupied countries, mounting guerrilla campaigns against the occupiers. The Nazi response was brutal. Captives were summarily executed, as here at Ralja in Yugoslavia. Sometimes reprisals took the form of mass murder, with whole communities wiped out.

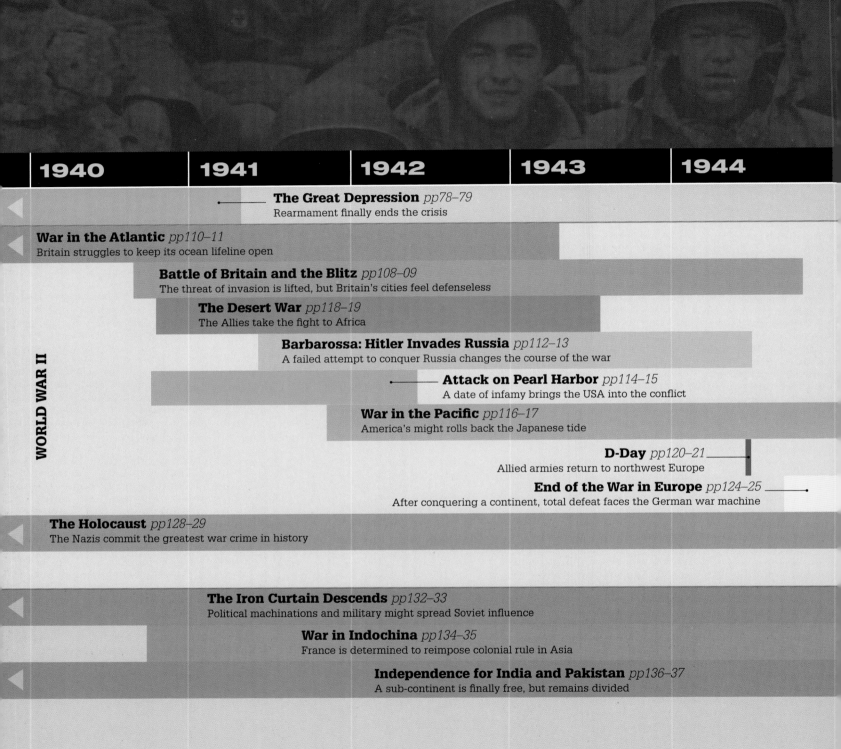

1940-49

1945   1946   1947   1948   1949

Nuclear Bombs Dropped on Japan *pp126–27*
The ultimate weapons are unleashed

Berlin Blockade *pp140–41*
The USSR tests the West's resolve

Israel Declares Statehood *pp142–43*
A dream is realized, but others fear the price

China Goes Red *pp144–45*
A second great nation joins the Communist bloc

McCarthyism *pp152–53*
A witch-hunt for hidden communists in America's "Red Scare"

Battle of Britain and the Blitz

1940–1944

From summer 1940 Britain came under air attack from the German Luftwaffe. In the Battle of Britain, Germany failed to win command of the air, but British cities were devastated in the Blitz.

08/13/1940

DEFENSES SCRAMBLE
To meet the German air attack in summer 1940, Royal Air Force (RAF) Fighter Command relied on Hurricane and Spitfire aircraft. When pilots at RAF bases received the order to "scramble," they had about five minutes to get airborne. The aircraft rapidly gained altitude and intercepted Luftwaffe bombers.

09/07/1940

BOMBING LONDON
In the Battle of Britain, the Germans initially targeted air bases and radar stations, but on September 7 they launched their first mass bombing raid against London. More than 300 Heinkel and Junkers bombers took part in the raid. Beginning in daylight and continuing into the night, the bombings caused 1,600 civilian casualties.

11/14/1940

BOMB DAMAGE IN COVENTRY Many British cities outside London were heavily bombed during the Blitz, including Liverpool, Glasgow, Hull, Plymouth, Birmingham, Coventry, and Belfast. A single raid on Coventry in November 1940 killed more than 500 people, rendering a third of the city's houses uninhabitable and destroying the historic cathedral.

04/11/1941

GOING UNDERGROUND
From October 1940 to May 1941, cities in Britain were battered by repeated German night bombing raids with incendiary and explosive devices. Many Londoners sought safety by sleeping in Underground subway stations, as well as in specially built shelters. Every man, woman, and child had to be prepared to seek cover when the warning sirens sounded.

04/23/1941

ROYAL VISIT
King George VI and his wife raised civilian morale by continuing to live in London throughout the Blitz and by visiting bombed-out areas after raids. The warm reception given to the King and to Prime Minister Winston Churchill on such visits was a sign of popular support for the war.

05/10/1941

LONDON BURNING
The worst night of the Blitz over London came on May 10, 1941. Firefighters were overwhelmed by the scale of the attacks. The Houses of Parliament were wrecked, stations put out of action, and 3,000 people killed or injured. But this was the last major raid of the Blitz. German aircraft were subsequently transferred to support the invasion of the Soviet Union.

WARTIME POSTER
This poster encouraged British people to buy war bonds to finance the building of bombers.

08/15/1940

RADAR STATION Britain's sophisticated coastal radar stations tracked incoming German aircraft, giving vital early warning of imminent raids.

08/18/1940

GERMAN LOSSES
In August and September 1940, the Luftwaffe sought to drive the RAF from the skies "in the shortest possible time" as a prelude to a land invasion of Britain. But in the aerial war of attrition, the RAF shot down more aircraft than it lost. Hitler abandoned his invasion plans and the Luftwaffe switched from daylight attacks to night raids on cities—the Blitz.

12/29/1940

ST. PAUL'S AMID FLAMES In December 1940 much of the historic City of London was burned down in an incendiary raid that started almost 1,500 fires. St. Paul's Cathedral, although struck by an incendiary bomb, survived almost unscathed.

CHILD'S PLAY This World War II version of the card game Happy Families was adapted to reflect life during the Blitz.

> **Never** in the field of human conflict was **so much** owed by **so many** to **so few**.
>
> BRITISH PRIME MINISTER CHURCHILL, REFERRING TO PILOTS OF FIGHTER COMMAND, AUGUST 20, 1940

06/22/1944

FLYING BOMBS
In summer 1944 Germany renewed its air offensive against London using V1 flying bombs. Arriving by day and night, these pilotless aircraft, packed with explosives and controlled by a primitive guidance system, caused large-scale damage and loss of life. Their effect was eventually reduced by improving air defenses and the capture of their launch sites.

11/25/1944

MISSILE DESTRUCTION
From September 1944 London was also subjected to attack by V2 ballistic missiles. Traveling faster than the speed of sound, these missiles struck without warning. Fortunately for the British, V2s were inaccurate and many went astray; only 500 had hit London by the war's end. In all about 8,000 Britons were killed by V1s and V2s, compared with 52,000 killed by conventional bombing.

War in the Atlantic

1939–1943

The Germans were quick to realize the strategic importance of victory over the Allied fleets in the Atlantic. Both Britain and the Soviet Union received essential food, fuel, and war material by sea, and trade routes had to be protected against German surface ships and U-boats (submarines) at all costs. If the Germans could successfully disrupt Allied shipping, Britain would be starved out of the war.

1939

ATLANTIC MERCHANT CONVOYS From the start of the war the British Navy organized merchant ships into convoys that were escorted across the ocean by naval vessels. Convoys could sail no faster than their slowest ship, and at first there was a shortage of both escort vessels and trained crew.

1940

U-BOAT BASE IN OCCUPIED FRANCE After the Germans defeated the French in June 1940 they moved their submarines to ports along France's western coast, much closer to Atlantic sea lanes. Submarine commander Admiral Karl Dönitz established his headquarters at Lorient in Brittany.

1941

AMERICA JOINS THE ATLANTIC WAR US vessels began escorting convoys of merchant ships even before America formally declared war on Germany in December 1941. Depth charges—explosives dropped into the sea—were used to attack German U-boats.

1941

BRITAIN FACES RATIONING As German submarines took their toll on imported supplies, the British people suffered shortages of essential goods. Gasoline was not available for private driving and food sales were strictly controlled using ration coupons to ensure that no one was undernourished.

1941

DEPTH CHARGES German U-boats inflicted heavy losses in 1940 and 1941, sinking more than 1,000 ships. British and Canadian vessels struck back, locating U-boats with sonar and attacking them with depth charges.

> **"**
> The **enemy** knows all our **secrets** and we know **none of his**.
> **"**
>
> KARL DÖNITZ, GERMAN NAVAL COMMANDER, 1943

1942

U-BOAT ATTACKS INCREASE After America's entry into the war, losses of merchant ships increased sharply. Attacking at night in packs, U-boats sank twice as many ships as in 1941. However US shipyards were mass-producing 20 cargo ships a week to replace the vessels lost.

1943

1939

THE SINKING OF GRAF SPEE

The German battleship *Admiral Graf Spee* preyed on merchant ships in the South Atlantic. After clashing with British warships at the Battle of the Plate River, it was forced into port at Montevideo, Uruguay. Badly damaged, it was sunk by its own commander.

1941

BISMARCK IS DESTROYED

The British Royal Navy's first attempt to intercept Germany's prized battleship *Bismarck* ended in disaster when *HMS Hood* (right) was sunk by *Bismarck*'s guns. After a frantic search, the *Bismarck* was located, and sunk with air-launched torpedoes and gunfire.

1942

ARCTIC CONVOYS

The most arduous escort duty was protecting convoys carrying military equipment to the Soviet Union's Arctic ports. Freezing weather made a sailor's life hard, even in the absence of enemy action. Losses were sometimes heavy, as in the case of the ill-fated Convoy PQ-17, which lost 24 of its 35 merchant ships.

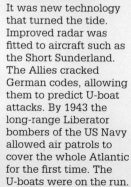

FUNNY FOOD

British people became used to unfamiliar foods. Dried eggs came in a tin, bread was a standardized gray National Loaf, beer was diluted, and precooked Spam replaced much of the fresh meat supply.

NEW DEFENSES

It was new technology that turned the tide. Improved radar was fitted to aircraft such as the Short Sunderland. The Allies cracked German codes, allowing them to predict U-boat attacks. By 1943 the long-range Liberator bombers of the US Navy allowed air patrols to cover the whole Atlantic for the first time. The U-boats were on the run.

1943

U-BOATS TAMED

In Spring 1943 Allied shipping losses peaked, but so did the sinking of U-boats. Using improved technology and tactics, escort ships and aircraft imposed heavy losses. U-boats were temporarily withdrawn for repairs, and would never again seriously threaten the Allied war effort.

Barbarossa: Hitler Invades Russia

1941–1944

In June 1941 Adolf Hitler launched Operation Barbarossa, the invasion of the USSR. His forces overran large tracts of territory, but failed to crush the Soviet Red Army. Instead, Hitler's armies were destroyed as Stalin's forces fought back.

06/22/1941

WHIRLWIND ATTACK About 4 million soldiers took part in the German invasion, which started on June 22, 1941. German heavy weaponry and blitzkrieg tactics shattered Soviet defenses along the entire border, from the Baltic to the Black Sea.

09/07/1941

SOVIET TROOPS CAPTURED Trapped in large encirclements, vast numbers of Soviet soldiers were captured by the Germans. Carried off to camps, more than 2 million had died in captivity by early 1942 due to maltreatment and systematic massacre. This was in line with Nazi policy, which planned to kill 30 million "excess" Soviet citizens.

09/08/1941

LENINGRAD UNDER SIEGE Inhabitants of Leningrad (modern-day St. Petersburg) endured bombardment and starvation after the Germans laid siege to the city. The siege lasted 872 days and cost a million civilian lives.

12/05/1941

ENDURING THE COLD As the advancing Germans reached the outskirts of Moscow in December 1941, the harsh Russian winter set in. German troops, most without winter equipment, suffered bitterly from the cold. A counteroffensive drove the Germans back from Moscow, which was never taken.

07/17/1942

ADVANCE TO STALINGRAD Through 1942 the Soviet Union suffered heavy losses of men and territory. In August German forces advancing deeper into Russia launched an attack on Stalingrad, on the Volga River. Soviet General Georgii Zhukov prepared a rescue mission, encircling the Germans inside the city.

07/01/1943

SOVIET RESISTANCE German-occupied areas in the Soviet Union saw bands of partisans (resistance fighters) waging guerrilla warfare. They disrupted German supply routes and communications. The German response was brutal; they not only publicly executed captured guerrillas but also massacred thousands of peasants in collective reprisals.

08/23/1943

SWIFT ADVANCE The assault took the Soviets completely by surprise. The Germans gained huge tracts of land before the Soviets could respond.

KEY

→ German/Axis advances
— Front line June 21, 1941
— Front line Sept 1, 1941
— Front line Nov 15, 1941
— Front line Dec 5, 1941

(map labels: FINLAND, Helsinki, Tallinn, Leningrad, Baltic Sea, Riga, USSR, Moscow, Smolensk, EAST PRUSSIA, Minsk, Warsaw, BYELORUSSIA, POLAND, Kiev, HUNGARY, UKRAINE, Rostov, ROMANIA, Sea of Azov, CRIMEA, Black Sea, Sevastopol)

08/23/1942

DEFENDING THE CITY The Germans entered Stalingrad in August 1942. Determined Soviet troops defended the city building by building, until Zhukov's trap cut off the Germans from the rear.

01/31/1943

FIELD MARSHAL SURRENDERS Trapped inside Stalingrad, with supply lines cut off, German soldiers began to starve and freeze to death. Despite orders from Hitler to fight to the last man, German Field Marshal Friedrich Paulus surrendered on January 31. He survived the war, but almost all the 100,000 soldiers taken prisoner with him died in captivity.

VICTORY AT KURSK At Kursk in western Russia, the Soviets and Germans fought the largest armor battle in history, with around 8,000 tanks deployed. Despite sustaining heavy losses, the Soviets were victorious, and their drive westward became unstoppable. By summer 1944 the Red Army had entered Poland and was approaching the German frontier in East Prussia.

06/22/1944

TECHNICAL ADVANTAGE The Soviet victory depended on their ability to mass-produce effective armaments. Weapons such as the truck-mounted Katyusha rocket launchers were cheap, easy to manufacture, and devastating in battle.

„КРАСНАЯ АРМИЯ СОВМЕСТНО С АРМИЯМИ НАШИХ СОЮЗНИКОВ СЛОМАЕТ ХРЕБЕТ ФАШИСТСКОМУ ЗВЕРЮ". (И. Сталин).

UNITED IN BATTLE A Russian poster depicts Britain, the Soviet Union, and the USA united in the fight against Hitler. The British and Americans supplied their Soviet allies with large quantities of supplies vital to the war effort.

Attack on Pearl Harbor

1941

On December 7, 1941, Japan launched a surprise attack on the American base at Pearl Harbor, Hawaii. The raid brought the United States into war not only against Japan, but also against Germany and Italy.

> …a **date** which will **live in infamy**…
>
> US PRESIDENT FRANKLIN D. ROOSEVELT, DECEMBER 8, 1941

09/27/1940

JAPAN JOINS THE AXIS
Japan signed a Tripartite Pact with the Axis powers, Nazi Germany and Fascist Italy. Japan's relations with the United States were strained due to America's opposition to Japan's war of conquest in China. The Japanese alliance linked the gathering storm in the Pacific and Asia to the ongoing war in Europe.

03/11/1941

12/07/1941

CAUGHT UNAWARE
It was a relaxed Sunday morning for the US personnel at Pearl Harbor. Although tensions with Japan were high, there had been no declaration of war and defenses were not on alert. The first wave of Japanese bombers surprised American battleships lined up at anchor with guns unmanned.

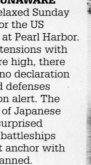

12/07/1941

FINAL STRIKE A second wave of 170 Japanese aircraft completed the devastation. Torpedoes and bombs sank or wrecked 18 American warships, including five battleships. Japan had succeeded in temporarily putting the US Pacific Fleet out of action, opening the way for conquests in the Pacific and Southeast Asia.

12/08/1941

MOURNING THE DEAD More than 2,000 Americans died in the Pearl Harbor attacks. The USA formally declared war on Japan, and Germany in turn declared war on America.

02/15/1942

MALAYA AND THE PHILIPPINES INVADED
At the same time as the Pearl Harbor attack, Japan invaded the Philippines and the British colony of Malaya. In February 1942 the Japanese captured the British base at Singapore. Captured British and Commonwealth soldiers and civilians were treated harshly by the Japanese.

04/03/1942

DEATH MARCH IN BATAAN After the Bataan Peninsula in the Philippines fell to the Japanese in April 1942, American and Filipino prisoners of war were subjected to a brutal forced march. Thousands died of maltreatment, hunger, and exhaustion. The death march further embittered Americans toward the Japanese.

"ARSENAL OF DEMOCRACY"

In December 1940, US President Franklin D. Roosevelt declared that America must become an "arsenal of democracy" and equip Britain to fight Germany. American factories increased output of arms and munitions, supplied to the British without payment—but the USA stayed out of the war.

10/18/1941

TOJO COMES TO POWER In July the US imposed an oil embargo on Japan, in response to its takeover of French Indochina. Unable to continue its war in China without oil, Japan had to either abandon its imperial ambitions or fight America. In October, General Hideki Tojo was appointed prime minister to prepare for war.

12/07/1941

TAKING OFF Japanese Admiral Isokuru Yamamoto devised a plan for naval aircraft to destroy the US Pacific Fleet at Pearl Harbor in Hawaii. Six Japanese aircraft carriers crossed the Pacific Ocean unobserved. At dawn on December 7, 1941, the Japanese launched the first wave of attacks, deploying 183 bombers and torpedo aircraft from 250 miles (400 km) north of Hawaii.

12/07/1941

AIRFIELDS BOMBED The aircraft that should have defended Pearl Harbor were caught on the ground, as the Japanese bombed and strafed the airfields. More than 300 American aircraft were destroyed or damaged. The US Navy's aircraft carriers were away at sea at the time, and luckily avoided destruction.

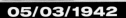

05/03/1942

BACKLASH AGAINST JAPANESE AMERICANS Some 120,000 American citizens of Japanese origin lived on the Pacific Coast. Under Executive Order 9066, signed by President Roosevelt in February 1942, these Japanese Americans were forcibly relocated to internment camps for the duration of the war. This contrasted starkly with the treatment of Americans of German or Italian origin.

...we here highly resolve that these dead shall not have died in vain...

REMEMBER DEC. 7th!

DEFIANT RESPONSE American citizens were urged to remember the "sneak attack" on Pearl Harbor to encourage them in the war effort.

War in the Pacific

1941–1945

After the attack on Pearl Harbor in December 1941, a Japanese tide of conquest unfurled over Southeast Asia and the Pacific. However, from mid-1942 an American-led fight back first halted Japanese expansion and then reversed it. As the war drew closer to Japan, the fighting increased in ferocity.

04/18/1942
DOOLITTLE RAID
Seeking revenge for Pearl Harbor, a US Air Force Lieutenant-Colonel named Jimmy Doolittle led 16 bombers in a raid on Japanese cities. Although all of the aircraft were destroyed, American casualties were light, and the success of the mission boosted American morale.

08/07/1942
AMERICANS LAND ON GUADALCANAL
In August 1942 US troops landed on Guadalcanal in the Solomon Islands. The Japanese counter-attacked with aircraft and warships. Japanese soldiers landed on the island and fierce battles were fought around the American airstrip, Henderson Field.

11/16/1942
AUSTRALIANS IN NEW GUINEA
Australian forces played a major role in the Pacific war. In New Guinea, they fought the Japanese along the Kokoda Trail, a track through disease-ridden jungle and across steep mountains. Their victory at Milne Bay is credited as the first land defeat of Japan in the war.

02/01/1944

CAPTURING ISLANDS
Under Admiral Nimitz, US forces began an effective campaign to capture the Pacific island by island, driving ever closer to Japan. The Americans repeatedly overcame ferocious Japanese resistance. Few prisoners were taken as many Japanese soldiers preferred suicide to surrender.

WARTIME PROPAGANDA
A poster boasts of American courage following the attacks on Pearl Harbor.

06/19/1944

10/20/1944
THE RETURN OF MACARTHUR
When the Japanese conquered the Philippines in 1942, US General Douglas MacArthur promised to return to the islands. His vow was fulfilled on October 20, 1944, during the landings on Leyte Island. Fighting in the Philippines continued until the end of the war.

10/23/1944
KAMIKAZE ATTACKS
During the naval battle of Leyte Gulf, Japanese soldiers adopted suicide tactics. Using their aircraft as flying bombs, they attempted to crash into the decks of US warships. These kamikaze ("divine wind") attacks were extremely effective, sinking dozens of ships by the war's end.

06/07/1942

BATTLE OF MIDWAY
In June 1942, the US and Japanese fleets clashed at the Battle of Midway. Dive-bombers destroyed four Japanese carriers and a cruiser. Although the Americans lost *USS Yorktown*, overall the battle was a triumph for the US Navy, and a disaster for the Japanese—a turning point in the war.

06/28/1942

CAMPAIGN IN BURMA
The Japanese army advanced into Burma, threatening British-ruled India. The Chindits, special forces of the British Army of India, were sent into the Burmese jungle to carry out guerrilla warfare behind Japanese lines. The Allies did not reoccupy Burma until the summer of 1945.

01/12/1943

US INDUSTRY
By 1943 American factories and shipyards were fully geared up for war. A target of building 27,500 naval aircraft was met and surpassed. Dozens of new carriers were built to operate the planes. Japan simply could not compete, its forces declining as American naval power grew.

BATTLE OF THE PHILIPPINE SEA
In June the Americans landed on Saipan in the Mariana Islands. Japan sent a fleet of carriers to attack US warships supporting the landings. It was a disaster for the Japanese—600 of their aircraft were shot down in what became known as the Marianas Turkey Shoot. The American fleet suffered minimal damage.

> On Iwo Island, **uncommon valor** was a **common virtue**.

FLEET ADMIRAL CHESTER W. NIMITZ, SPRING 1945

02/23/1945

BATTLE OF IWO JIMA
Nimitz's island-hopping strategy culminated in the first attack on Japanese home soil, at the island of Iwo Jima. US Marines suffered 26,000 casualties in the battle, before raising the American flag in victory.

The Desert War

1940–1943

The deserts of North Africa saw fierce tank battles as the Axis and Allies fought for control of the Mediterranean and the Suez Canal. Although the campaign made a legend of German Field Marshal Erwin Rommel, his Axis forces were finally overpowered, allowing the Allies to protect their oil supplies in the Middle East and drive Italy out of the war.

09/13/1940

MUSSOLINI IN EGYPT
In June 1940 Italian dictator Benito Mussolini took his country into World War II as an ally of Nazi Germany. In September Italian forces advanced across the border from Libya, then an Italian colony, into Egypt, where British troops were stationed to guard the Suez Canal.

04/11/1941

TOBRUK UNDER SIEGE Rommel's advance left Australian troops besieged at the Libyan port of Tobruk. Despite German air attacks, they held out until the siege was lifted.

05/01/1942

MALTA BOMBED
The Mediterranean island of Malta was a vital base for Britain's Royal Navy and a threat to Axis supply lines to North Africa. German and Italian air forces bombed the island throughout 1941–1942, and convoys carrying supplies to the island came under heavy attack. Although the bombings caused heavy damage, Malta survived the onslaught.

11/04/1942

VICTORY AT EL ALAMEIN
The offensive at El Alamein was a hard-fought battle against well-prepared Axis defenses. After 12 days' struggle through lines of anti-tank guns and minefields, the Eighth Army drove Rommel's forces in headlong retreat westward. The battle cost Montgomery more than 13,000 casualties, but Axis losses were much higher.

> "We are going to **finish** with this chap **Rommel once and for all**.
>
> **GENERAL BERNARD MONTGOMERY, COMMANDER OF BRITISH EIGHTH ARMY, AUGUST 1942**

01/10/1941

ITALIANS SUFFER DEFEAT British and Commonwealth forces counterattacked. By January 1941 the Italians were retreating across Libya and thousands were taken prisoner.

03/11/1941

ROMMEL ARRIVES IN AFRICA To rescue Mussolini's troops, in March 1941 Hitler sent Field Marshal Erwin Rommel to North Africa at the head of the Afrika Korps, a force of German tanks. Under Rommel's inspired leadership, the Germans and Italians reversed the tide of war in the desert.

05/26/1942

FREE FRENCH FIGHTERS The battle of Gazala, fought in the Libyan desert in May–June 1942, was a decisive victory for Rommel's tanks, which outfought their British opponents. During the battle the Free French brigade, part of the British Eighth Army, displayed outstanding courage at Bir Hakeim, holding out for 16 days against superior forces.

10/23/1942

MONTGOMERY TAKES COMMAND In August 1942 General Bernard Montgomery took command of Eighth Army, which had been driven back to El Alamein, deep inside Egypt. Montgomery restored the troops' morale, repelled an Axis attack at the battle of Alam El Halfa, and meticulously prepared for a large scale offensive.

11/08/1942

AMERICANS IN AFRICA In November 1942 a largely American force landed on the North African coast, in Algeria and Morocco. The Americans were led by Major General George S. Patton, known to his men as "Old Blood and Guts." The landings brought US troops into combat with German and Italian forces for the first time.

05/13/1943

AXIS SURRENDER Trapped between Montgomery's and Eisenhower's armies, the Axis forces retreated into Tunisia, where they fought a determined defensive campaign. In May 1943, after Rommel had been pulled out, the remaining Axis troops surrendered. Almost 250,000 became prisoners of war.

07/09/1943

ALLIES INVADE SICILY Victory in North Africa provided the springboard for Allied landings on the Mediterranean island of Sicily in July 1943. The island was captured after five weeks of hard fighting. This successful Allied invasion of Italian territory eventually led to the overthrow of Mussolini. He was replaced as head of government by Marshal Pietro Badoglio, who signed an armistice with the Allies in September.

MONTGOMERY'S BANNER
The Desert Rat was the famous emblem of the British 7th Armored Division, which fought in all the major battles of the North African campaign.

D-Day

1944

By the summer of 1944, after months of secret planning and a massive buildup of forces, the Allies were ready to launch the invasion that would liberate Western Europe from German occupation. The date of the invasion, June 6, would go down in history as D-Day.

GENERAL EISENHOWER
US General Dwight D. Eisenhower was in overall command of the Allied forces in Europe.

GENERAL MONTGOMERY
British General Bernard Montgomery commanded the ground troops in the largest amphibious invasion in history.

02:00

06:30

DEFENSIVE LINE The German forces were protected by an extensive system of trenches, barbed wire, and bunkers. They defended with grim determination.

06:31

NORMANDY BEACHES
The Allies landed on five codenamed beaches: Sword and Gold for the British; Juno for the Canadians; and Omaha and Utah for US forces.

KEY
→ Allied landing/advance
▲ Allied parachute landing
— Allied front line June 7, 1944

Cherbourg
English Channel
US 1ST ARMY
BRITISH 2ND ARMY
UTAH
OMAHA
GOLD
JUNO
SWORD
St Mère Eglise
Lion-sur-Mer
Pointe du Hoc
Bayeux
Vierville
Arromanches
Caen
FRANCE

08:30

CONSOLIDATING THE BEACHES
Eventually the Americans overwhelmed the defenses at Omaha, and all five beaches were in Allied hands. Later in the morning, the first of a vast array of supply ships, protected from air attack by barrage balloons, began pouring vital reinforcements ashore.

> ❝ The **free men of the world** are marching together to **victory**. ❞
>
> **US GENERAL DWIGHT D. EISENHOWER, JUNE 6, 1944**

11:00

16:00

AIR ATTACK The D-Day operations began early on June 6 when three Allied airborne divisions landed by parachute and glider behind enemy lines. Their job was to destroy German artillery batteries that threatened the mission, as well as capture and hold key bridges until the main forces arrived. A massive air assault was also launched to soften German defenses.

03:00

CROSSING THE CHANNEL The largest armada in history, a fleet of about 7,000 ships, left ports in southern England to ferry the main Allied army to France. By dawn on June 6, off the Normandy coast, thousands of troops clambered into landing craft, ready to launch their attack.

07:30

THE STRUGGLE BEGINS After naval bombardment further weakened the defenses, Allied land forces advanced. The British and Canadians reported victory at Sword, Juno, and Gold. US forces at Utah also achieved a swift victory, but those landing at Omaha suffered as strong winds battered the landing craft and beach defenses took their toll.

07:30

FIERCE FIGHTING At Omaha, US forces were met by a storm of fire from defenders on the cliffs. Casualties were horrendous as they struggled to wade ashore.

BEACHES OF BLOOD Success came at a terrible cost, with 2,500 Allied dead and another 7,500 wounded, but Allied commanders had expected far greater losses. After treatment on the beaches, most of the wounded were soon on ships back to hospitals in southern England. The Germans had lost about 9,000 men in their frantic defense of the coastline.

12:30

ADVANCING INLAND As reinforcements arrived, the five Allied divisions moved inland to meet up with the paratroopers that had landed earlier. While British forces moved to reinforce the Allied eastern flank against counterattacks from elite German tank units, US forces spread out to the west.

THE BREAKOUT By the end of D-Day, a total of 150,000 Allied troops had disembarked onto the Normandy beaches. Over coming days they would move to capture surrounding territory, linking the separate beachheads to create a platform for further advance. The liberation of occupied Europe had begun.

HOPEFUL HEADLINES Newspapers across the Allied countries rejoiced at the news of D-Day. Optimism for an early end to the war grew with the capture of Paris in August.

1945

The Ashes of Dresden

Between February 13 and 15, 1945, Allied bombers dropped thousands of tons of incendiary and high-explosive bombs on the German city of Dresden. The bombs created a firestorm, a self-sustaining furnace in which hot air rushing upward sucked in cold air from the surrounding area. Eyewitnesses recall victims fainting from lack of oxygen, or being dragged into the flames by the force of the storm. The heat of the blaze melted glass and even metal. When the fires died, they revealed a devastated city. The Rathausturm (City Hall tower) miraculously remained standing. At its top a sandstone sculpture representing the figure of kindness looked down on the ashes. The attack on Dresden was controversial even at the time, with critics accusing the Allies of seeking revenge for the Blitz over British cities. Dresden today is a bustling modern city, but the scars of 1945 will never completely disappear.

End of the War in Europe

1944–1945

By 1945 Germany had clearly lost the war in Europe, but Hitler wanted a fight to the death. Invaded from east and west, Germany suffered massive destruction before surrendering.

12/16/1944

BATTLE OF THE BULGE In 1944 the Germans launched a final offensive against Allied positions in France and Belgium. American troops bore the brunt of this surprise attack, halting the German advance. The battle ended in a decisive victory for the Allies.

02/21/1945

CIVILIANS FLEE As the Soviets advanced, vast numbers of civilians fled toward the west using any means of transportation they could find.

04/25/1945

ELBE MEETING In March 1945 the Western Allies crossed the Rhine, while the Soviets advanced into Germany from the east. American and Soviet troops met and posed for photographs on the Elbe River in April. The Soviets were then left to overcome the final resistance of the Nazi regime in Berlin.

04/30/1945

SOVIETS CAPTURE BERLIN At the end of April victorious Soviet troops raised the Red Flag over the Reichstag building in Berlin. To avoid capture, Hitler killed himself inside his Berlin bunker on the same day.

05/04/1945

GERMANY SURRENDERS Admiral Hans-Georg von Friedeburg signed the surrender of German forces in northern Germany on May 4, 1945. The unconditional surrender of all German forces was completed at ceremonies in the city of Reims in France, on May 7, and in Berlin on May 8.

FALLEN NAZI EMBLEM This Nazi emblem was found in the rubble of the Reich Chancellory. All symbols of Hitler's regime were removed by the victorious Allies during their "de-Nazification" of Germany.

02/03/1945

RULING THE SKY

By 1945 Allied bombers had overwhelmed German defenses, pummeling targets at will. Refusing to admit defeat, Hitler mobilized the elderly and children for the defense of his crumbling Reich. Industry was kept functioning by building factories underground and using slave labor.

02/13/1945

DRESDEN DESTROYED In one of the most controversial acts of the war, Allied bombers pounded Dresden for two days and nights. The resulting firestorm killed an estimated 25,000 civilians, and reduced the historic city center to rubble.

04/28/1945

MUSSOLINI EXECUTED

Benito Mussolini was the first Axis dictator to die. He was captured by communist resistance fighters and shot. His body was hung upside-down in the forecourt of a Milan gasoline station, alongside his mistress Clara Petacci and other executed Fascists. Thousands of Fascists around Italy were purged, and political unrest reached boiling point.

08/05/1945

VE DAY CELEBRATION Proclaimed Victory in Europe Day, May 8, 1945 was the occasion for joyous celebrations in all Allied capitals. However, the triumph was missed by one of its chief architects—US President Franklin Roosevelt, who died on April 12.

> ## The **flags of freedom** fly all over Europe.
>
> **US PRESIDENT TRUMAN,
> VE DAY SPEECH, MAY 8, 1945**

Nuclear Bombs Dropped on Japan

1945

Scientists knew it was possible to create a massive explosion through nuclear fission. In 1942 the USA initiated the top secret Manhattan Project to build an atom bomb. This huge scientific and industrial effort reached fruition in 1945.

03/09/1945

> We have discovered the **most terrible bomb** in the history of the world.

PRESIDENT TRUMAN'S DIARY ENTRY, JULY 16, 1945

07/27/1945

HIROHITO CONSIDERS PEACE Japanese Emperor Hirohito believed his country must seek peace, but a majority in his government still wanted a fight to the death.

08/06/1945

CLUELESS CREW
The crew of the B-29 bomber *Enola Gay* was assigned to drop the first atom bomb on the city of Hiroshima. The bomber took off from Tinian Island in the Marianas on August 6, 1945. Only then did the commander inform his men of the nature of the weapon they were carrying.

08/06/1945

HIROSHIMA DESTROYED The blast wave from the explosion flattened an area of 5 sq miles (12 sq km) in the center of the city. Violent winds spread destructive firestorms, completing the devastation.

08/09/1945

NAGASAKI BOMBED
Since the Japanese made no move to surrender, the USA dropped a second atom bomb on the city of Nagasaki on August 9, 1945. Although this bomb was even more powerful, the devastation was less total, because parts of Nagasaki were sheltered from the full effect of blast and radiation by surrounding hills.

08/11/1945

MASSIVE DEATH TOLL
Tens of thousands were killed immediately by the nuclear bombs. Others died of severe burns and exposure to deadly levels of nuclear radiation. Although the exact death toll, including deaths from the long-term effects of radiation, is not certain, it almost certainly exceeds 200,000.

RAIDS OVER JAPAN
From March 1945, the USA started intensive bombing raids against Japanese cities, using high-altitude B-29 bombers capable of dropping massive bomb loads. A single raid on Tokyo in March 1945 is believed to have killed as many as 100,000 people in a firestorm started by incendiary bombs.

07/16/1945

TESTING THE BOMB
In July the first atomic device was tested at Alamagordo in the New Mexico desert. Robert Oppenheimer, the scientific director of the Manhattan Project, led the examination of twisted wreckage at ground zero. The power of the explosion had exceeded expectations.

07/26/1945

POTSDAM CONFERENCE
The war had ended in Europe, but Japan refused to surrender. In July US President Harry S Truman met leaders of the other Allied nations for a conference at Potsdam in Germany. On July 26 they issued a declaration calling on Japan to surrender or face "utter destruction." Unaware of the atom bomb's existence, the Japanese failed to agree terms of surrender.

08/06/1945

ATOM BOMB DROPPED
The atom bomb, known as "Little Boy," was released from an altitude of 31,000 ft (9,500 m) at 8.15 am. It detonated over the center of Hiroshima in a blinding flash of light and heat that vaporized everything on the ground below. The blast, equivalent to about 14,000 tons of TNT, threw up a swirling mushroom cloud that towered over the city.

SECOND BOMB Codenamed "Fat Man," the plutonium bomb dropped on Nagasaki was more powerful than "Little Boy," which contained uranium.

09/02/1945

JAPANESE SURRENDER
Despite the bombings the Japanese government remained split on whether or not to surrender, but Emperor Hirohito pressured them to give in. The decision to surrender was made on August 14 and announced to the people the following day. The official surrender document was signed on board USS *Missouri* on September 2, bringing World War II to a close.

The Holocaust

1938–1945

From 1933, Jews living in Germany were subjected to harassment, discrimination, and segregation. During World War II, Nazi anti-Semitism culminated in a systematic attempt to exterminate the entire Jewish population of Europe, a Holocaust in which an estimated 5.7 million people were killed.

11/09/1938

KRISTALLNACHT During the night, Nazi stormtroopers and civilians attacked Jewish shops, homes, and synagogues throughout Germany and Austria. Thousands of Jews were arrested and taken to concentration camps. It was dubbed "Kristallnacht" (Crystal Night) because of the number of smashed windows, and marked an escalation in mistreatment of the Jews.

09/21/1939

GHETTOIZATION OF JEWS When Germany conquered Poland in 1939, Polish Jews were herded into ghettos. Those who did not die there through hardship or random killings were sent to extermination camps.

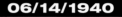

06/14/1940

YELLOW BADGE From 1941, Jewish people under Nazi rule were required to wear a yellow Star of David sewn on their clothes.

01/20/1942

THE FINAL SOLUTION At the Wannsee Conference in Berlin in January 1942, leading Nazis and German civil servants discussed the systematic extermination of all Jews in German-occupied Europe. Their plan—known as the Final Solution—was an industrialized system of death camps, where prisoners could be exterminated en masse, to speed up the genocide.

07/16/1942

07/23/1942

MASS DEATH When trainloads of Jews arrived at the camps, some were taken off to work as slave laborers. The rest were led directly to gas chambers, where they were killed. Working was the only chance of survival, but conditions in the camps were appallingly harsh.

04/29/1944

FANATIC Among the most infamous prosecutors of the Final Solution was Adolf Eichmann. In April 1944 he organized the deportation of more than 430,000 Jews from Hungary to Auschwitz. He continued his work even after the Nazi government had called a halt to the killings.

11/13/1938

KINDERTRANSPORT

After Kristallnacht, German and Austrian Jews were desperate to escape persecution, but many countries refused to accept Jewish refugees. Some 10,000 Jewish children escaped to Britain, leaving their parents behind, in a program known as Kindertransport, and a similar program was organized in the USA.

> We had the **moral right**, we had the **duty**… **to destroy** this people [the Jews]…

SS CHIEF HEIMLICH HIMMLER, OCTOBER 1943

SLAVE LABOR

Jewish prisoners were taken to concentration camps, where they were forced to work without pay. The German chemical company IG Farben, for instance, established a factory at Auschwitz to capitalize on prisoner labor. Working and living conditions were harsh, food supplies inadequate, and punishments savage.

09/29/1941

MASSACRES IN EASTERN EUROPE

In June 1941, Germany invaded the Soviet Union. Death squads were sent into occupied territory to round up and kill political dissidents. In September 1941, 33,000 Jews were killed in two days at Babi Yar in Ukraine. They were buried in mass graves.

ROUNDED UP TO DIE

Jews were brought from all over Europe to the death camps. In July 1942, 13,000 Jews were arrested in Paris with the support of the pro-Nazi Vichy government. They were sent to Auschwitz for extermination. Conditions on the long journey across Europe were horrendous, and many died packed into cattle trucks.

01/27/1945

LIBERATION In 1944–1945, advancing Allied armies overran the camps, liberating the survivors. They were shocked by what they found: the deathly starvation and mistreatment of the survivors, and evidence of mass murder on an unprecedented scale.

1945

Holocaust Victims

The Nazi policy of mass extermination gave rise to a brutal practical problem: how to achieve the killing and disposal of millions of human beings. The Nazis' Final Solution was murder on an industrial scale: factories devoted to death, and to the destruction of corpses. Perhaps the most infamous extermination camp was at Auschwitz-Birkenau in southern Poland, where 1.3 million people are thought to have been killed and cremated. Victims were stripped of their belongings, and rooms full of discarded shoes, pairs of glasses, and even human hair stood as testament to the staggering number of dead. It is thought that approximately 5.7 million Jews were killed in the Holocaust, along with an estimated 5 million gypsies, Soviet prisoners, Slavs, political dissidents, and homosexuals. The vast number of deaths, and the astonishing, dehumanizing brutality of the killings, would permanently alter mankind's perception of evil.

The Iron Curtain Descends

1939–1950

Stalin used the outbreak of World War II to seize control of Eastern Poland. Following Hitler's invasion of Russia in 1941, the USSR joined the fight against Germany, and as the Red Army drove the German invaders back, Stalin tightened his grip on Eastern Europe.

1939

NAZI–SOVIET PACT
A week before the German invasion of Poland, Hitler and Stalin agreed a non-aggression pact. It included secret terms to divide Eastern Europe between Germany and the USSR. The pact was signed by Soviet foreign minister Vyacheslav Molotov and Hitler's negotiator Joachim von Ribbentrop.

1940

FOREST MASSACRE
Stalin was quick to eliminate potential resistance. Soviet secret police carried out a mass execution of 22,000 Poles, including 8,000 prisoners of war. Mass graves were discovered in Katyn Forest, Belarus, by the Nazis in 1943, but the USSR denied the atrocity until 1990.

1940

WAR IN THE SNOW
Stalin's forces marched on to Finland, but the tiny Finnish army resisted bravely. Although forced to sue for peace, Finland retained independence with minimal loss of territory. The following year, Hitler's armies turned on the Soviet Union, and Stalin turned to the Allies.

1945

YALTA CONFERENCE As the Red Army marched on Berlin, Stalin met with Churchill and US President Franklin D. Roosevelt at Yalta, Ukraine. Churchill and Roosevelt remained wary of the communist leader. As negotiations continued over coming months, the lines were drawn for an ideological division between communist east and democratic west.

1945

YUGOSLAVIA GOES RED As the Nazis were driven back, partisan fighters in eastern Europe and the Balkans welcomed Soviet troops as liberators. Many of them were supporters of communism, such as Marshal Tito, the Yugoslavian leader, who became head of a federal communist state in 1945.

1949

1939

POLAND DEFEATED
Following the Nazi invasion, the Soviet Red Army moved into Eastern Poland on September 17. Polish resistance collapsed and the country was divided into German and Russian zones, in accordance with the Nazi–Soviet Pact.

1944

MOSCOW TALKS
As German defeat became more likely, the Allied leaders met in Moscow to discuss the future. British Prime Minister Winston Churchill jotted down an informal agreement for the division of Europe between the Soviets and the West after the war.

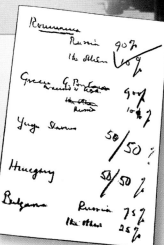

> ## Never mind. We'll do it **our own way** later.
>
> **STALIN TO SOVIET FOREIGN MINISTER MOLOTOV, ON THE YALTA AGREEMENT, FEBRUARY 1945**

1946

SOVIET GERMANY
With the final defeat of the Nazis, Germany was divided. East Germany became a Soviet-occupied zone. In 1949, it became the German Democratic Republic, a satellite state of the USSR, with most of its political and economic processes under Soviet control.

KEY
- Soviet territory
- Soviet-dominated communist states by 1949
- Members of NATO 1949
- Independent communist state
- — Iron Curtain in 1949
- • Cities divided into zones of occupation

SOVIET EXPANSION
Stalin resolved that Russia would never be invaded again. By 1948, the USSR lay behind a wall of communist states, forming an east–west divide that Churchill labeled the Iron Curtain.

THE EASTERN BLOC EXPANDS
Communist parties in Hungary, Bulgaria, and Romania mounted aggressive propaganda campaigns, calling for closer union with the USSR. Soviet agitators stirred up unrest, and anti-Soviet parties were subject to persecution. Communist movements were accused of falsifying election results and suppressing opposition.

1950

SOVIET CULTURE
By 1950, Soviet-backed regimes were in place across Eastern Europe. Contact with the west was tightly controlled, as were political and cultural expression. Monuments such as the Palace of Science and Culture in Warsaw, Poland, were a constant reminder of Soviet dominance.

FINLAND

UNITED KINGDOM

NORWAY

SWEDEN

Baltic Sea

ESTONIA

LATVIA

LITHUANIA

DENMARK

NETHERLANDS

IRELAND

BEL.

LUX.

WEST GERMANY

Berlin

EAST GERMANY

POLAND

BYELO-RUSSIA

U S S R

CZECH.

Vienna

UKRAINE

ATLANTIC OCEAN

FRANCE

SWITZ.

AUSTRIA

HUNG.

ROMANIA

YUGOSLAVIA

Black Sea

ITALY

BULGARIA

SPAIN

Mediterranean Sea

ALBANIA

GREECE

TURKEY

PORTUGAL

War in Indochina

1940–1954

France had ruled Indochina (present-day Vietnam, Cambodia, and Laos) since 1887. Heading the fight for liberation was a group of exiled nationalist revolutionaries, most notably communist leader Ho Chi Minh. After joining the fight against Japanese occupation during World War II, he and his allies saw an opportunity to free their country from colonial rule.

FRENCH INDOCHINA
France ruled south Vietnam as a colony. Central and north Vietnam, Laos, and Cambodia were protectorates. The French exploited the region for cash crops such as cotton, severely reducing food production. Their policies were bitterly resented by the local population.

05/19/1941

VIET MINH FOUNDED
Returning to Vietnam after 30 years, Ho Chi Minh set up the headquarters of the Viet Minh (League for the Liberation of Vietnam) at Bac Bo, near the Chinese border, to fight a guerrilla war against the Japanese. After Japan's surrender in World War II, the Viet Minh occupied Hanoi, where Ho Chi Minh proclaimed the Democratic Republic of Vietnam.

10/05/1945

FRENCH RETURN
The first French troops arrived in Saigon in 1945 to reimpose French colonial rule. The SS Île-de-France, an ocean liner, was used to convey later reinforcements. Negotiations over France's recognition of the Democratic Republic of Vietnam broke down when a French cruiser shelled the port of Hai Phong in November 1946.

12/19/1946

06/13/1949

HOSTILITIES CONTINUE French armed forces continued their campaign against the Viet Minh. In an attempt to undermine Ho Chi Minh's authority, the French persuaded Bao Dai, the last emperor of Vietnam, to return as head of a puppet state with limited independence.

01/18/1950

CHINA ENTERS THE FRAY The People's Republic of China, established in 1949, formally recognized Ho Chi Minh's government. The war entered a new phase as communist China supplied the Viet Minh with military advisors and weapons, enabling them to renew attacks against the French.

11/14/1953

PLAN TO END THE WAR The French established an outpost at Dien Bien Phu, near the border with Laos. Six parachute battalions were dropped into the area, to begin setting up a base surrounded by seven fortified strongpoints. The plan was to lure the Viet Minh to attack, and destroy them in the crossfire.

> ## "
> The **French** are... **weak** ... they will have to go because the **white man** is **finished** in Asia.
>
> **HO CHI MINH, MARCH 1946** "

03/13/1954

THE BATTLE BEGINS
General Giap moved around 40,000 men into the hills surrounding Dien Bien Phu, using peasants on bicycles to carry artillery guns piece by piece up the mountains. His initial artillery attack took the French completely by surprise. The Viet Minh captured one strongpoint after another, forcing the French to surrender in May.

HO CHI MINH

Born in Annam in 1890, Ho Chi Minh (birth name Nguyen Sinh Cung) became a communist while working in Paris after World War I.

09/22/1940

JAPAN IN INDOCHINA During the Second Sino-Japanese War, Japan invaded Vietnam across the Chinese border to cut off China's supply lines. Bicycle troops, used extensively by the Japanese in their jungle campaigns, were among the first to enter. More troops came ashore at Hai Phong on the Gulf of Tonkin and began to advance on Hanoi. The pro-Axis Vichy French authorities negotiated a ceasefire that allowed the Japanese to occupy military bases in Indochina.

WAR OF RESISTANCE

Ho Chi Minh called for a popular rising against the French and withdrew the Viet Minh to Bac Can in the northern mountains. The French took possession of Hanoi and other major cities, but their forces were continually harassed by Viet Minh guerrillas, who moved freely at night. The guerrillas were led by General Vo Nguyen Giap.

10/07/1947

OPERATION LEA French paratroopers were employed in a major assault to encircle Viet Minh guerrilla positions in the north. Ho Chi Minh and General Giap narrowly escaped capture, but the operation was a strategic failure and was abandoned after two months.

07/21/1954

FRENCH LEAVE

This humiliating defeat forced the French out of Indochina. However, the West remained fearful of communist rule and stepped in to support Vietnamese opposition to Ho Chi Minh. At a peace deal signed in Geneva, Vietnam was divided into communist North and pro-Western South.

VICTORY POSTER

This Viet Minh poster celebrating the victory of Dien Bien Phu, depicts a soldier with a dove of peace sitting on his shoulder.

135

Independence for India and Pakistan

1939–1948

By 1945 British control over India was severely weakened. Mahatma Gandhi's policy of nonviolent resistance had amassed a huge following, and the British Indian Armed Forces threatened strikes and mutiny. The newly elected Labour government in Britain decided to push ahead with Indian independence. However, any settlement would have to satisfy both Hindus and Muslims.

03/23/1940

LAHORE RESOLUTION
Unlike the Congress, the Muslim League supported the British war effort. Meeting at Lahore in Punjab, it adopted Muhammad Ali Jinnah's resolution that Muslims should have separate states in the northwest and the northeast of India, where they formed the majority population. This decision widened the split with Congress leaders.

08/08/1942

QUIT INDIA In August 1942 Gandhi and Nehru launched the Quit India Movement, calling for civil disobedience to upset the British war effort. The movement gained massive popularity, and Indians across the country abandoned their jobs to join the protest. Congress leaders were immediately imprisoned and held without trial for two years.

08/16/1946

SECTARIAN RIOTS
The Muslim League was determined that any independent nation should provide a separate homeland for Muslims. When the Congress rejected this plan, the situation turned violent. More than 4,000 people were killed in Calcutta on a day of riots. Gandhi pleaded with both sides to stop the fighting.

> " At the **stroke of the midnight** hour, when the world sleeps, **India will awake** to life and **freedom**. "
>
> FIRST INDIAN PRIME MINISTER JAWAHARLAL NEHRU, AUGUST 14, 1947

08/15/1947

INDIAN INDEPENDENCE
Huge crowds gathered outside the Constituent Assembly in Delhi to hear Nehru's Independence Day speech after he was sworn in as Prime Minister by Mountbatten. Liaquat Ali Khan had become the Prime Minister of Pakistan after a similar ceremony in Karachi, its capital city, the previous day.

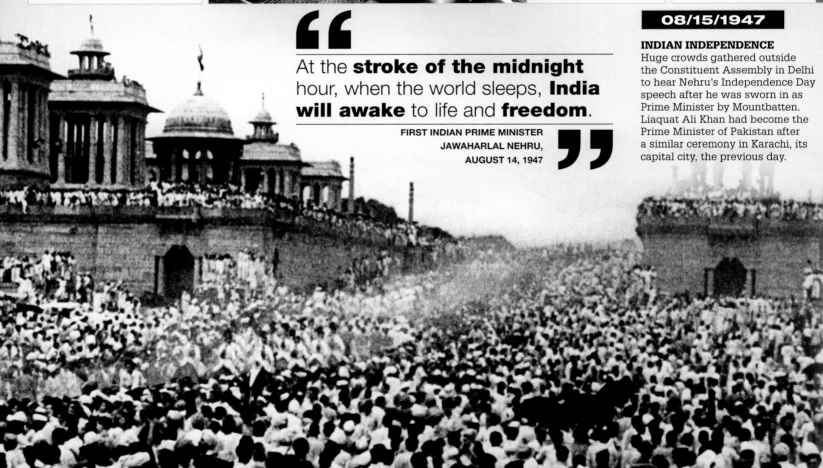

JAWAHARLAL NEHRU
Leader of the Indian National Congress, Nehru was at the forefront of the struggle for independence.

MUHAMMAD ALI JINNAH
Jinnah, head of the Muslim League, was determined that independence should include a separate state for the Muslims.

09/03/1939

INDIA IN WARTIME
On the outbreak of World War II, Britain unilaterally declared India's entry into the war without consulting Congress leaders. More than 2.5 million Indian soldiers fought with the British Army in many parts of the world. The decision caused widespread anger, and many Congress leaders withdrew from the government in protest.

07/03/1947

PARTITION PLAN
Lord Louis Mountbatten, appointed Viceroy of India in March 1947, announced that the country would be partitioned into separate states for Hindus and Muslims. He had reached this plan amid growing violence between the religious groups. Independence was to be established in August.

PAKISTAN IS BORN
Under the partition agreement, Muslim majority areas in the northwest and northeast formed the state of Pakistan. The new country came into being on August 14, 1947, a day before India gained independence. The name Pakistan derives from two Urdu words, *pak* meaning pure, and *stan* meaning country.

10/15/1947

MILLIONS DISPLACED The hastily arranged partition left millions of Muslims and Hindus stranded on the wrong side of the new borders, leading to a massive transfer of about 14 million people.

10/29/1947

OUTPOURING OF
VIOLENCE Punjab was divided in two, leaving one half in India and the other in Pakistan. Sikhs were caught in the middle of fierce religious rioting and suffered a large number of casualties. Many people were slaughtered on both sides of the border, and bodies were laid in mass graves.

01/30/1948

REVERED LEADER
Jinnah was honored as *Quaid-e-Azam*, Great Leader, in Pakistan. His face was ubiquitous, appearing on all currency notes and coins.

GANDHI
ASSASSINATED At the height of the violence, Gandhi was walking to a prayer meeting when he was shot three times in the chest. His killer was Nathuram Godse, a Hindu extremist who believed that Gandhi had betrayed his people. Nehru addressed the nation that evening, as Gandhi lay in state: "The father of our nation is no more."

A CENTURY OF

Cars

As objects of mass consumption and a symbol of personal freedom for millions of owner-drivers, automobiles became a defining feature of progress in the 20th century. Unfortunately, even as they increased mobility, cars were also using up finite resources of petroleum and contributing to the degradation of the natural environment. Developing cars that would provide a satisfactory performance without guzzling gas and causing excessive pollution posed a critical challenge.

EARLY CARS As seen on this French poster, early in the century cars were expected to be driven by a uniformed chauffeur and left their wealthy passengers exposed to the elements.

1900–1910 At the start of the century, automobiles were toys for the wealthy. They provided fun outings for rich families and excitement for amateur sportsmen in perilous road races. The authorities, regarding cars as a dangerous nuisance, tried to impose impossibly strict safety regulations. In 1901 the speed limit in Britain was 14 mph (22 kph), while in Connecticut, it was 15 mph (24 kph). By 1910 the gasoline-driven internal combustion engine, offering better performance and a compact design, had established its superiority over electric and steam engines. Cars took on a standard layout that would last for decades, with the engine at the front and rear-wheel drive.

TRAFFIC JAMS By the 1930s dense traffic was already posing problems in major cities such as London, requiring innovations including traffic lights and pedestrian crossings.

1910–1940 Price was the key to popular motoring. Using mass production, car maker Henry Ford cut the cost of his Model T from more than $800 in 1910 to $290 by the 1920s. By 1929 the USA had almost 30 million cars, five times as many as the rest of the world. But driving was still largely unregulated, and 29,000 people were killed on American roads in 1930. Building roads specifically designed for cars, such as interstate highways in the USA and German autobahns, increased speed and reduced accidents. Meanwhile, motor

1900s

GORDON BENNETT CUP The fastest competitors in the prestigious Gordon Bennett Cup race, held in France, achieved average speeds above 43 mph (70 kph) over almost 342 miles (550 km) of mountain roads.

1910s

FORD MODEL T Henry Ford's Model T was the first automobile to be manufactured on a moving assembly line. Built in 93 minutes, it was cheap enough to be affordable to the wider public; 15 million were sold by 1927.

1920s

RILEY BROOKLANDS Racing cars continued to capture the popular imagination. British manufacturer Riley had a series of successes in the 1920s with models such as the Brooklands, which was driven by both men and women racers.

1940s

WARTIME WILLYS JEEP The US Army entered World War II with the Willys Jeep as its new four-wheel drive, general-purpose vehicle. In the course of the war, more than 600,000 Jeeps were manufactured by Willys, and also by Ford.

HEAD TURNER The 1959 Cadillac Series 62 was the epitome of design excess, with tall tailfins designed to attract maximum attention.

racing flourished with the creation of annual classics, such as the Le Mans 24-hour race.

1940–1970 From the 1940s American car makers turned their backs on stripped-down simplicity and began mass-marketing cars that were big and flamboyant, with flashy chrome bumpers and tailfins. Relatively cash-strapped, Europe became the leader in cheap, economical cars, from the Volkswagen Beetle to the British Mini. European car makers pushed innovative design features, including rear engines and front-wheel drive. Well made and suited to crowded

cities, these cars began to sell in the USA, as did the Toyotas and Datsuns of a rapidly expanding Japanese car industry. By the 1960s, fins were out and high-powered sports cars were in.

1970– Mounting safety concerns marked the end of an era of relatively

The **car** has become an article of **dress without** which we feel… **unclad**.

MEDIA THEORIST
MARSHALL MCLUHAN,
1968

8,000

The approximate number of cars worldwide in 1900. By 2000 there were about 500 million cars.

unregulated, carefree motoring. Safety features such as seatbelts and airbags, as well as tighter speed limits, were introduced, reducing road deaths. Oil crises and growing environmental awareness forced car makers to address issues of fuel economy and pollution. Alternatives to the internal combustion engine began to be seriously explored, especially electric cars. Ownership of cars continued to expand worldwide and Asian countries, such as South Korea and India, became

major car producers. Many people still loved automobiles for speed and style, paying high prices for supercars by manufacturers such as Ferrari and Lamborghini. By the end of the 20th century, even the standard family car was a marvel of modern technology.

HYBRID POWERPLANT The Toyota Prius hybrid car combines an internal combustion engine with electric motors. This reduces fuel consumption and harmful emissions.

1950s

CITROËN DS A masterpiece of automotive design, the Citroën DS caused a sensation with its streamlined body shape and innovative hydropneumatic suspension, which provided a smoother ride than any previously experienced.

1960s

PORSCHE 911 Introduced at the Frankfurt Motor Show, its sleek lines, air-cooled engine mounted at the rear, and independent rear suspension made the Porsche 911 an instant classic. It went on to become one of the longest lasting production sports cars.

1980s

JEEP CHEROKEE The launch of the Jeep Cherokee marked the advent of the sports utility vehicle (SUV), a car with four-wheel drive and the chassis of a light truck. It became the vehicle of choice for suburban dwellers with large families.

2000s

LAMBORGHINI MURCIÉLAGO The new millennium brought a surge in supercars—high-speed, glamorous models sold at a price only the super-rich could afford. The Murciélago accelerates from 0 to 60 mph (0–100 kmh) in less than 4 seconds.

Berlin Blockade

1948–1949

After World War II, the victorious Allies divided Germany into four zones, controlled by the USA, USSR, France, and Britain. Deep within the Soviet zone, the capital, Berlin, was also divided four ways. In 1948 tension mounted over moves to unify West Berlin (the British, French, and American areas). The Soviet response was to try to squeeze the Allies out, bringing the city to its knees.

06/24/1948

06/26/1948

AIRLIFT MISSION The only way into West Berlin was by air. The Western Allies formed an ambitious plan to airlift enough food and fuel to supply the entire blockaded area. The scene was set for the largest aerial supply operation in history. On June 26, the first C–47 Dakotas carrying supplies landed at Berlin's Tempelhof and Gatow airports.

06/26/1948

ESSENTIAL SUPPLIES ARE DELIVERED As each plane landed in Berlin people rushed to unload it. Supplies included everything the trapped Berliners needed to survive: bags of flour, gasoline, groceries, medical supplies, and coal.

10/15/1948

COMBINED TASK FORCE The British and American air forces combined to become an Airlift Task Force. Despite shortages and hardship, Berliners remained in good spirits. Pilots dropped candy to children who cheered as the planes flew overhead.

> " We had **no guns**, only **flour**. "
>
> UNKNOWN AIRLIFT PILOT

02/22/1949

THE BLOCKADE BEGINS

The Soviet plan was simple, swift, and effective. In one night, troops blocked road, river, and rail links, sealing off all access to West Berlin. Electricity, food, and fuel supplies were abruptly severed, leaving the inhabitants facing starvation. At the city's borders an uneasy stand-off began between Soviet and Western troops.

07/12/1948

CONSTRUCTION OF NEW RUNWAY

When the airlift began there were only two airfields in Berlin. By July 1,000 tons of supplies were being delivered every day, and the runways struggled to cope. Men and women from across the blockade zone joined in the construction of a new runway at Tempelhof to facilitate the relief effort.

09/18/1948

RECORD DAY

On September 18, 900 flights delivered 7,000 tons of supplies—a new record. The landings were achieved despite rain, fog, high winds, and constant harassment from Soviet fighter planes. The airlift was now supplying the city with enough fuel as well as food. The blockade was failing.

12/20/1948

OPERATION SANTA CLAUS The airlift, initially planned to last a few weeks, was now in its sixth month. In the lead up to Christmas the Allies carried out Operation Santa Claus, bringing presents to the children of West Berlin. Thousands flooded the airfields to receive gifts of toys and candy.

THE MILLIONTH TON

In February 1949 the millionth ton of supplies arrived in Berlin. To commemorate this occasion a symbolic sack of grain was handed to the West Berliners. By this stage a flight was reaching the city every 36 seconds. Efforts to boost morale culminated in the Easter Parade, when 13,000 tons of coal were flown into the city in one day.

05/12/1949

SOVIETS LIFT THE BLOCKADE

The airlift had succeeded beyond all expectations. Despite all their efforts, the Soviet forces had to back down and the blockade was finally lifted. After 11 months of canned food Berliners were ecstatic, and thousands gathered in the streets to celebrate and thank the Western forces.

Israel Declares Statehood

1946–1949

After the horrors of the Holocaust, the international community was determined to find displaced Jews a homeland. Many refugees headed for British-administered Palestine, believing it to be the land promised to them by God. When the United Nations partitioned Palestine into Jewish and Arab states it fueled Arab anger, and two bitterly opposed peoples found themselves side by side in the most volatile region in the world.

05/01/1946

11/30/1947

ISRAELIS CELEBRATE
As the crisis escalated, Britain decided to hand over the problem to the United Nations. On November 29, 1947 the UN General Assembly voted to partition Palestine into Jewish and Arab sectors. The next day, Jews celebrated ecstatically, while Arabs violently opposed the solution.

ISRAELI FLAG
The flag of the new state of Israel shows the Star of David, an ancient symbol of Judaism.

12/16/1947

BRITISH CIVILIANS EVACUATED
After the plans for Palestine were revealed, terrorist attacks intensified. In response, Britain evacuated all of its nonessential citizens, including many who had lived in Palestine for their whole lives.

PARTITION OF PALESTINE
The UN General Assembly decided that Palestine would be divided into Jewish and Arab states, with Jerusalem as an international city.

UN PARTITION PLAN 1947
- Proposed Arab State
- Proposed Jewish State
- Proposed International zone

LEBANON

SYRIA

Haifa
Nazareth

West Bank

Mediterranean Sea
Tel Aviv
Jericho
Jerusalem
Gaza Strip
Hebron
Dead Sea
Gaza

Beersheba

E G Y P T   TRANSJORDAN

Eilat

04/20/1948

BRITISH LEAVE
A force of 100,000 British troops had been tasked with holding the line between Arabs and Israelis in Palestine, and many were killed in the crossfire. In April 1948, they were finally given the order to withdraw. Exhausted and demoralized, they returned home.

05/14/1948

05/15/1948

ARAB-ISRAELI WAR
The day after the creation of Israel, it was invaded by Egypt, Lebanon, Syria, Transjordan, and Iraq. The first Arab-Israeli War had begun. Israel defended itself and expanded its territory. Within months the Arab forces were crushed, both militarily and psychologically.

JEWISH REFUGEES
Boatloads of Jewish refugees arrived in Palestine after the war. The British were caught between Jewish demands for their own land and Arab nationalists who resented the newcomers. Despite pressure from the USA, the British severely restricted Jewish immigration—largely because of Arab objections.

07/22/1946

KING DAVID HOTEL BOMBING
Tensions quickly turned to violence. A Jewish underground army, Haganah, accused the British of bias toward the Arabs. They mounted a campaign of terrorism, and in July 1946 blew up the King David Hotel in Jerusalem with the loss of 91 lives.

01/06/1948

VIOLENCE ESCALATES
Terrorist attacks by Arabs were met with increasing violence from Jews. In January, Haganah terrorists killed 26 Palestinians in a car bomb attack in Jaffa, and residents were forced to flee after a huge explosion rocked the Semiramis Hotel in Jerusalem.

JEWISH STATE PROCLAIMED
Israel was proclaimed on May 14, 1948 by David Ben-Gurion, the de-facto leader of the Jews in Palestine, a few hours before the British Mandate expired at midnight. The early proclamation shocked the international community, sending a strong message that the new state would manage its own affairs.

> "
> We consider that the **United Nations** ideal is a **Jewish ideal**.
> "
>
> **DAVID BEN-GURION, ISRAELI LEADER, TIME MAGAZINE, AUGUST 16, 1948**

06/20/1948

ALTALENA SINKS
Crowds gathered to watch the wreckage of the cargo ship *Altalena* near Tel Aviv in June 1948. On board were immigrants, as well as arms and fighters for the Irgun, a splinter group of the Jewish Haganah. David Ben-Gurion, fearful of a violent uprising against the new Israeli state, had ordered the ship to be destroyed.

06/29/1949

CEASEFIRE
In 1949 Israel concluded peace treaties with all of the warring Arab nations apart from Iraq. Egypt and Israel also signed a ceasefire that left Egypt occupying the Gaza strip. Israel had made substantial gains but thousands of Palestinians had become refugees and terrorist attacks continued.

China Goes Red

1946–1949

At the end of World War II China descended into chaos. The reluctant cooperation between Nationalists and Communists to fight the Japanese invasion of 1937 evaporated overnight, as both sides scrambled for territory. The communist People's Liberation Army, led by Mao Zedong, saw a chance to seize power.

CHINA DIVIDED By 1946 the Communists were in control of north and central China, while the Nationalists commanded the south of the country.

12/31/1946

COMMUNIST TACTICS Outnumbered by the KMT, Mao adopted a policy of avoiding Nationalist-held cities so as not to lose men in engagements that they could not win. Instead, he concentrated his forces in rural areas to drum up additional support. By the end of the year PLA numbers had risen to 2 million.

03/19/1947

FALL OF YAN'AN Ever since the Long March of 1936, Yan'an had been the center of Communist power in China, and soldiers of the PLA used it as a training base. In early 1947 it was stormed by the Nationalists, but Mao had received prior warning of the attack. He abandoned the city and withdrew his forces into the surrounding mountains to regroup.

10/19/1948

01/04/1949

NATIONALISTS CRUSHED After losing the decisive battle of Huai-Hai in January 1949, Nationalist morale collapsed. US President Truman withdrew all aid to Chiang Kai-shek, and Nationalists fled as the PLA entered the capital, Nanjing.

04/20/1949

YANGTZE INCIDENT On its way up the Yangtze River to rescue embassy staff in Nanjing, British naval vessel *HMS Amethyst* was fired upon by Communists from the shore, killing 22 crew members. The vessel was stranded upriver for 100 days before making a successful dash for the sea.

05/25/1949

SHANGHAI IS TAKEN The KMT's last stronghold, Shanghai, fell after heavy street-fighting. Nationalists surrendered to the PLA at bayonet point. Chiang Kai-shek went on the run, joining 2 million Nationalist refugees on the island of Taiwan. There he established the Republic of China and continued to claim sovereignty over mainland China.

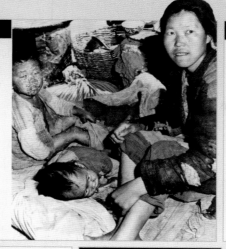

06/26/1946

CIVIL WAR RESUMES
Breaking an uneasy ceasefire, Nationalist leader Chiang Kai-shek launched a massive offensive against the People's Liberation Army (PLA) of Mao Zedong in Manchuria. The Nationalist Kuomintang (KMT) army outnumbered the PLA by more than three to one.

07/15/1946

WIDESPREAD FAMINE
People were starving in China's Nationalist-held cities as a result of war-induced famine and soaring inflation caused by Chiang Kai-shek's disastrous economic policies. The Nationalist regime was riddled with corruption and relied on massive loans from the United States to fight the war.

12/07/1946

BUILDING SUPPORT
The Communists were quicker than Chiang Kai-shek to gain popular support. They welcomed defectors from the KMT and won control of the countryside by promising land to the peasants. Anti-Nationalist protests, such as the burning of KMT banners and symbols, became increasingly common.

SIEGE OF CHANGCHUN
After a five-month siege of the city of Changchun in northeast China, Nationalist defenders surrendered to the PLA. The Communists had cut off all supply routes to the city the previous May, and as a result an estimated 150,000 civilians, unable to escape, died of starvation by the end of the siege.

12/31/1948

DEATH BY FIRING SQUAD In areas that remained under KMT control, reprisals against alleged communist sympathizers were brutal. The streets of Shanghai saw summary executions.

Now the **people's war** has been **won**.

MAO ZEDONG, CHAIRMAN OF THE CHINESE COMMUNIST PARTY, OCTOBER 1, 1949

10/01/1949

PEOPLE'S REPUBLIC OF CHINA Mao changed the country's capital to Beijing, and in front of a huge crowd in Tiananmen Square he formally proclaimed the birth of the People's Republic of China on October 1. Communists had taken control of the most populous country in the world.

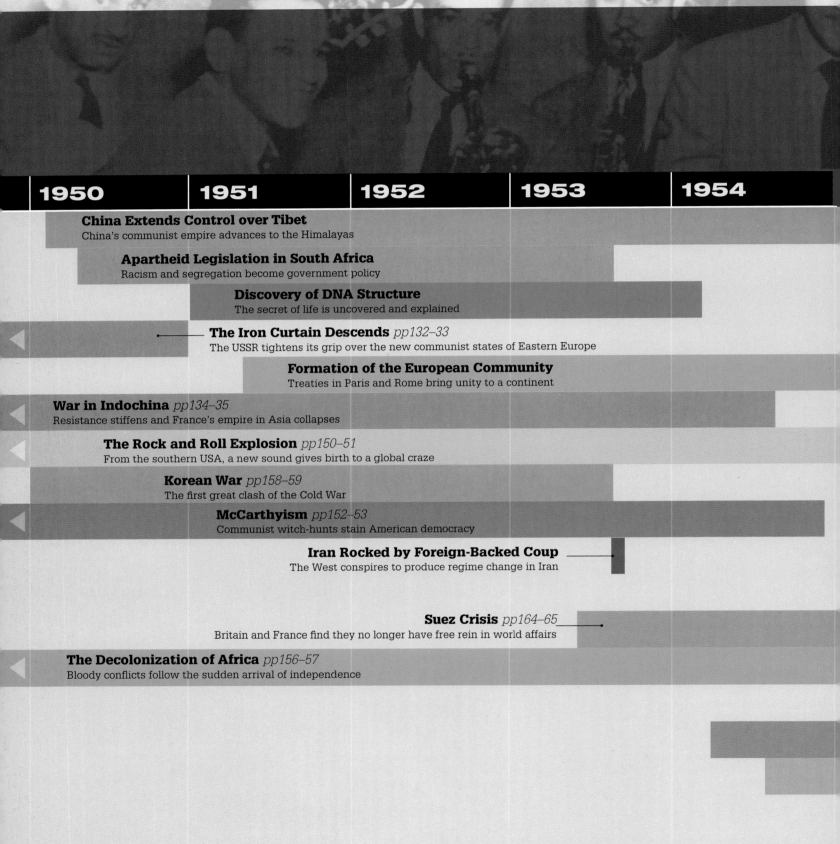

1950	**1951**	**1952**	**1953**	**1954**

China Extends Control over Tibet
China's communist empire advances to the Himalayas

Apartheid Legislation in South Africa
Racism and segregation become government policy

Discovery of DNA Structure
The secret of life is uncovered and explained

The Iron Curtain Descends *pp132–33*
The USSR tightens its grip over the new communist states of Eastern Europe

Formation of the European Community
Treaties in Paris and Rome bring unity to a continent

War in Indochina *pp134–35*
Resistance stiffens and France's empire in Asia collapses

The Rock and Roll Explosion *pp150–51*
From the southern USA, a new sound gives birth to a global craze

Korean War *pp158–59*
The first great clash of the Cold War

McCarthyism *pp152–53*
Communist witch-hunts stain American democracy

Iran Rocked by Foreign-Backed Coup
The West conspires to produce regime change in Iran

Suez Crisis *pp164–65*
Britain and France find they no longer have free rein in world affairs

The Decolonization of Africa *pp156–57*
Bloody conflicts follow the sudden arrival of independence

1950-59

Hungarian Revolution *pp162–63*
Dissent in the Soviet empire is crushed

War in Algeria *pp168–69*
France vows to keep Algeria French

Che Spreads the Revoluton *pp170–71*
The rise and fall of an iconic freedom fighter

The Struggle for Civil Rights *pp180–81*
African-Americans seize the day in the campaign for equality

Cuban Missile Crisis *pp174–75*
The world holds its breath as superpowers clash

War in Vietnam *pp184–85*
North and South collide, setting the scene for long and bloody conflict

Space Race *pp200–01*
Humanity takes its first steps toward the stars

SLEGS BLANKES
EUROPEANS ONLY

1951

Fighting Apartheid

The 1948 general election victory of South Africa's National Party saw a succession of new laws designed to disenfranchise and segregate the country's majority black population. By 1951, the system, known as apartheid, had strengthened and extended the existing powers and privileges of the white minority of largely Afrikaaners. The new regime officially segregated residential areas, education, transportation, and health provision, with blacks and others now classified as nonwhite, isolated in the worst land with no political representation and poor public services. The regime provoked massive resistance from black South Africans, with numerous uprisings and protests, such as this occupation of white-only railroad cars, but as opposition became more violent it was met with extreme state repression and a further diminution of rights. It was not until 1994 that the apartheid system was finally overthrown.

The Rock and Roll Explosion

1949–1960

The 1940s saw a mingling of black and white cultures in the USA, with music by black artists increasingly popular among white audiences. But it wasn't until the 1950s that these influences came together to create a new style that would change the face of popular music.

12/10/1949

THE FAT MAN
Fats Domino achieved national stardom with his single "The Fat Man." His rolling piano style and wah-wah vocals were a departure from the swing and blues styles popular at the time. Although still regarded as "black" rhythm-and-blues music, it laid the foundation for a new style.

07/30/1954

THE KING Elvis Presley burst onto the scene at the Shell Theater in Memphis. His energetic, theatrical style was revolutionary for a white singer at the time, and he would become the iconic rock and roll performer.

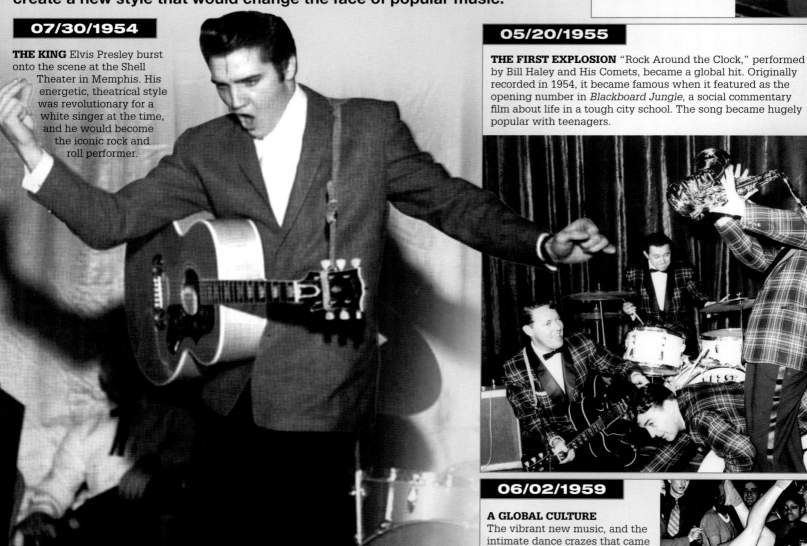

05/20/1955

THE FIRST EXPLOSION "Rock Around the Clock," performed by Bill Haley and His Comets, became a global hit. Originally recorded in 1954, it became famous when it featured as the opening number in *Blackboard Jungle*, a social commentary film about life in a tough city school. The song became hugely popular with teenagers.

06/02/1959

A GLOBAL CULTURE
The vibrant new music, and the intimate dance crazes that came with it, spread across the world. They targeted a newly emerging teenage market that had more money and independence than ever before. In Britain, a generation of fans dressed in Edwardian clothes and styled themselves as "Teddy boys." It was even reported that Elvis records were for sale on the black market in the USSR.

NEW TECHNOLOGY
In 1949, the first 45 rpm single was produced. Light and durable, the new records could be stacked more efficiently into jukeboxes.

12/30/1952

BRIDGING THE RACE GAP
Chuck Berry joined Johnnie Johnson in playing "white" country-and-western music to predominantly black crowds. His success marked a growing trend toward integration of white and black music in the USA, and record producers began looking for a white performer to bridge the gap from the other side.

01/01/1956

A NEW CELEBRITY
Teenage fans became infamous for their screaming devotion to rock and roll stars. Traditionalists worried about loose morals and changing values, fearing the corruption of the young. This marked the beginning of the split between youth and the Establishment that would eventually lead to the counter-culture revolution of the 1960s.

> It's the **rhythm** that gets to the kids—they're starved of music they can **dance** to, after all those years of crooners.
>
> DISC JOCKEY ALAN FREED, 1956

09/02/1956

THE CRAZE SPREADS
Paramount Theater in New York showcased the wave of acts in this new genre. Rock and roll had gone from a musical experiment, largely confined to the south of the country, to a national craze in just a few short years. The number of fans continued to expand quickly in the USA and across the world.

03/12/1957

HERE'S LITTLE RICHARD
In March, Little Richard released his debut album, featuring some of his biggest hits. An innovative and charismatic performer, Little Richard brought white and black audiences together in concert venues that had previously been segregated.

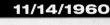

11/14/1960

GOT SOUL
Ray Charles won a Grammy Award for his pioneering song "Georgia on My Mind," the latest in a series of hits in a new "soul" genre that followed on from Chuck Berry's use of gospel musical stylings with secular, often suggestive lyrics. Ray Charles would go on to inspire a new generation of musicians.

12/31/1960

THE END OF THE BEGINNING
By 1960, the scene was changing. Elvis had returned from a spell in the army, but chose to focus on acting over music. With the deaths of superstars Buddy Holly and Eddie Cochran, and Little Richard's retirement to become a preacher, the pioneers began to be replaced. They had inspired a new wave of artists, including female singers such as the Supremes and Aretha Franklin. Rock and roll had created a new form of expression, and music would never be the same again.

McCarthyism

1947–1954

As the Cold War deepened, fears grew in America that Soviet spies might have infiltrated the government and military, ready to bring down the system from within. Senator Joe McCarthy mounted a crusade to hunt down subversive elements, but his campaign quickly turned into a witch-hunt that undermined the very liberties it was intended to protect.

03/21/1947

LOYALTY OATH Stung by criticism that he was soft on communists, US President Truman proposed that all federal employees should be required to swear loyalty to the United States. The Senate had already formed the House Committee on Un-American Activities (HUAC) to investigate subversive elements.

08/05/1948

THE NET WIDENS Many of the cases brought by HUAC relied on hearsay, and the truth of the allegations was never confirmed. Alger Hiss, a State Department official, appeared before a grand jury to deny charges of espionage. Hiss was later found guilty of perjury, but was never proven to have spied.

02/09/1950

MCCARTHY'S LIST Joe McCarthy, then a relatively unknown senator from Wisconsin, was determined that HUAC investigations should go further. At a speech in West Virginia, he waved aloft a list of 205 people working in the State Department whom he accused of being members of the Communist Party.

01/13/1953

HOOVER HELPS McCarthy found further support from FBI director J. Edgar Hoover, who passed confidential material to him and the HUAC during the early 1950s.

02/18/1953

ARMY ROW McCarthy's campaign grew bolder. During a Senate inquiry into subversion in the army, he caused outrage by telling General Ralph Zwicker he was not fit to wear army uniform and had the intelligence of a five-year-old child. McCarthy's critics accused him of bullying and trying to suppress freedom of speech.

04/22/1954

10/27/1947

THE STARS PROTEST
HUAC had the power to blacklist those suspected of communist sympathies, preventing them from working. When a swathe of Hollywood actors, writers, directors, and producers were accused, the glitterati came out in protest as Humphrey Bogart led a parade of stars to Washington to sit in on HUAC proceedings.

11/25/1947

"HOLLYWOOD TEN"
At one HUAC hearing, 10 witnesses, citing the right to freedom of speech, refused to answer the question: "Are you now or have you ever been a member of the Communist Party?" They were blacklisted and never worked again.

03/30/1951

NUCLEAR SECRETS
McCarthy's fears seemed grounded as Ethel and Julius Rosenberg were sentenced to death for passing atomic secrets to the Soviet Union. Many Americans had been shocked in 1949 when the USSR detonated its first atomic bomb, far sooner than expected, further fueling anti-communist fears.

COMMUNIST PARANOIA
This anti-communist comic book was published in the USA in 1947. More than 4 million copies were printed. Nightmarish depictions of a Communist takeover played on the widespread fears over Red penetration into American society.

02/22/1953

BROADWAY CRITIC
The film and theater communities continued to protest what they saw as an attempt to limit political freedom. Arthur Miller's play *The Crucible*, depicting 17th-century witch trials, was seen as a critique of McCarthy's methods. Miller was later investigated by the HUAC.

AS SEEN ON TV
As McCarthy's investigation of the Army continued, the hearings were shown in full on live television. For the first time, American families were able to see McCarthy's tactics for themselves. The broadcasts undermined McCarthy's accusations. Already under attack in the media, his popularity declined sharply.

12/02/1954

FALL FROM GRACE The Senate voted to censure McCarthy for abuse of power. He was forced to abandon his campaign, and died less than three years later.

> Until **this moment**, Senator, I think I never really gauged your **cruelty**.

ARMY COUNSEL JOSEPH WELCH, IN A TELEVISED CLASH WITH McCARTHY, JUNE 9, 1954

1952

Thermonuclear Dawn

On November 1, 1952, the USA detonated the first hydrogen bomb over Enewetak Atoll in the Pacific Ocean. The new weapon was vastly more powerful than anything seen before, dwarfing even the atomic bombs dropped on Hiroshima and Nagasaki in 1945. As tensions mounted in the Cold War between the USA and the USSR, both sides entered an arms race, constructing vast arsenals of weapons of mass destruction. The proliferation of nuclear devices spread fear across the world. By the 1980s, both sides possessed stockpiles sufficient to kill the entire population of the Earth several times over. And yet, despite near misses such as the Cuban Missile Crisis of 1962, nuclear armageddon never came. Some historians argue that the destructive power of the bomb was so great that neither side dared to use it. The Cold War stayed cold, because the consequences of open conflict had become unthinkable.

The Decolonization of Africa

1939–1965

The European powers who ruled Africa were weakened after World War II and under pressure from the US and USSR to end colonialism. Yet African nations experienced independence with varying degrees of success.

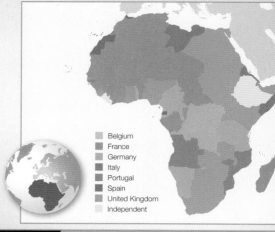

Belgium
France
Germany
Italy
Portugal
Spain
United Kingdom
Independent

GHANAIAN FLAG The colors of Ghana's flag represent the country's resources and struggle for independence: green for lush vegetation; gold for mineral wealth; and red for blood shed in the fight for Ghanaian freedom.

03/06/1957

06/30/1960

CONGO INDEPENDENCE DAY For countries such as Congo, the road to independence was less secure. Joyous crowds gathered to witness King Baudouin of Belgium hand over power.

07/05/1960

STRUGGLE FOR INDEPENDENCE
A general election had taken place only one week earlier. The winner was revolutionary activist Patrice Lumumba, who struggled to form a coherent government. Chaos followed within days of the independence ceremony, as the army mutinied against the last few Belgian officers.

> We are **proud** of this **struggle**, of tears, of fire, and of **blood**.

PATRICE LUMUMBA, CONGO'S FIRST PRESIDENT, ON THE FIGHT FOR INDEPENDENCE, JUNE 30, 1960

07/14/1960

MILITARY INTERVENTION A UN force was deployed to keep the peace, but became embroiled in a succession of battles and ceasefires. Unhappy with the UN's failure to use direct force, Lumumba accepted military aid from Russia and sent troops into Katanga.

09/14/1960

PATRICE LUMUMBA OUSTED In September 1960, Lumumba was overthrown by one of his army officers, Joseph Mobutu. The US government secretly supported Mobutu, who was seen to be more friedly to the West. Lumumba was eventually captured by Tshombe's soldiers, and dragged on to a plane where he was beaten and executed.

COLONIAL BORDERS OF AFRICA
By 1913 Africa was divided between seven European powers. Rich in natural resources, and with an abundant supply of cheap labor, the land was prized by its colonial rulers. Indigenous Africans were generally excluded from government posts, education, and training, and anticolonial feeling grew rapidly.

09/01/1939

SERVICE IN WORLD WAR II Regiments from some African colonies fought for their European rulers during World War II. Fighting an unknown enemy in the service of colonial powers, many returned home determined to seek independence.

03/06/1957

A NEW GHANA
The African struggle for self-rule began in the British Gold Coast. In 1951, activist Kwame Nkrumah won the country's first election, despite being in jail. On his release, he formed a government and, in 1957, became prime minister of the new Ghana—the first sub-Saharan colony to gain independence.

RAISING THE FLAG
On March 6 the church bells rang out across the Ghanaian capital, Accra. The British Union Jack flag was lowered in the square outside parliament, and the green, gold, and red colors of the new Ghanaian nation were hoisted. More than 100,000 people were present at the formal flag-raising ceremony.

03/06/1957

CELEBRATION OF INDEPENDENCE
Celebrations erupted across Ghana. Workers were given the day off, and many—dressed in traditional costume—daubed themselves with the colors of the new flag and danced in street parades. Pioneers of a revolution, their joy inspired other African nations to seek widespread change.

07/11/1960

KATANGA BREAKS AWAY
The province of Katanga declared independence from Congo under pro-Western leader Moise Tshombe. He appealed to the Belgians for assistance. Lumumba saw this as an attempt by Belgium to hold on to the richest part of the country, and sought UN backing to expel Belgian forces.

11/24/1965

GENERAL MOBUTU SEIZES POWER
Mobutu became leader in 1965. He Africanized his name to Mobutu Sese Seko, renamed the country Zaire, and proceeded to rule with an iron fist for 30 years. All political opposition was banned, and he amassed a huge personal fortune, spawning a system of corruption that left his people impoverished. Zaire became virtually bankrupt, despite its vast natural resources.

Korean War

1950–1953

In 1948 communist leader Kim Il-sung, supported by the Soviet Union, established the People's Democratic Republic of Korea in North Korea. With the USA backing an anti-communist regime in South Korea, the stage was set for the first significant armed conflict of the Cold War.

06/25/1950

LIGHTNING INVASION
North Korea launched a surprise attack on South Korea. Its army of 90,000 soldiers was equipped with Soviet-made tanks and artillery. South Korea had no tanks and very few anti-tank weapons. Expecting little resistance, the North Korean army rapidly advanced south.

09/19/1950

UPBEAT MOOD IN THE UN CAMP
The success at Inchon turned the tide of the war. MacArthur's troops broke the North Korean communication lines. By September 29 UN forces had retaken Seoul, the South Korean capital. On October 9 MacArthur sent his army into North Korea.

10/18/1950

TRUMAN MEETS MACARTHUR
US President Harry S. Truman met MacArthur on Wake Island in the Pacific to discuss the progress of the war. MacArthur assured the President that the North Korean army had been destroyed. He did not believe that China would carry out its threat to intervene.

12/08/1950

UN FORCES RETALIATE By this time, some 340,000 UN soldiers were fighting alongside the South Koreans. However, despite some successes during which Chinese and North Korean troops were captured, the Chinese advance was unstoppable.

02/16/1951

BOMBING NORTH KOREA Between January and March 1951, the US Air Force escalated its bombing campaign on North Korea, flattening 18 of its 22 major cities. Napalm, an inflammable liquid, was used, and Truman later said that he had considered employing the atomic bomb.

06/28/1950

UN COMES TO THE AID OF SOUTH KOREA
Fifteen nations, including the USA, Britain, and Australia, responded to the UN's call to send troops to defend South Korea. By early July US B-26 planes were making bombing raids behind North Korean lines. One of the raids targeted the railroad bridge on the Han River, halting the approaching North Korean army.

09/15/1950

UN FORCES LAND AT INCHON The North Korean army had kept UN forces confined to Pusan in the southeast peninsula. On September 15 US General Douglas MacArthur, in command of the combined UN force, made a daring landing of two divisions at Inchon, a port some 150 miles (240 km) behind enemy lines, breaking the stranglehold.

11/01/1950

CHINA ENTERS THE WAR Chinese troops launched a surprise offensive on the UN forces, secretly crossing the Yalu River, the border between China and North Korea. On November 1 the Chinese army inflicted a major defeat on American troops at the Battle of Unsan and forced them to retreat.

THE 38TH PARALLEL
Established as the dividing line between North and South Korea at the end of World War II, the 38th parallel was restored as the line of demarcation in 1953. This map shows the extent of North Korean penetration in the first phase of the war, and the depth of the US-led UN counteroffensive.

CHINA — USSR

NORTH KOREA
● Pyongyang
Imjin
Sea of Japan (East Sea)
38th Parallel
—— Ceasefire line
—— Limit of North Korean advance
—— Limit of UN advance
● Inchon
SOUTH KOREA
Yellow Sea
● Pusan
JAPAN

...we **must win**. There is **no substitute** for **victory**.

UN COMMANDER GENERAL MACARTHUR, MARCH 20, 1951

04/11/1951

MACARTHUR SACKED
In a sudden move, Truman recalled MacArthur, who had made no secret of his desire to actively pursue a war of aggression against communist China. The news was greeted with outrage by right-wing groups in the USA, but General Matthew Ridgeway, who replaced MacArthur, did much to restore the confidence of the soldiers fighting under his command.

04/22/1951

BATTLE OF THE IMJIN RIVER By mid-April UN troops were back in the area of the 38th parallel when the Chinese launched their offensive against Seoul. The British Gloucestershire Regiment took heavy losses in an attempt to halt their advance at the Imjin River. By May the UN front line had moved just north of the 38th parallel and the war entered a prolonged stalemate.

07/27/1953

ARMISTICE SIGNED An armistice was signed after months of negotiation. A demilitarized zone (DMZ) was established at the 38th parallel and a UN commission was set up to monitor the peace.

KOREAN SERVICE MEDAL More than 1.2 million South Korean and UN soldiers served in the Korean War, many of whom were awarded the Korean Service Medal.

1953

Conquest of Everest

The dream of standing on the roof of the world was finally realized on May 29, 1953. Mount Everest, the world's highest peak, was successfully climbed for the first time by New Zealander Edmund Hillary and Nepalese Sherpa Tenzing Norgay. For more than 30 years a succession of expeditions, principally British, had attempted to conquer mountaineering's ultimate challenge, but while some came agonizingly close, none was known to have reached the peak and safely returned to base camp. By May 27, 1953, two members of an expedition led by Colonel John Hunt, the ninth British team to take on Everest, had turned back just short of the summit as they ran out of time and oxygen supplies. Two days later, Hillary and Norgay made their team's final ascent from the South Col route. At 11:30 am they arrived at the summit. They briefly paused to take photographs that soon after their descent were seen around the world.

Hungarian Revolution

1956

The death of Joseph Stalin in 1953 brought hopes of liberal reform throughout the Soviet bloc. In Hungary, Imre Nagy, who believed in communism "with a human face," replaced Stalinist hard-liner Matyas Rakosi as Prime Minister. His promise of reform made him a popular leader, but was resisted by supporters of the USSR. As the Soviets sought to tighten their grip on Eastern Europe, liberals in Hungary began to demand change.

10/06/1956

ACT OF DEFIANCE The body of former Foreign Minister Laszlo Rajk, executed in 1949, was reburied in a ceremony attended by 100,000 mourners. Rajk had been executed on charges of espionage, and the large crowds at his funeral were a sign of widespread anti-Soviet feeling.

10/23/1956

PUBLIC PROTEST In an act of solidarity with the Polish people, about 20,000 protesters, mostly students, gathered to lay a wreath at the statue of Josef Bern, Polish-born hero of the Hungarian Revolution of 1848. They marched to Radio Budapest, calling for the withdrawal of Soviet troops from Hungary. Thousands more joined the protests, burning Soviet flags.

10/23/1956

STATUE OF STALIN FALLS In Budapest, demonstrators toppled a giant statue of Stalin, built in 1951 to mark the dictator's 70th birthday. The 30 ft-(9 m-) high monument was dismantled and dragged through the streets.

10/24/1956

TANKS ON THE STREET Faced with total loss of control, the USSR had to act. At 2:00 a.m., on the orders of Defense Minister Georgy Zhukov, Soviet tanks entered Budapest and took up key positions around the city. As conflict seemed imminent, Nagy was appointed Prime Minister to placate the demonstrators. Appealing for calm, he promised political reform.

10/25/1956

TROUBLE FLARES The violence worsened as Soviet troops fired on protestors outside the Parliament building. Insurgents took to the streets, hurling Molotov cocktails at the tanks.

10/30/1956

SOVIETS BACK DOWN The USSR agreed to tolerate Nagy's new government, and the fighting petered out. Soviet tanks withdrew from Hungary, watched by anxious crowds.

11/01/1956

A STEP TOO FAR The new government announced its decision to withdraw from the Soviet bloc and become a democracy, and a neutral party in the Cold War. Soviet tanks soon began to mass once again on the Hungarian border. Nagy appealed to the UN for assistance against Soviet aggression.

10/19/1956

POLISH RESISTANCE
The Hungarians took inspiration from Poland, where reformist leader Wladyslaw Gomulka (seen addressing a crowd) had been confirmed as First Secretary despite Soviet opposition. When the USSR threatened to use troops against militant strikers. Gomulka made it clear that the Polish army would fight back if Soviet troops advanced.

10/23/1956

SYMBOL OF THE REVOLUTION
Insurgents cut out the insignia of the communist party to restore the old Hungarian national flag.

POLICE RESISTANCE A crowd attempting to take control of Budapest radio station was shot at by the Hungarian secret police. The rebels reacted angrily and members of the secret police were rounded up and imprisoned or executed.

10/27/1956

> **"** ... it is **possible** that I shall **only** be able to **stay at my post** for one or two **hours**. **"**
>
> **IMRE NAGY'S LAST BROADCAST, NOVEMBER 4, 1956**

BRIEF RESPITE The swearing-in of Nagy's government brought a temporary lull in the violence. He pledged that Soviet tanks would be withdrawn, prisoners released, and the secret police disbanded.

11/04/1956

THE TANKS COME BACK About 1,000 Soviet tanks rolled into Budapest just before dawn, this time using brute force to crush the Hungarian Army and civilian resistance. Nagy broadcast his final appeal for help at 5:15 a.m. Less than three hours later, Radio Hungary was silenced.

11/11/1956

THE REVOLUTION ENDS Up to 200,000 refugees fled across the border to Austria as the Soviet-backed regime of Janos Kadar took full control. Thousands of civilians had been killed or wounded in the Soviet crackdown, and an unknown number ended up in Soviet jails.

Suez Crisis

1953–1956

In 1950 Egypt still bore marks of its colonial past. An Anglo–French company owned the Suez Canal—a vital international waterway linking Europe and Asia. Britain maintained an army presence there to protect it. On July 23, 1952 a group of nationalist army officers, led by General Neguib, overthrew the corrupt, pro-British regime of King Farouk.

06/22/1953

06/27/1956

EGYPT TAKES OVER THE SUEZ CANAL At a speech in Alexandria, Nasser shocked the world by announcing the nationalization of the Suez Canal, to provide revenue for the Aswan Dam. Egyptian troops swiftly took position, cutting off British and French control.

08/16/1956

CRISIS TALKS
Twenty-two nations attended a conference in London to discuss the Suez Crisis but failed to find a diplomatic solution. In October Britain and France, with the most to lose from Nasser's seizure of the canal, agreed to a secret plan with Israel to invade Egypt and secure the canal zone.

11/04/1956

ANTI-WAR PROTEST
Nearly 30,000 people attended a rally in London's Trafalgar Square to hear Labour politicians condemn the invasion of Egypt. The Suez Crisis sharply divided political opinion in Britain. Still clinging to ideas of empire, right-wing Conservatives, backed by the British press, supported the government's policy.

11/05/1956

PORT SAID ATTACKED Ignoring UN calls for a ceasefire, a Franco–British force assaulted Port Said. However, after a threat from the USA to withhold financial loans, Britain backed down. Nasser had won.

11/21/1956

UN TROOPS LAND IN EGYPT
After a ceasefire agreement on November 7, a UN Emergency Force was dispatched to Suez to keep the peace.

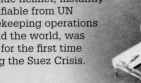

PEACEKEEPER HELMET
The blue helmet, instantly identifiable from UN peacekeeping operations around the world, was worn for the first time during the Suez Crisis.

CAIRO REJOICES

A year after the military coup, Egypt established itself as a republic. Muhammad Neguib, soon to become the country's first president, drove through the streets of Cairo. Beside him was Colonel Gamal Nasser, his junior partner in the army coup. Within months, Nasser began to elbow out Neguib from power.

10/23/1954

MAN AT THE TOP
Nasser's popularity grew after he had negotiated the withdrawal of British troops from Egypt. Under the agreement, all British forces would leave the country by June 1956. Three weeks later Nasser overthrew Neguib to become president. His aim was to modernize Egypt and make it leader of the Arab world.

09/27/1955

US CANCELS SUPPORT
Building the Aswan Dam over the Nile River was a key project in Nasser's plans of modernization. However, by 1955 his growing friendship with China and the Soviet Union drove a wedge between Egypt and the USA. US President Dwight D. Eisenhower cancelled a $56 million grant to help build the dam.

10/29/1956

INVASION Israeli forces moved into the Sinai desert and raced toward the canal. Britain and France carried out bombing raids against Egyptian air force bases.

10/31/1956

CANAL BLOCKADE
Nasser responded by sinking 47 ships in the Suez Canal, immediately blocking it to international shipping. The canal was the main supply route for Gulf oil to Europe, and this action led to emergency gasoline rationing.

> **"**
>
> I've just never seen great powers make such **a complete mess** and **botch of things**.
>
> **US PRESIDENT EISENHOWER, ON HEARING OF THE BRITISH AND FRENCH INVASION OF THE CANAL ZONE, NOVEMBER 5, 1956**
> **"**

A CENTURY OF

Cinema

A staggering half a million movies have been produced in the 11 decades since cinema began. A novelty at the turn of the century, the first 30 years saw an unprecedented period of growth. Films went from silent to talkies, short to feature length. They created stars, and found their way around the world. Cinema has been both an art form and a pioneer of new technology. From the first flickering images, it has grown into a multi-billion dollar entertainment industry.

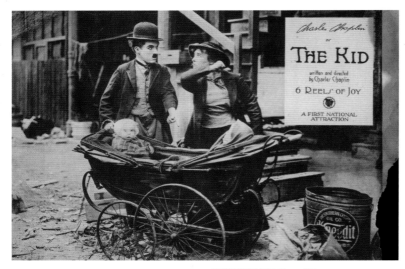

SILENT STAR One of the most famous early stars, Charlie Chaplin was a genius of the silent screen.

1900–1920 Early movies were crude, short, and seen as "low" culture. This all changed when D. W. Griffith's civil war epic *Birth of a Nation* opened in 1915, with three hours of action, close-ups, and sweeping shots. As World War I raged in Europe, the USA dominated cinema. Hollywood, a quiet suburb of Los Angeles, became the center of the industry and the home of the stars.

$2.8 BILLION

The worldwide box-office takings of *Avatar*, released in 2009, smashed all records. It used groundbreaking motion-capture and 3-D techniques.

1920–1950 Film blossomed as a serious art form in the 1920s and nowhere more so than in Germany and Russia. Sergei Eisenstein used new editing techniques in films such as *Odessa Steps*, while German Expressionists used sets to reflect the characters' moods. Films were still silent until the small Hollywood studio Warner Bros took a gamble on *The Jazz Singer* in 1927. The first "talkie,"

it revolutionized the industry. The Golden Age of Hollywood arrived in 1939 when films such as *Gone With the Wind* and *The Wizard of Oz* thrilled global audiences. By World War II, cinema-going was a well-established pastime. Both sides used official and unofficial propaganda films to maintain

SIREN OF THE SCREEN Sex symbol Marilyn Monroe was the perfect weapon to win audiences away from television.

EARLY MOVIE CAMERA
The French pioneered film making, developing early cameras such as this silent Pathé model, mounted on a tripod.

FIRST TALKIE
The Jazz Singer, starring the most popular singer of the day, Al Jolson, was the first full-length talking film. By 1930 the silent film was finished.

DISNEY ANIMATION
Walt Disney created animated cartoons that were distributed all over the world, cementing Hollywood's monopoly of the movie industry.

WAR MORALE-BOOSTING
Film made a huge contribution to the war effort, raising morale among both soldiers and the people back home.

popular support for the war effort. British studios won hearts and minds with *Went the Day Well* and *Henry V*. In the USA, hard-boiled crime fiction gave rise to film noir, which explored the dark side of the American dream.

1950–1960 During the communist scare in the USA, many leading figures in the arts were investigated for "un-American" activities. Some fled to Europe. Those who stayed kept to safe, nonpolitical films. Cinema also had to compete with a new medium: television. Epics such as *Ben Hur* set out to show that movies were bigger and better,

GOING FOR GOLD The first Oscars were handed out in 1929 at a ceremony hosted by actor Douglas Fairbanks.

while *Mary Poppins* and *The Sound of Music* appealed to family values.

1960–1970 By the end of the 1960s, big Hollywood movies cost a fortune to produce. Small, independent films reflected a decade of social change, and European film-makers such as Federico Fellini and Ingmar Bergman swapped Hollywood glamour for gritty realism. Influenced by Japanese director Akira Kurosawa, actor Clint Eastwood and director Sergio

BOLLYWOOD BOOM India, home to Bollywood, has developed the largest film industry in the world, making more than 800 movies a year.

Leone redefined the Western, turning clean-cut cowboys into brooding anti-heroes.

1970– Hollywood struck back with new advances in special effects. *Star Wars* and *Jaws* impressed and terrified audiences. People flocked to see Pixar Studio's computer-generated film *Toy Story* (1995). Blockbusters got bigger. In 1997, *Titanic* broke all box-office records, marrying cutting-edge special effects with a classic story of love and loss. As the

century came to a close, digital technology made film-making cheaper and easier. Hollywood still dominated, but had to compete with European cinema, independent films, movies made for the internet, and the massive presence of Bollywood in India. With seemingly endless ideas and innovation, cinema remains the defining art form of the modern world.

> " This film cost **$31 million**. With that kind of money I could have **invaded some country**. "

ACTOR AND DIRECTOR CLINT EASTWOOD ON *GRAN TORINO*, 2008

1950s

DRIVE-IN MOVIES
Drive-in movies were a huge attraction for the new teenage market. They showed low-budget films and sci-fi "quickies" that would appeal to young people.

1960s

CINEMASCOPE EPICS
Television had an adverse effect on cinema attendance. Hollywood responded with cinemascope, which showed films such as *Ben Hur* in a wide-screen format.

1980s

STAR WARS FRANCHISE
The epic sci-fi *Star Wars* movies launched a new era of profitable franchises. Rather than stand-alone films, producers wanted sequel after sequel.

1990s

COMPUTER GENERATED
Toy Story, the first completely computer generated 3-D film, was a huge commercial success.

War in Algeria

1956–1962

Algeria had high hopes of winning independence from France after World War II. When it did not materialize, war broke out between Algerian nationalists and French settlers. In 1958 a crisis developed as sections of the French army mutinied, the government in France collapsed, and thousands of settlers in Algeria were killed. In an attempt to gain peace, French war hero Charles de Gaulle was brought back into power.

09/30/1956

FRENCH CRACKDOWN Terrorist attacks by Algerian nationalists were on the rise. In 1956, 500,000 French soldiers were sent to the country. The heavy-handed crackdown provoked a backlash and resistance groups became more violent, setting the stage for a protracted civil conflict.

03/16/1958

TERRORIST ATTACKS IN PARIS The conflict spread to France, where police rounded up thousands of people for identity checks because they were thought to be of "Algerian" appearance. Terrorist attacks by the FLN led to escalating violence on the streets of Paris.

05/13/1958

POLICE TACKLE PROTESTERS Paris remained defiant. Right-wing extremists marched to demand that Algeria stay French. Dozens were arrested as the demonstration turned ugly.

05/14/1958

DE GAULLE READY TO ASSUME POWERS As the situation became desperate, the spotlight fell on the hero who had liberated France in World War II. General Charles de Gaulle, the wartime leader of the Free French, was seen to be the only one who could guide the country. He duly told the nation that he was at their disposal.

05/29/1958

PRESIDENT COTY MEETS POLITICIANS Newspaper and television journalists waited to capture every moment as developments rapidly unfolded in the French parliament. On May 28 the government resigned, and the following day President René Coty called upon politicians to accept Charles de Gaulle as Prime Minister.

06/01/1958

DE GAULLE APPOINTED PRIME MINISTER Charles de Gaulle accepted Coty's offer and became Prime Minister elect, but he drove a hard bargain. He asked for unrestricted powers for a period of six months and the authority to draft a new constitution for the French Republic. On June 2, 1958 the National Assembly accepted his terms.

01/29/1960

DE GAULLE PROMISES INDEPENDENCE De Gaulle had a tricky task. The army and the *pieds-noirs* believed he would support their demands, while Algerian nationalists felt that he might grant them independence. In 1960, to the horror of settlers, he committed France to the goal of emancipating Algeria. Throughout 1961 there were further coup attempts and de Gaulle narrowly escaped assassination.

07/05/1962

ALGERIAN INDEPENDENCE In a referendum, France voted to grant Algeria its independence, and in 1962 France and the FLN signed a treaty ending colonial rule. Almost a million Europeans soon fled Algeria for France. Algerians celebrated, but thousands had lost their lives in the conflict, and relations between Paris and Algeria remained strained.

>
> **I open the door of reconciliation.**
>
> **CHARLES DE GAULLE,
> FRENCH PRIME MINISTER,
> JUNE 4, 1958**

02/01/1958

GUERRILLA WAR
At the beginning of 1958 Algeria was rocked by a series of terror attacks. The guerrilla war was led and coordinated by the National Liberation Front (FLN), the main nationalist movement in the country. They picked up recruits and began focusing on terrorism in key cities.

05/16/1958

CIRCULATION ROUTIERE

FRENCH SETTLERS STAGE A REVOLT
The *pieds-noirs*, French settlers in Algeria, were taking matters into their own hands. They were furious with the French government for not taking more positive action to stop the FLN and their nationalist revolt. In May, their leaders, backed by the French army and military police, staged a coup and demanded the return of de Gaulle.

05/23/1958

CALLING DE GAULLE
A revolutionary government for Algeria was set up in defiance of Paris, led by the army. They had heard that other candidates for Prime Minister were being considered, but insisted that they would maintain their posts until de Gaulle led them to victory over Algerian nationalists.

06/04/1958

DE GAULLE IN ALGERIA
Shortly after becoming Prime Minister, De Gaulle visited Algiers, the capital of Algeria, where he was greeted by cheering crowds.

Che Spreads the Revolution

1954–1968

After World War II, Latin America saw a growth in political activism and a demand for change. Che Guevara, an Argentine revolutionary, believed that only armed struggle could solve the problems of poverty and inequality in the region.

03/07/1954

12/02/1956

CUBAN REVOLUTION

When Castro launched his attack on the Batista regime, Che joined him in the front line. They landed on the coast of Oriente Province on December 2, 1956, but most of the revolutionaries were either captured or killed. Castro and his men retreated to the Sierra Maestra Mountains to the south.

07/26/1958

01/01/1959

REBELS TAKE CUBA

By January 1, 1959 Castro's small guerrilla force overpowered the 30,000-strong Cuban army and Batista was forced to flee. The victorious rebels entered the capital Havana the next day. Castro became Prime Minister and his regime was recognized by the US government.

07/10/1965

AFRICAN OUTING

In 1965 Che traveled to Congo to foment a rebellion against the authoritarian regime of President Mobutu Sese Seko. Che was initially impressed by rebel leader Laurent Kabila, but rebel forces were divided by internal rivalries, and Che lost faith in the revolt.

10/08/1967

CAPTURED IN BOLIVIA

Intending to spark a new revolution, Che traveled to Bolivia with 50 volunteers in 1966. Largely spurned by the local population, he was captured by government forces on October 7, 1967 and executed the next day on the orders of Bolivia's military ruler General René Barrientos.

GUATEMALA TURNING POINT Ernesto "Che" Guevara visited Guatemala in 1953 to participate in the new social reforms of President Jacabo Arbenz. However, within a year of Che's arrival, Arbenz was unseated by Colonel Carlos Castillo Armas, in a coup backed by the CIA. Che fled to Mexico during the coup, angry at seeing Guatemala's populist dream crushed by outside forces.

06/07/1956

MEETING WITH CASTRO In Mexico City, Che met Cuban revolutionary Fidel Castro. Castro was in self-imposed exile, having been released from prison after attempting to overthrow Cuban dictator Fulgencio Batista's regime in 1953. He formed the 26th of July Revolutionary Movement, supported by his brother Raul and Che, who had become a committed Marxist. Together they plotted revolution in Cuba.

ARMED GUERRILLA STRUGGLE Although Batista's troops crushed the initial uprising, Castro and Che, along with 12 others, began recruiting a peasant army. They harassed the government with guerrilla attacks and gained widespread attention and support. The movement expanded and Che proved himself to be a ruthless soldier.

> " The **revolution** is not an apple that falls **when it is ripe**. You have to **make it fall**. "
>
> CHE GUEVARA, QUOTED IN
> *INTERCONTINENTAL PRESS*, 1965

12/12/1964

SPREADING THE SOCIALIST MESSAGE Following the Cuban revolution, Castro declared his willingness to support revolutionaries around the globe. Che was the most visible advocate of this commitment. He travelled widely, attending UN summits and meeting world leaders, advocating armed struggle for socialism. Che became a hero of left-wing intellectuals and radical youth around the world.

08/13/1968

FACE OF GLOBAL PROTESTS As 1968 became a year of mass protests around the world, the face of Che Guevara became ubiquitous. In Mexico City, students campaigning against the one-party rule of the government carried banners bearing his image. Here as well as in protests across the globe, Che was held up as a heroic example of revolutionary reform.

HONORED MEMORY In Cuba, Che remains a national hero and is still widely revered. His face appears on the 3 Peso banknote. His body is interred in a grand mausoleum in the Cuban city of Santa Clara.

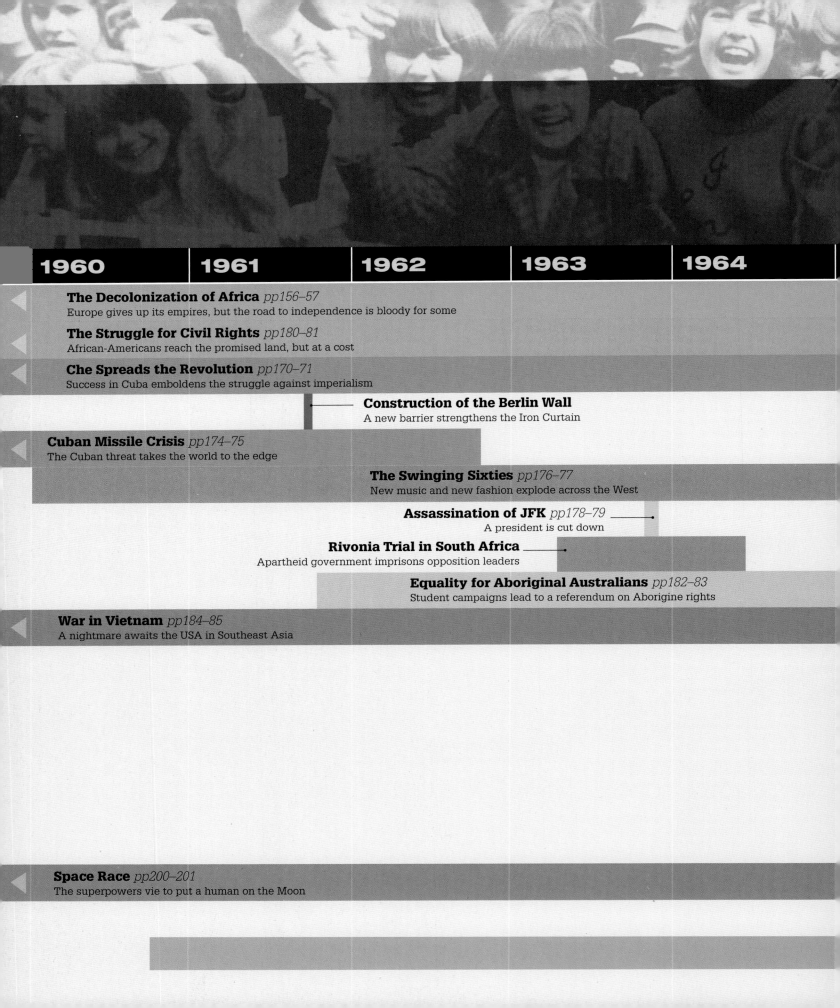

1960	**1961**	**1962**	**1963**	**1964**

The Decolonization of Africa *pp156–57*
Europe gives up its empires, but the road to independence is bloody for some

The Struggle for Civil Rights *pp180–81*
African-Americans reach the promised land, but at a cost

Che Spreads the Revolution *pp170–71*
Success in Cuba emboldens the struggle against imperialism

Construction of the Berlin Wall
A new barrier strengthens the Iron Curtain

Cuban Missile Crisis *pp174–75*
The Cuban threat takes the world to the edge

The Swinging Sixties *pp176–77*
New music and new fashion explode across the West

Assassination of JFK *pp178–79*
A president is cut down

Rivonia Trial in South Africa
Apartheid government imprisons opposition leaders

Equality for Aboriginal Australians *pp182–83*
Student campaigns lead to a referendum on Aborigine rights

War in Vietnam *pp184–85*
A nightmare awaits the USA in Southeast Asia

Space Race *pp200–201*
The superpowers vie to put a human on the Moon

Greek Military Coup
Army colonels seize power and suppress democracy

Cultural Revolution in China *pp188–89*
Thousands are persecuted as Mao seeks to regain power

Six-Day War *pp190–91*
Israel destroys its enemies but gains little security

Biafran War
West Africa's cruel and bloody civil war

The Year of Protests *pp196–97*
Students and workers seek to overthrow the French state

Prague Spring *pp198–99*
A brief moment of Czech freedom is crushed by Soviet tanks

The Troubles in Northern Ireland *pp212–13*
Sectarian violence verges on civil war

Division of Cyprus *pp222–23*
Independence does not solve Cypriot problems

Cuban Missile Crisis

1959–1962

When Fidel Castro's revolutionary regime in Cuba took delivery of Soviet missiles, it provoked a showdown with the USA that brought the world to the brink of nuclear conflict.

HOSTILE NEIGHBOR The establishment of missile launch sites in Cuba, 90 miles (144 km) off the coast of Florida, would have brought major US cities within the range of Soviet nuclear warheads.

– – US naval blockade of Cuba
– – Range of Soviet missiles
→ Route of ships carrying missiles from USSR

04/15/1961

INVASION BEGINS The attack began with air raids on Cuban airfields. Two days later the brigade of exiles landed at the Bay of Pigs, on the south coast of Cuba, and were decisively defeated by Castro's forces.

04/21/1961

UNDER ARREST Nearly 1,200 of the invaders were captured by Castro's troops in Cuba. About 100 were killed, and some managed to escape to sea. The Bay of Pigs fiasco propelled Castro closer to the USSR, and was a huge embarrassment to US President John F. Kennedy, who had ordered the attack.

10/14/1962

HARD EVIDENCE Bad weather delayed the surveillance flight until October 14. Flying low over western Cuba, the U-2 spy plane obtained clear photographic evidence of medium-range missile sites within striking distance of major US cities.

10/22/1962

KENNEDY'S WARNING Kennedy responded by going public. In a television address seen around the world, he announced the presence of missiles and ordered a naval blockade to prevent Soviet ships from reaching Cuba. Military action seemed inevitable. The world held its breath as two nuclear superpowers prepared for war.

10/27/1962

DAYS OF CRISIS The tension mounted as, in the middle of urgent negotiations between Washington and Moscow, an American U-2 spy plane was shot down over Cuba, killing the pilot. Nuclear conflict became a terrifying possibility.

04/23/1959

MOST WANTED
Cuban Prime Minister Fidel Castro was a thorn in the side of the US government. He had taken power in Cuba by ousting the pro-American Batista dictatorship in 1955, and openly mocked CIA plans to kill him. In March 1960 US President Dwight D. Eisenhower approved a CIA plan to invade Cuba.

04/01/1961

ARMED AND READY
The CIA's activities were well known to Cuban intelligence. All Cuban workers, including women, were armed and organized into defense groups. The CIA, meanwhile, recruited anti-Castro exiles, who were secretly trained in camps in Guatemala in preparation for the invasion of Cuba.

07/12/1962

WEAPONS AGREEMENT
In 1962 the USA placed medium-range Jupiter missiles, armed with nuclear warheads, in Turkey, threatening Soviet interests. In response, Soviet leader Nikita Khrushchev persuaded Castro to allow Soviet strategic nuclear weapons to be based on Cuba.

09/28/1962

ARMS TO CUBA
US intelligence discovered that the Soviet ship *Kasimov*, photographed off Cuba, was carrying IL-28 Beagle bombers capable of bearing nuclear warheads. Fearing a Soviet arms buildup, Kennedy ordered a U-2 spy plane to fly over and observe activity in Cuba.

> ❝
> We've been **eyeball to eyeball**, and I think the other fellow **just blinked**.
>
> **US SECRETARY OF STATE DEAN RUSK ON HEARING THAT THE SOVIET SHIPS HAD TURNED BACK, OCTOBER 1962**
> ❞

11/09/1962

WEAPONS LEAVE CUBA Faced with the threat of nuclear war, the two sides reached a compromise. In return for Kennedy's promise not to invade Cuba, Khrushchev agreed to remove the missiles. The crisis was over. Observed by American naval ships, Soviet freighters, carrying missile systems, sailed away from Cuba.

The Swinging Sixties

1960–1969

The 1960s were an era of enormous change. Europe emerged from the shadow of World War II, and economic growth was widespread. At the same time, the Cold War was beginning to take hold, with proxy conflicts in Korea and Vietnam. A fresh optimism, and increasing affluence, saw the emergence of new music, politics, and fashion. Suddenly anything seemed possible.

1962

THE BEATLES EMERGE
A young band from Liverpool made a name for themselves playing gigs at The Cavern Club. The Beatles would go on to become the most famous band in music history. Not long after this early appearance, drummer Pete Best was replaced by Ringo Starr, completing the iconic lineup.

1964

BRITISH INVASION If American rock and roll had dominated the music scene of the 1950s, the Sixties belonged to British performers. First The Beatles, then bands such as The Who and The Rolling Stones conquered the American airwaves and crossed the Atlantic to perform to hysterical crowds.

1964

REBELS WITHOUT A CAUSE Teenagers in Britain rebelled against the post-war austerity of their parents. London became the center of the Mod subculture, which was all about clothes, clubs, Jamaican music, and mopeds. Their bitter rivals were the Rockers, who rode motorcycles and listened to rock and roll.

1967

PURPLE HAZE
In the USA, Jimi Hendrix transformed guitar music. His sensational, jazz-influenced style made him one of the most innovative and influential musicians of his day.

UNDERGROUND PRESS
New publications defied censorship laws and traditional notions of propriety. One of the most famous was *OZ*. Its London offices were often raided and its staff prosecuted for obscenity.

1963

SECOND WAVE FEMINISM
Activist Betty Friedan published *The Feminine Mystique*, renewing the campaign for gender equality. The new movement did much to give women control of their own social and sexual lives, fighting the assumption that a woman should be dependent on her husband.

1964

THE NEW LEFT
Music and art became increasingly political. Performers such as Bob Dylan advocated a new left-wing politics that empowered the individual, rejecting both the conservatism of the USA and the authoritarian socialism of the USSR.

1964

WARHOL POP ART
Art moved away from ivory towers with the rise of Pop Art, which was mass-produced, commercial, and witty. Established artist Andy Warhol put himself at the forefront of the movement. He was fascinated by celebrity culture and his studio, the Factory, became famous for its star-studded parties.

1965

MINISKIRT IN FASHION
British designer Mary Quant shocked the Establishment by launching the miniskirt, which left the wearer's legs exposed up to the mid-thigh. Despite, or perhaps because of, the initial scandal, the "Quant look" was soon seen throughout the world. London became the center of the global fashion industry. Twiggy, one of Quant's early models, became a star, popularizing a new, more androgynous look for women.

1967

SUMMER OF LOVE
Popular resistance to the Vietnam War, fear of the nuclear arms race, and a new interest in drugs and Eastern philosophy combined to form the hippie movement. Its followers encouraged people to turn away from warfare and embrace peace, love, sexual freedom, and psychedelic drugs.

1969

LENNON BED-IN
Beatle John Lennon and his new wife Yoko Ono joined the calls to "give peace a chance." They invited the press to two week-long bed-in protests.

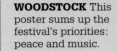

WOODSTOCK This poster sums up the festival's priorities: peace and music.

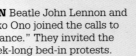

> ❝
> The **answer**, my friend, is **blowing** in the **wind**.
>
> BOB DYLAN, ON MAINSTREAM POLITICIANS, 1969
> ❞

1969

MUSIC LEGEND
For three days and nights, thousands partied at the open-air Woodstock Music Festival in Sullivan County, New York. An estimated 400,000 people listened to the greatest musicians of the day perform live. The festival came to epitomize the Sixties, even as they gave way to a new, more cynical decade.

Assassination of JFK

1963

Young, dynamic, and hard-working, John F. Kennedy was a popular president. But his career was cut tragically short on November 22, 1963 when, during a campaign visit to Texas, he was assassinated in full view of watching cameras.

JOHN F. KENNEDY

John F. Kennedy was the youngest person and the first Roman Catholic to be elected President of the USA.

12:30

SHOTS FIRED As the open limousine slowed to pass the Texas School Book Depository, three shots rang out. Kennedy slumped forward, hit in the head and neck. Sitting just in front, Governor of Texas John Connally was also struck.

12:30

RUSH TO HOSPITAL Immediately Secret Agent Clint Hill leapt into the car to shield the President. The driver accelerated toward nearby Parkland Memorial Hospital. They arrived in just a few minutes, but there was little the medics could do. Kennedy's injuries were too severe.

> " Let us strive to build **peace**… in the hearts and minds of **all our people**. "
>
> PRESIDENT J. F. KENNEDY, SPEECH TO THE UN, SEPTEMBER 1963

THE GUN THAT KILLED A PRESIDENT
This Mannlicher-Carcano rifle was hidden in the Texas School Book Depository. Lee Harvey Oswald's palm print was later found on the barrel.

11/23/1963

AMERICA STUNNED
The news of Kennedy's death left the nation in shock, and the story of his death dominated the headlines. Oswald had been charged with the murder of President Kennedy just before midnight. He denied the charges. A former Marine, he had lived in the USSR and his wife was Russian.

11/23/1963

11:40

ARRIVAL IN DALLAS
Kennedy was planning to run for re-election in 1964, and his visit to Dallas was designed to gather support. He and his wife Jacqueline disembarked from Air Force One at Love Field airfield, just outside the city. The pink outfit and pillbox hat Jackie Kennedy was wearing would become fixed in people's recollections of the day's tragic events.

12:15

MOTORCADE SETS OFF Kennedy's visit was due to start with a grand procession by motorcade through the city, ending at the Dallas Trade Mart. The journey was expected to take 45 minutes, and the route had been widely advertised in Dallas newspapers to allow crowds to gather by the roadside to greet the President.

13:48

DEATH ANNOUNCED
Fighting back emotion, CBS anchorman Walter Cronkite removed his glasses to inform the nation that President Kennedy had died of his wounds at 13:00 Central Standard Time. His body was taken back to Air Force One. The killing was one of the first national news stories to be broken on television.

13:50

OSWALD ARRESTED
Less than an hour after Kennedy's death, police arrested Lee Harvey Oswald, who was hiding in a theater. Oswald had killed a police officer at 13:15. Police discovered that he worked at the Texas School Book Depository, identified by witnesses as the source of the shots, and where his rifle had already been found.

14:38

JOHNSON SWORN IN
Vice President Lyndon B. Johnson was sworn in as the 36th President of the United States on board Air Force One. At his side stood Jackie Kennedy, still wearing her blood-stained pink outfit. The plane took off for Washington, carrying the casket containing Kennedy's body back to the White House.

THE KILLER KILLED
As Oswald was being transferred to the county jail, a Dallas nightclub owner named Jack Ruby ran forward and shot him in the stomach. Oswald died almost immediately. Ruby's motives for killing Oswald remain unclear. He was arrested, but died of pneumonia in 1966, before his case could come to trial.

11/25/1963

A NATION MOURNS
More than 800,000 people lined the streets of Washington for Kennedy's funeral and millions more watched on television. Kennedy's body was interred in Arlington National Cemetery, Virginia. The ceremony was attended by 19 heads of state, and the President's widow and children.

11/29/1963

OFFICIAL INVESTIGATION
President Johnson appointed Chief Justice Earl Warren to head an investigation into the assassination. Reporting 10 months later, Warren concluded that Oswald acted alone in killing Kennedy, and Ruby acted alone in killing Oswald. A further inquiry suggested that at least two gunmen fired at the President, but could not identify any definitive evidence of conspiracy. Many Americans still believe that the investigations were seriously flawed.

The Struggle for Civil Rights

1954–1965

Until the 1960s many African-Americans faced daily discrimination and segregation. Protest groups emerged to challenge inequality, but the struggle for basic rights would be long and hard.

07/12/1954

LYNCH MOBS White supremacist groups in the Southern states were notorious for acts of violent repression. In the worst cases, black people could be summarily hanged for an alleged crime, sometimes with the collaboration of local police.

09/04/1957

INTEGRATED SCHOOLS, When a landmark ruling by the US Supreme Court banned segregation in public schools, nine black students tried to attend a white school at Little Rock, Arkansas. Riots erupted as Governor Orval Faubus ordered the National Guard to stop the students. The Governer's orders were overturned by President Eisenhower, who sent paratroopers to ensure that local forces complied.

02/01/1960

10/01/1962

UNIVERSITY RIOTS
Two people were killed and dozens injured in riots at the University of Mississippi when James Meredith became the first black student to attend. President Kennedy addressed the nation urging peace and asking advocates of segregation to respect the law. Meredith was escorted to his first class by US Marshalls through a crowd of several hundred jeering students.

04/12/1963

POLICE BRUTALITY
Civil rights marches in Birmingham, Alabama, led by Martin Luther King, became pivotal to the campaign. Police used tear gas, fire hoses, dogs, and baton charges to suppress the protests. As images of the brutality were broadcast around the world, sympathy for the civil rights movement spread.

06/11/1963

GOVERNOR RESISTS
The Governor of Alabama, George Wallace, blocked the entrance to the University of Alabama in a symbolic attempt to prevent two black students from enrolling. President Kennedy demanded he step aside, aligning himself solidly with the civil rights movement.

06/21/1964

MURDERS INVESTIGATED The tide had turned. When three civil rights workers were murdered in Mississippi, federal investigators brought 18 people, including the local sheriff, to trial. Seven were jailed.

08/06/1965

MILLIONS FREE TO VOTE With the passing of the Voting Rights Act, black people across the southern states were finally free to register to vote, without restriction or fear of intimidation. The Civil Rights Act of the previous year had outlawed racial discrimination.

MEDAL OF HONOR
In 1999, Rosa Parks was honored with a Congressional Award.

12/01/1955

ROSA PARKS TRIUMPHS

A number of African-American groups fought against discrimination using a policy of nonviolence. On December 1, 1955 a seamstress named Rosa Parks boarded a bus in Montgomery, Alabama. She was a member of the National Association for the Advancement of Colored People (NAACP) and when the bus filled up, refused to give up her seat for a white person. She was arrested.

12/05/1955

BUSES BOYCOTTED

In response to the arrest of Rosa Parks local activists organized a boycott of the bus system. A group calling itself the Montgomery Improvement Association was established. Its charismatic president, Reverend Martin Luther King, was instrumental in leading the boycott. Their campaign drew attention and support from across the nation.

RESTAURANT SIT-IN Four black students in North Carolina defied racial segregation in restaurants by sitting at a white-only counter. Their action triggered a wave of "sit-ins" in restaurants across the South.

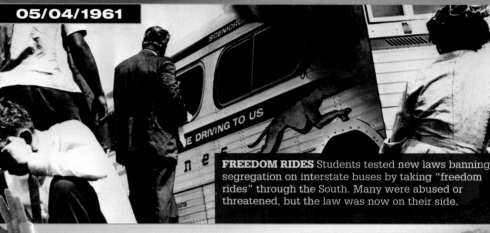

05/04/1961

FREEDOM RIDES Students tested new laws banning segregation on interstate buses by taking "freedom rides" through the South. Many were abused or threatened, but the law was now on their side.

08/28/1963

"I HAVE A DREAM"

In one of the campaign's defining events, almost 300,000 activists marched in Washington. Martin Luther King inspired the crowd with a speech setting out his vision of a country without racial prejudice. Five years later, King was assassinated.

> **I have a dream** that my four little children will one day live in a nation where they will **not be judged** by the **color of their skin**, but by the content of their **character**.
>
> MARTIN LUTHER KING, JR,
> AUGUST 28, 1963

Equality for Aboriginal Australians

1939–2008

The first whites in Australia left a legacy of discrimination against the indigenous Aborigines. They were herded onto reserves and denied ownership of their ancestral lands. Their struggle for equality would be long and hard.

09/01/1939

WARTIME SERVICE Although Aborigines were not recognized as Australian citizens, two Aboriginal military units were established during World War II, and Aborigines served as formally enlisted soldiers, sailors, and airmen. They hoped that victory would grant them a new political voice.

09/04/1951

Homes Are Sought For These Children

STOLEN GENERATION The government adopted a policy of assimilation for Aborigines in the belief that their lives would be improved by being "more white." As many as one in ten Aboriginal children were removed from their families and put into white homes. They became known as the Stolen Generation.

YIRRKALA BARK PETITION In 1963 Aborigines presented the government with a petition calling for land rights.

10/21/1961

ABORIGINAL RIGHTS Charles Perkins, one of only two Aboriginal students at the University of Sydney, became a leading advocate of Aboriginal rights. He spoke at the Federal Council for Aboriginal Advancement in 1961, emphasizing land rights, social injustice, education, and health.

02/20/1965

FREEDOM RIDE Charles Perkins sought ways to publicize the plight of the Aboriginal people. In February 1965 he organized university students from Sydney to set off on a "freedom ride." They traveled around the country towns of New South Wales to campaign and witness the levels of inequality.

05/27/1967

REFERENDUM ON ABORIGINE RIGHTS A referendum was held to give Aborigines citizenship rights. The "yes" vote was more than 90 percent. The Prime Minister also established an Office of Aboriginal Affairs.

07/23/1972

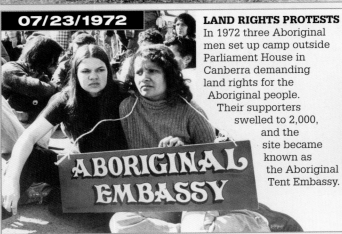

LAND RIGHTS PROTESTS In 1972 three Aboriginal men set up camp outside Parliament House in Canberra demanding land rights for the Aboriginal people. Their supporters swelled to 2,000, and the site became known as the Aboriginal Tent Embassy.

10/26/1985

ULURU RETURNED In 1985 Ayers Rock, considered sacred to Aborigines, was returned to them. Its name was changed to Uluru.

01/26/1988

ABORIGINES PROTEST AT BICENTENARY In 1988, Australians gathered to celebrate the bicentenary of the arrival of white settlers. But for Aborigines, it symbolized the anniversary of an invasion. Many gathered in Sydney to protest, and more than 40,000 joined a march—the largest for Aborigine rights in Australian history.

10/27/1949

LIMITED VOTING RIGHTS GRANTED The Australian Aborigines League (AAL) fought to end all forms of discrimination. In 1949 the Commonwealth Electoral Act was amended to give the vote to Aborigines who had served in the war. For AAL secretary Doug Nicholls it was an historic moment.

> " The **time has now come** for the nation to turn a **new page**.
>
> KEVIN RUDD,
> AUSTRALIAN PRIME MINISTER,
> FEBRUARY 13, 2008 "

08/26/1999

MOTION OF RECONCILIATION Between 1997 and 1999, state governments apologized to the Stolen Generation. The government offered a motion of reconciliation on August 26, 1999, expressing "sincere regret" and calling for official recognition of the suffering of the Aborigines.

04/13/2008

OFFICIAL APOLOGY Prime Minister Kevin Rudd made an unequivocal formal apology in Parliament to the Aborigine people in a televised broadcast beamed live across the country.

War in Vietnam

1955–1968

With the French driven out of Indo-China, Vietnam was partitioned between communist North, under Ho Chi Minh, and the Republic of Vietnam in the South. The USA was determined to prevent the spread of communism across the border. As they prepared to prop up the ailing South Vietnamese government, the scene was set for what would become one of the defining struggles of the Cold War.

02/12/1955

COMMUNIST ALLIANCE Ho Chi Minh (right) sought aid from Mao Zedong, leader of China, in his campaign to unify Vietnam as a communist state.

06/11/1963

CRISIS IN THE SOUTH Buddhist monks burned themselves to death in protest against the oppressive rule of Ngo Dinh Diem, who was widely seen as a puppet of the USA. Diem also repeatedly postponed a referendum on union with the North, which he feared would lead to communist rule.

08/02/1964

GULF OF TONKIN INCIDENT The aircraft carrier USS *Maddox* exchanged fire with North Vietnamese torpedo boats. The facts of the incident are still disputed, but it gave the USA cause to hugely escalate its military involvement in support of the government of South Vietnam.

NORTH VIETNAM
CHINA
• Dien Bien Phu
Hanoi •
Gulf of Tonkin
Thanh Hoa •
LAOS
• Vinh
• Vientiane
• Dong Hoi
• My Lai
• Hue
• Da Nang
THAILAND
SOUTH VIETNAM
Qui Nhon •
CAMBODIA
Na Trang •
Phnom Penh •
• Saigon
South China Sea
Gulf of Thailand

KEY
■ North Vietnam
■ South Vietnam
— Demilitarized zone

VIETNAM After the First Indo-China War, the former French colony was divided into North and South Vietnam, Cambodia, and Laos.

06/18/1965

AERIAL ASSAULT By this time, conventional NVA forces had joined the Viet Cong campaign. The US Air Force began an intensive programme of air attacks designed to destroy NVA infrastructure. Bombs were also dropped on neutral Laos along the route of the Ho Chi Minh trail, used as a supply route by North Vietnamese forces.

CRUDE GRENADE The Viet Cong ingeniously improvised weaponry using basic materials at hand.

01/30/1968

THE TET OFFENSIVE US and ARVN forces were stunned when the NVA and VC launched surprise attacks across the south. More than 80,000 troops hit more than 100 targets in the largest offensive of the conflict so far. What had begun as civil unrest was now full-scale war, and years of bloody fighting would follow.

05/19/1959

GUERRILLA WAR IN SOUTH VIETNAM
Protests and political action against South Vietnam's autocratic ruler Ngo Dinh Diem developed into armed resistance, openly supported from North Vietnam by Ho Chi Minh. The country moved toward a bloody civil war. The USA was not involved in fighting, but sent a large number of military advisers.

06/04/1961

HIGH STAKES
US President John F. Kennedy feared that neighboring states such as Laos and Cambodia would become communist if Ho Chi Minh succeeded in taking over all of Vietnam. Seeing the crisis as a crucial test of US resolve in the Cold War, he promised aid to South Vietnam.

01/02/1963

TENSION MOUNTS
As violence mounted, South Vietnamese forces (known as the ARVN) were caught in desperate fighting against a communist guerrilla army known as the Viet Cong (VC). At the same time, they nervously awaited an invasion by the North Vietnamese Army (NVA).

03/08/1965

US FORCES ARRIVE
A force of 3,500 American marines landed to defend US Air Force bases from Viet Cong attack. US troop numbers escalated to 200,000 by December. US General William Westmoreland proposed a swift campaign to neutralize pockets of Viet Cong, driving them out of populated areas.

03/24/1965

OPTIMISTIC BEGINNINGS At first, morale was high among US troops, who believed superior resources and technology would give them an easy victory.

05/17/1965

CAUGHT IN THE MIDDLE Guerrilla attacks by the Viet Cong put the civilian population at risk from both terrorism and brutal reprisals by the ARVN. The delocalized nature of Viet Cong forces meant that civilians were often caught in the crossfire, and the death toll swiftly mounted.

02/22/1967

SEARCH AND DESTROY
The US ground operation was designed to be highly mobile, using small search-and-destroy teams transported by helicopter. But in hostile jungle terrain US troops were vulnerable to hit-and-run ambush tactics, and struggled to engage Viet Cong guerrillas.

> If they want to **make war** for 20 years then **we shall** make war…
>
> **HO CHI MINH, DECEMBER 1966**

1965

Beatlemania

By the mid-1960s, The Beatles had charmed the world with their music and their personalities. For three years after releasing their first single, their every movement seemed certain to be accompanied by crowds of screaming young girls and admirers, a phenomenon dubbed "Beatlemania." Their charm and talent had even won over the older generation, and seemingly the Establishment, too, determined to be associated with their youthful brilliance and global success. On October 26, 1965, the four musicians were rewarded for their achievements in a manner that was unheard of for mere musicians of such youth, each receiving the order of Member of the British Empire (MBE). Their visit to Buckingham Palace, London, where they received their decorations from Queen Elizabeth II, was a major news event and desperate policemen struggled to hold back the crowds of hysterical fans that had gathered outside.

Cultural Revolution in China

1966–1976

In the 1960s, Mao felt the need to reinforce his hold on power. He ordered a campaign to stamp out "antiquated" ideas and customs. This Cultural Revolution quickly became a political witch-hunt on an unprecedented scale.

MAO ZEDONG

Mao had ruled China since 1949, and had a fanatical following among the people.

1966

1966

RED GUARD RALLY In August Mao greeted a rally of almost a million student followers in Beijing's Tiananmen Square. With Mao's blessing, the students formed the Red Guards, who would be at the forefront of Mao's campaign to eradicate reactionary capitalist elements.

1966

PURGE OF INTELLECTUALS
Schools and colleges were closed as the Red Guards set about ridding Chinese society of elitist academics. Scientists, teachers, scholars, writers, and managers suffered public humiliation and savage beatings. Many were killed or committed suicide.

无产阶级文化大革命万岁!

1972

A **proletarian** party must **get rid** of the stale and take in the **fresh air**

MAO ZEDONG,
AUGUST 1968

1976

DEATH OF MAO
Chairman Mao died on September 9 at the age of 82, and China entered a prolonged period of mourning. He had named a loyal follower, Hua Guofeng, as his successor, but many believed that Jiang Qing, Mao's wife and the architect of the Cultural Revolution, would take power.

PERSONALITY CULT

At the age of 72, Mao was eager to dispel any notion that he was unfit to rule. He participated in a highly publicized mass swim in the Yangtze River, where his followers claimed he covered an incredible 9 miles (15 km). This athletic display was the start of a campaign to turn popular support into a cult of personality.

1966

SPREADING THE WORD Mao's political sayings were collected in a volume known as *The Little Red Book*. Printing presses were pushed to the limit, churning out millions of copies. Lin Biao, head of the Chinese People's Liberation Army and Mao's greatest ally, insisted that every soldier should read it.

1967

THE LOST GENERATION

Millions of young people from the cities were sent to work side by side with peasants in the countryside. Mao believed this would build a new, classless society, but in practice only poor and politically undesirable students were affected. The wealthy and well-connected could usually find ways to stay at home. Schools remained closed, depriving a whole generation of education.

NIXON IN CHINA

The wider world remained largely unaware of events in China. Zhou Enlai, Chinese Premier since 1949, even arranged an official visit by Richard Nixon, President of the USA, China's most hated foe. However, behind the scenes Mao's health was failing, and the political élite were preparing to battle to succeed him.

THE LITTLE RED BOOK

This collection of quotations from Mao's speeches and writings was the foundation of his personality cult. Every Red Guard carried a copy, and extracts were displayed on vast posters.

1976

THE TABLES ARE TURNED Against all expectations, Hua ordered the arrest of Jiang Qing and her followers, a radical faction known as the Gang of Four. Their downfall was enthusiastically welcomed in Beijing, and marked the end of the excesses of the Cultural Revolution.

1976

RADICALS ON TRIAL

The Gang of Four were tried and convicted of anti-party activities. Jiang Qing was the only one to offer any defense. The four became scapegoats, leaving Mao's reputation officially unblemished, but the scars of his last years in power would take decades to fade.

Six-Day War

1967

In the late 1960s tensions were on the rise again between Israel and its Arab neighbors. Egyptian President Gamal Abdel Nasser campaigned to unify the Arab world, with opposition to Israel among his rallying calls. Palestinian guerrilla groups began carrying out attacks against Israel. However, when Arab forces prepared to mount an assault, the ferocity of Israel's response would take them completely by surprise.

05/16/1967

MILITARY BUILDUP Falsely informed by the USSR that Israel was planning to invade Syria, Nasser began to move troops into the Sinai Peninsula. He demanded the withdrawal of the UN Emergency Force deployed in Sinai and the Gaza strip since 1956, in the aftermath of the Suez Crisis. The UN agreed to his demands.

06/05/1967

ISRAEL STRIKES FIRST At 7:45 a.m. the Israeli air force launched a massive attack on Egyptian airfields, destroying most of Egypt's bombers and half of its fighter jets. Just 19 Israeli planes were lost in the onslaught.

06/05/1967

WAR IN SINAI Along with the air attack, three Israeli divisions of tank, infantry, and paratrooper brigades moved swiftly into Sinai. The Israeli attack concentrated all its efforts on breaking through the heavily fortified Egyptian positions in Sinai and the Gaza Strip. By June 6 its tanks had penetrated deep into the desert.

06/06/1967

> **Israel** [will] **stop at nothing** to cancel the blockade... President Nasser should have **no illusions**.
>
> ISRAELI PRIME MINISTER LEVI ESHKOL, ON THE CLOSURE OF THE STRAITS OF TIRAN, MAY 19, 1967

UZI SUBMACHINE GUN Named in honor of its designer, Major Uziel Gal, the Uzi submachine gun had a high rate of fire and was standard issue for frontline Israeli soldiers in the Six-Day War.

10/06/1967

GOLAN HEIGHTS CAPTURED Syrian shelling from Golan Heights, the high rocky plateau overlooking northern Israel, was intense. Once the war in Sinai ended, Israel diverted resources to the northern battle zone. The Heights were taken on June 10.

05/23/1967

TENSIONS MOUNT
An estimated 40,000 Egyptian troops and 500 tanks poured into the Sinai Peninsula. Nasser closed the Straits of Tiran to Israeli shipping, thereby blockading the port of Eilat, Israel's only access to the Red Sea, and stopping the flow of oil from its main supplier, Iran.

05/25/1967

ARAB ALLIANCE
Nasser's calls for a pan-Arab alliance against Israel began to bear fruit. King Hussein of Jordan signed a mutual defense pact with Egypt, and Jordanian tanks moved toward the West Bank. The buildup of Arab forces on Israel's borders continued as Iraq joined the military alliance. Israel's frantic quest for an international diplomatic solution failed. War now seemed inevitable.

06/05/1967

BATTLE FOR JERUSALEM
Ignoring Israeli pleas that Jordan should remain neutral, King Hussein ordered the Jordanian army to shell targets in Israeli-held West Jerusalem and the suburbs of Tel Aviv. Israel launched a fierce counterattack and two days later, Israeli paratroopers took the Old City of Jerusalem.

EGYPTIAN ROUT
Egypt's military chief Field Marshal Mohamed Abdel Hakim Amer ordered all units to retreat. Thousands were killed, others surrendered as the Egyptian army raced back, pursued by Israeli forces. The war in Sinai was over. Israel had won complete control of the Sinai Peninsula, threatening Egypt's control of the Suez Canal, a vital trade link.

06/07/1967

WEST BANK SEIZED
Although capturing the West Bank was not part of Israel's original strategy, Israeli forces continued to advance after taking the Old City of Jerusalem. Jordanian forces retreated across the Jordan River and by the end of June 7 the entire West Bank was in Israeli hands. Palestinian civilians surrendered to Israeli soldiers.

06/11/1967

ISRAELIS CELEBRATE
A ceasefire was reached on June 11, after six days of incessant fighting. Claiming to have acted in self-defense, Israel had doubled its territory at the expense of its Arab neighbors. It acquired the West Bank, Gaza Strip, Golan Heights, and Sinai. Israeli soldiers celebrated the victory on the streets of Jerusalem.

ISRAEL AFTER 1967
Israel had captured vast swathes of Arab territory. More than 600,000 Palestinians living in the West Bank came under Israeli administration.

Israel 1949

Area occupied by Israel after 1967 war

- - - Disputed frontier

Beirut
Damascus
LEBANON
Golan Heights
SYRIA
Mediterranean Sea
Tel Aviv
Gaza Strip
West Bank
Jerusalem
Gaza
Dead Sea
ISRAEL
Suez Canal
JORDAN
EGYPT
Suez
Sinai
Eilat
Straits of Tiran
Gulf of Suez
SAUDI ARABIA
Red Sea

A CENTURY OF

Music

The 20th century produced a bewildering and diverse range of music, from pure beauty to pure noise. It was an era of contrasts, with some artists sticking to their roots and others overturning tradition. As musical influences from all over the world met, genres became more diverse. Social and political identity became tied to musical taste. By the end of the century, as new technology made distribution easier, music stars were some of the world's richest and most influential people.

1910–1930 Classical music was already in a state of flux when, on May 29, 1913, *The Rite of Spring* premiered in Paris. A ballet score composed by Igor Stravinsky, it was a new musical idiom. Its debut, with its crashing discordant notes, caused a riot. Nothing, it seemed, would be the same again, and after World War I, everything, including music, had to be reconstructed. This was helped by the rise of popular music such as blues and jazz. Jazz emerged from New Orleans, but Chicago in particular became its home, where stars such as Billie Holiday, Ella Fitzgerald, and Nat King Cole rose to prominence.

1930–1940 As German composer Kurt Weill debuted his socially critical operas to Berliners, American audiences welcomed big musicals on Broadway, many of which also tackled contemporary issues. *Showboat* depicted interracial marriage, while *Porgy and Bess* was born out of the experiences of the Great Depression.

WAR MUSIC World War I inspired patriotic tunes to improve morale, such as this American song about the departure of troops to Europe.

JAZZ ROYALTY American band leader William "Count" Basie directs his jazz orchestra, formed in the 1930s.

4.86 MILLION

Number of sales of *Candle in the Wind*, Elton John's 1997 song on the death of Princess Diana. It was the biggest selling single of all time.

1920s

RADIO The radio had a revolutionary effect on Western culture and brought jazz and blues directly into people's homes.

1930s

JAZZ One of the founders of jazz, Louis Armstrong turned it into an international sensation.

1940s

CROONERS The 1940s was the age of crooners such as Frank Sinatra.

1950s

JUKEBOX The jukebox was synonymous with rock and roll, played on the new 45 rpm records.

NEW SOUND Electric guitars redefined music for the 20th century. Les Paul created many of the earliest models, including this 1940 prototype.

1940–1970 In 1943 *Oklahoma!* heralded the age of the big musical. But while parents swayed to the sound of Julie Andrews (*The Sound of Music*, 1959), their kids were dancing to a different tune. American popular music exploded. Charlie Parker experimented with bebop, James Brown mixed gospel with blues, Elvis Presley played rock and roll, and Johnny Cash established himself as king of country. America dominated the music scene into the early 1960s until The Beatles crossed the Atlantic and stormed the US charts. Times were changing. Teenagers listened to Bob Dylan, and gained a social conscience. Then during the hippy era, they tuned in and dropped out as drug-inspired music by artists such as Jimi Hendrix fueled nonconformist counter-culture.

1970–1990 Electronic music produced a rhythmic, pared-down sound, but the stars of the 1970s were dancers. Disco was born in New York at clubs where DJs played nonstop dance tracks. It was all getting too comfortable. Punk rock bands such as The New York Dolls and the Sex Pistols delighted in offending, reflecting the discontent among bored, unemployed youth. Rap, hip hop, and house music were all influenced by punk. It was all about attitude and what you had to say.

1990– The rage fizzled out. Nirvana captured the plight of disillusioned youth, and *Smells like Teen Spirit* became an anthem for the loser generation. In the 21st century, digital music

ELECTRONIC MUSIC
Will.i.am from the Black Eyed Peas hosts a club night in 2010 where electro is the new disco.

> "
> If I hadn't heard **rock and roll** on the radio, I would have had **no idea** there was **life** on this **planet**.
> "

offers an incredible range of musical choice at the touch of a button. The huge budgets of major studios create multi-million dollar sales for artists such as Beyoncé and Lady Gaga. At the same time, the internet and indie labels offer even amateur musicians an audience, and a shot at the big time.

1960s

BEATLEMANIA
At the height of their fame, The Beatles released the seminal *Sergeant Pepper* album, which kicked off the "summer of love" across Europe and the US in 1967.

1970s

GLAM ROCK
Led by singers such as David Bowie, glam rock was camp, over the top, and sardonic.

1980s

POP ICONS Pop stars such as Madonna took the world by storm, helped enormously by the video revolution.

2000s

MP3 PLAYER The introduction of MP3 players—such as the iPod in 2001—changed the way we listen to music.

1967

Flower Power

Driven by a belief that perhaps they really could change the world, a million demonstrators descended on Washington in protest against the Vietnam War on October 20, 1967. The war was deeply unpopular, having claimed the lives of tens of thousands of young Americans. The demonstrators attempted to enter the Pentagon, which was surrounded by the National Guard. Influenced by civil rights leaders such as Martin Luther King and Gandhi, in a spirit of remarkable innocence and nonviolence, the protesters faced the guns and bayonets with flowers. In the end, violence prevailed: 100 people were injured during the march and the US Army did not withdraw from Vietnam for a further six years. Nevertheless, the demonstrations played their part in undermining support for the war, and the image of a girl clutching a flower in the face of armed soldiers became an enduring symbol of peaceful protest.

The Year of Protests

1968

In the spring of 1968, a single demonstration in Paris reverberated around the world. Workers and students took to the streets in cities from Rome, London, and Paris to Prague and Mexico City. The one cause they had in common was opposition to America's war in Vietnam, but many marched against authoritarian regimes and rigid systems of government. The largest of the demonstrations began with a small group of activists in the University of Paris. When police were called in to quell a rally, students and workers joined in mass protests that brought France to its knees.

03/22/1968

TROUBLE IN PARIS
At the University of Paris annex in Nanterre, a suburb on the west of Paris, students had been protesting against poor conditions on campus since 1962. When four students were arrested during an anti-war rally, 500 demonstrators stormed the building. They went on to form the March 22nd Movement.

04/11/1968

PLOT TO KILL RUDI DUTSCHKE In West Germany the anti-war protest movement was spearheaded by Rudi Dutschke, the charismatic head of the Socialist Students' Union. After a smear campaign in some newspapers, which branded him a "public enemy," he barely survived an attempt on his life.

05/06/1968

CONFRONTATION WITH POLICE
On Rue Saint-Jacques in central Paris, the situation became violent. Students returning from the disciplinary hearing clashed with police. A number of protestors were left unconscious and the streets were filled with smoke and tear gas.

05/13/1968

ONE-DAY STRIKE
Crowds arrived from all over Paris, inspired by the actions of students at the Sorbonne. For the first time workers and students united in a massive protest forcing the closure of airports and rail stations. Around 800,000 marched through the streets, demanding de Gaulle's resignation.

> " Be **realistic**, **demand** the **impossible**.
>
> **GRAFFITI IN PARIS, MAY 1968** "

03/16/1968

PROTESTS IN ITALY Demonstrations against police brutality took place in several universities across Italy in the winter of 1967. In March 1968 Rome University was closed and more than 400 students were arrested.

03/17/1968

PROTESTS REACH LONDON The movement spread to London as thousands gathered outside the US Embassy to demonstrate against the Vietnam War. It swiftly descended into chaos when mounted police charged at the demonstrators. Stones were thrown and hundreds of protestors were arrested.

05/02/1968

DANNY THE RED The movement soon had a leader in Daniel Cohn-Bendit, a young German studying sociology at Nanterre. He was already known for boycotting lectures and examinations. Branded in the press as "Danny the Red" for the color of his hair and left-wing politics, he was arrested after occupying the Nanterre Faculty.

05/03/1968

RING LEADERS ARRESTED The protest shifted to the heart of Paris when Cohn-Bendit was told to attend a disciplinary board in the center of the city. Thousands took to the streets under the full glare of the world's media. An embarrassed President Charles de Gaulle ordered the arrest of the ring leaders. Armed police charged at the students.

05/20/1968

SPREADING THE WORD Students spread their message through banners and newspapers. They demanded the release of their leaders and an end to the "police state." The message reached those outside Paris, and within a few days 8 million workers joined the strike in car plants and factories.

05/24/1968

FRANCE COMES TO A HALT Workers and students came together once again, bringing France to a standstill. Almost a third of the workforce came out on strike. Marchers gathered at the Arc de Triomph in Paris and were cheered by spectators who lined the streets. The state prepared to use brutal force to crush the revolt.

05/24/1968

STOCK EXCHANGE SET ON FIRE In a televised address to the nation, de Gaulle demanded that citizens back his program of reform. France was on the brink of civil war. Within minutes of the speech riots erupted. Armed with Molotov cocktails, the demonstrators in Paris set fire to the French stock exchange.

05/30/1968

THE REVOLUTION DIES Fearing the worst, the government announced an early election. Crowds gathered in support of the French president, and the movement lost steam. However, its impact had been profound. In the following months, student protests took place in Spain, Poland, Czechoslovakia, the USA, and Mexico, as the spirit of revolution crossed the globe.

Prague Spring

1968

Czechoslovakia, which had lived under communist rule since 1948, epitomized the conflict between repressive Soviet influence and popular demands for political reform. As the people sought new freedoms, they posed a challenge that the neighboring Soviet Union could not tolerate.

RESISTING RUSSIAN CONTROL Many Czechoslovakians had long resented Soviet inflence over their government, because the Czech Communist Party imposed censorship and curtailed political and economic freedom. Anti-Soviet opinion escalated and people took to the streets to show their discontent.

> **How** could they **do this** to me?

ALEXANDER DUBČEK, ON HEARING OF THE RUSSIAN INVASION, AUGUST 26, 1968

08/22/1968

WARSAW PACT SOLDIERS IN PRAGUE Thousands of Soviet troops and soldiers from other Warsaw Pact countries, including Poland, Hungary, and Bulgaria, moved into the capital city of Prague to crush the growing uprising along with all liberal reforms. Initially the troops were met with confusion and shock from residents, who threw stones at the tanks and organized more demonstrations asserting Czechoslovakian nationalism.

08/25/1968

WRITING ON THE WALL To mark their protest, residents of Prague wrote on a building wall, "Lenin, wake up, they've gone mad." Such graffiti was common as Czechoslovakians sent messages in Russian to the invaders. Hastily produced pamphlets and posters spread information about the occupation, imploring citizens to stay loyal to Dubček and resist the occupation peacefully.

08/26/1968

PRAGUE DEFIANT In a show of defiance, one man simply stood before a tank and defied the soldiers to shoot him in the chest. Such images of desperate people standing defenseless against the tanks drew worldwide sympathy for the rebellion.

01/05/1968

DUBČEK STEPS IN

The Czechoslovakian Communist Party leader Alexander Dubček tried to modernize the country by introducing free speech and freedom of assembly. He abolished censorship and granted the press unprecedented liberty. These reforms were later known as the "Prague Spring," and made Dubček a national hero.

07/21/1968

RUSSIAN TANKS ENTER
Russia became alarmed at the new liberalism. Despite attempts by Dubček to assure the Soviets that he was still loyal, Russia moved tanks up to the Czechoslovakian frontier and in July crossed the border. In protest, the Czechoslovakians staged a one-hour strike.

08/26/1968

PRAGUE IS OCCUPIED
Around 500,000 troops, mostly from the Soviet Union, poured into Czechoslovakia. They quickly surrounded all key party, government, army, and media buildings in Prague. There was no military resistance, but clashes between invading troops and civilians left 72 Czechoslovakians dead and hundreds badly wounded.

08/26/1968

THE UPRISING WANES Resistance was brave but futile. Dubček was arrested and taken to Moscow for negotiations. After signing the Moscow Protocols that reversed his reforms, he was allowed to remain in office until April 1969, when he was replaced, expelled from the Communist party, and given a job as a forestry official.

08/27/1968

REFUGEES FLEE
After Dubček's exit, officials of the communist party took over. Czechoslovakia witnessed a mass exodus, as thousands escaped to refugee camps in Austria and attempted to enter Western Europe. Citizens who stayed behind were forced to either toe the Soviet-led party line or live as outcasts, facing harassment by the state secret service.

01/16/1969

PROTESTS CONTINUE
Anti-Soviet protests continued. Riots erupted in 1969 when student Jan Palach burned himself to death in protest at the occupation. Humanitarian groups opposed the suppression of human rights. Nonetheless, Czechoslovakia remained a Soviet satellite state until 1989.

Space Race
1957–1969

As the Cold War took shape, the USA and USSR competed to be the first to send people and material into space. It was a struggle for prestige and military advantage between two ideological enemies, but also an incredible display of human ingenuity, bravery, and the will to explore and understand our universe.

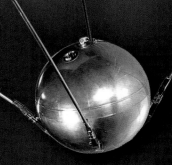

SPUTNIK 1 The first artificial satellite was the size of a basketball.

04/12/1961

FIRST MAN IN SPACE Once again the USSR achieved an early success when the cosmonaut Yuri Gagarin became the first human to travel to space. His spacecraft, *Vostok 1*, launched from Baikonur Cosmodrome and performed a single orbit of the Earth, landing after a flight of 108 minutes.

05/25/1961

KENNEDY UNDER PRESSURE In response, President John F. Kennedy promised that the USA would put the first human on the Moon.

06/22/1963

12/15/1965

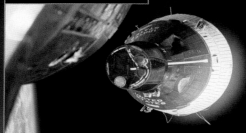

SPACE LINK-UP The rendezvous of *Gemini 6* and *Gemini* 160 miles (7,257 km) above the Earth, proved that spacecraft could manoeuvre and meet in space.

08/29/1966

EARTHRISE The world saw this iconic view of the Earth for the first time. It was taken as the unmanned *Lunar Orbiter 1* was about to dip behind the Moon during its 16th orbit. The US Lunar Orbiter Program mapped the Moon's surface to help find a suitable landing spot for the new *Apollo* spacecraft.

11/09/1967

MOON ROCKET US scientists faced the challenge of building a rocket powerful enough to reach the Moon and a spacecraft that could safely travel there and back. The Saturn V was the most powerful rocket ever made, and launched an unmanned spacecraft into Earth's orbit. It then provided an extra boost to send *Apollo* on a trajectory for the Moon.

12/24/1968

TO THE MOON *Apollo 8* was the first US mission to make the journey to the Moon. It tested the theory that a spacecraft could use the Moon's gravitational pull as it passed its far side to propel itself back into orbit. Ground control waited anxiously while the crew of Frank Borman, James Lovell, and William Anders were out of contact as they made the maneuver.

10/04/1957

THE RACE BEGINS The Space Age began with the USSR's *Sputnik 1*, the world's first artificial satellite. Launched by rocket from the Baikonur Cosmodrome, in Kazakhstan, the simple satellite took 98 minutes to orbit the Earth. It sent back valuable data on conditions in space and the upper atmosphere. Its success came as a surprise to the Americans, who were unaware of Soviet advances. They proceeded to speed up their own space program.

04/09/1959

THE MERCURY SEVEN

The American response came in the form of Project Mercury, designed to put the first human in orbit around the Earth. Candidates for the role were recruited from Air Force test pilots. The specifications included that they must be under 40, less than 5 ft 11 in (180 cm) tall, have a bachelor's degree, and have logged over 1,500 hours flying time, including jet qualifications. Just seven men were chosen.

RUSSIANS GRAB THE HEADLINES Still it was the Soviets who took the lead. Valery Bykovsky in *Vostok 5* set the record for the longest solo space flight of five days, and Valentina Tereshkova in *Vostok 6* became the first woman in space. The two cosmonauts were branded Russia's "Romeo and Juliet" space team. Soviet leader Nikita Khrushchev took full advantage of the propagada victory, joining the cosmonauts at a mass rally in Moscow.

06/03/1965

USA CLOSES THE GAP

Project Gemini saw the USA complete 10 piloted missions into space in 20 months. Ed White became the first American to walk in space when he exited his *Gemini 4* spacecraft for 21 minutes. He found the experience exhilarating. When he was ordered back into his spacecraft he is reported to have said "This is the saddest moment of my life."

01/27/1967

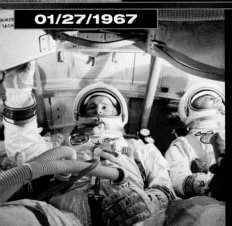

SPACE-RACE TRAGEDY Three US astronauts, Gus Grissom, Ed White, and Roger Chaffee, died when fire broke out on the *Apollo 1* spacecraft during tests at Cape Kennedy, Florida. The craft was designed for a manned flight to the Moon, and the disaster raised questions about whether crew safety was being compromised in the race to achieve a lunar landing.

07/20/1969

MAN ON THE MOON Neil Armstrong left *Apollo 11* to become the first man to walk on the Moon. Watched by millions around the world on live television, the historic event marked the end of the Space Race.

> That's one **small step** for [a] **man**, one giant **leap** for **mankind**.

NEIL ARMSTRONG, STEPPING ONTO THE MOON
JULY 21, 1969

1969

Moon Landing Broadcast

Hundreds of millions of people across the world gathered around television screens on July 20, 1969 to watch live broadcasts of the Apollo 11 *Eagle* lunar module as it touched down on the surface of the Moon. At the international arrivals building of New York's John F. Kennedy Airport, passengers were able to watch the historic moment on a large, temporary screen hanging high above them. Soon after the landing, astronaut Neil Armstrong descended the craft's steps to set foot on the lunar surface and become the first human on the Moon. He was followed by *Eagle* pilot Edwin "Buzz" Aldrin. Together they spent more than 21 hours on the Moon. Their arrival, and successful return, was the culmination of years of planning by a team of thousands, and fulfilled the vision of the late President Kennedy, who in 1961 had promised that a human would stand on the

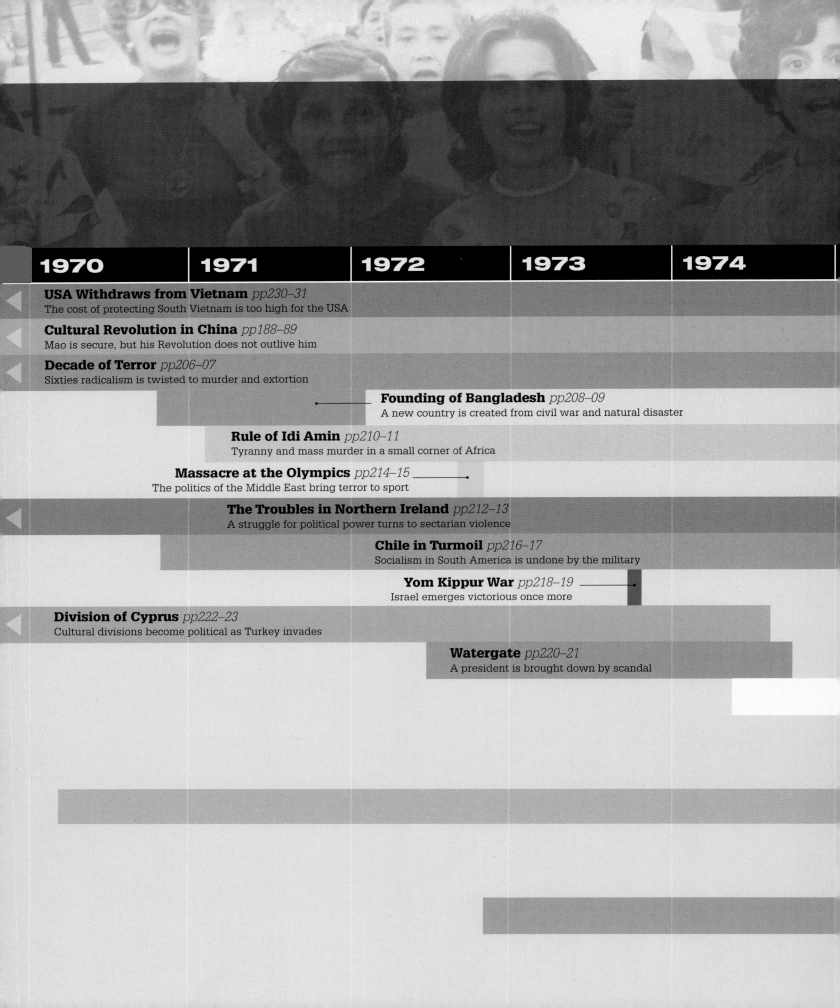

1970　　1971　　1972　　1973　　1974

USA Withdraws from Vietnam *pp230–31*
The cost of protecting South Vietnam is too high for the USA

Cultural Revolution in China *pp188–89*
Mao is secure, but his Revolution does not outlive him

Decade of Terror *pp206–07*
Sixties radicalism is twisted to murder and extortion

Founding of Bangladesh *pp208–09*
A new country is created from civil war and natural disaster

Rule of Idi Amin *pp210–11*
Tyranny and mass murder in a small corner of Africa

Massacre at the Olympics *pp214–15*
The politics of the Middle East bring terror to sport

The Troubles in Northern Ireland *pp212–13*
A struggle for political power turns to sectarian violence

Chile in Turmoil *pp216–17*
Socialism in South America is undone by the military

Yom Kippur War *pp218–19*
Israel emerges victorious once more

Division of Cyprus *pp222–23*
Cultural divisions become political as Turkey invades

Watergate *pp220–21*
A president is brought down by scandal

1970-79

Carnation Revolution *pp224–25*
Democracy comes to Portugal courtesy of military revolt

Lebanese Civil War *pp228–29*
Refugees and guerrillas pour in, fueling armed confrontation among rival factions

Angolan Civil War *pp232–33*
Violence follows Portugal's clumsy withdrawal from its old colony

Khmer Rouge *pp234–35*
A Marxist reengineering of society descends into genocide

Iranian Revolution *pp240–41*
The pro-Western shah is overthrown by religious fundamentalists

Iranian Hostage Crisis *pp242–43*
Radicalized students invade the US embassy in Tehran

Nicaraguan Revolution *pp244–45*
Nicaragua's right-wing dictator falls to armed rebellion

Soviet-Afghan War *pp238–39*
The USSR moves to control its Central Asian neighbor

Decade of Terror

1968–1978

The 1970s were marked by an escalation in terrorist attacks. One of the most terrifying groups to emerge was the left-wing Baader–Meinhof Gang from West Germany, later known as the Red Army Faction (RAF). Terrorism became international as the RAF allied with like-minded factions to conduct acts of violence around the world.

ANDREAS BAADER
Baader, the founder of the Red Army Faction, believed in violence to achieve revolution.

ULRIKE MEINHOF
The other half of the Baader–Meinhof duo, Meinhof was equally committed to waging war against the state.

06/18/1970

TERROR ACTIVITIES ON THE RISE The RAF decided they needed professional advice. In June 1970 Baader, Meinhof, and some of their associates trained at a Palestinian guerrilla base outside Amman, Jordan. On their return to Berlin, they mounted a series of bomb attacks against police, publishers, and US military bases.

06/01/1972

BAADER ARRESTED Baader was finally caught in Frankfurt during a shootout, along with fellow RAF members Jan-Carl Raspe and Holger Meins. He was brought down by a sniper bullet in his thigh. Despite this setback, a new generation of activists joined the RAF and their acts of terrorism continued.

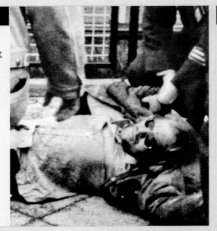

06/16/1972

MEINHOF CAPTURED Ulrike Meinhof set about signing up new recruits. By 1972, when she was finally arrested, the RAF was linked to dozens of bombings, along with the murders of several policemen. Meinhof, officially named Public Enemy No. 1, was sent to prison. Nonetheless, the RAF masterminded a new era of terror.

04/15/1974

PATTY HEARST SAGA Inspired by the RAF, the Symbionese Liberation Army, a left-wing radical group in the USA, achieved fame with the 1974 kidnap of heiress Patty Hearst. Brainwashed by her kidnappers, she began participating in their activities. Hearst was arrested and convicted for her role in a bank robbery. She served two years in jail but was later pardoned.

02/27/1975

POLITICIAN HELD HOSTAGE The chairman of Berlin's Christian Democrat Union (CDU), mayoral candidate Peter Lorenz was kidnapped by left-wing radicals of the 2 June Movement. They demanded the release of six terrorists and RAF members, who were duly freed and flown to Aden, Yemen.

04/24/1975

12/21/1975

OPEC STAFF TAKEN HOSTAGE A group of terrorists, led by Carlos the Jackal, stormed a conference of the Organization of the Petroleum Exporting Countries (OPEC) in Vienna and took more than 60 hostages. Carlos secured a $5 million ransom and a jet, which he used to flee to Algeria.

09/05/1977

INDUSTRIALIST HELD HOSTAGE In another bid to free its members from jail, German industrialist Hanns-Martin Schleyer was taken hostage by the RAF. His body was found a month later in the trunk of a car. The murder of Schleyer took place in what became known as the German Autumn of 1977, when attacks by the RAF reached a peak.

04/02/1968

STORES BOMBED Baader began his crusade by targeting places that he perceived as symbols of consumer capitalism. In 1968 he detonated homemade bombs in two Frankfurt stores, causing considerable damage. He was arrested but later escaped with the help of Ulrike Meinhof.

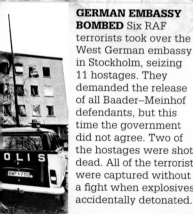

GERMAN EMBASSY BOMBED Six RAF terrorists took over the West German embassy in Stockholm, seizing 11 hostages. They demanded the release of all Baader–Meinhof defendants, but this time the government did not agree. Two of the hostages were shot dead. All of the terrorists were captured without a fight when explosives accidentally detonated.

06/27/1975

A NEW THREAT Palestinian campaigners against Israel increasingly turned to acts of terrorism. One infamous activist was Venezuelan-born Ilich Ramírez Sánchez, better known as Carlos the Jackal. He had a hand in many attacks on pro-Israeli businesses and individuals in Europe. In June 1975 he killed two French counterintelligence agents sent to question him, but his most notorious exploits were still to come.

> The **revolution** says: I was, I am, **I will be** again.
>
> **LAST STATEMENT OF THE RAF, APRIL 20, 1998**

10/18/1977

RAF LEADERS COMMIT SUICIDE After the attempted hijacking of another plane failed, RAF leaders Baader, Esslin, and Raspe gave up all hope of escape from prison and killed themselves in a suicide pact. Meinhof had committed suicide during her trial in 1976. But this was not the end of the group's activities. Baader and Meinhof became heroes for many young West Germans, and the RAF activities did not end until 1998, when it disbanded.

05/09/1978

MORO KIDNAPPING In Italy, the terrorist organization Brigate Rossi (the Red Brigades) sought to bring about armed revolution. Their highest-profile victim was Aldo Moro, former Prime Minister and leader of the Christian Democracy Party. Moro was kidnapped and held captive for 55 days, then executed. His body was found in the trunk of a car in Rome. Sporadic outbreaks of violence continued, until the collapse of communism in Europe considerably weakened revolutionary groups.

Founding of Bangladesh

1970–1972

When the small, economically disadvantaged province of East Pakistan broke away from West Pakistan to form Bangladesh, it sparked a wave of violence that precipitated an armed conflict between Pakistan and India.

WEST AND EAST PAKISTAN The creation of Pakistan in 1947 united two geographically separate Muslim regions. East Pakistan was formerly a part of Bengal.

03/23/1971

DISORDER GROWS
As resistance grew in East Pakistan, protesters, often armed with crude weapons, took to the streets of the capital, Dhaka, amid scenes of violence. President Yahya Khan prepared for a military crackdown, flying in large detachments of troops from West Pakistan to take control of the situation.

03/26/1971

CALL FOR FREEDOM
Sheikh Mujib was arrested in the early hours of March 26. Shortly afterward, a Bengali army officer, Ziaur Rahman, seized the radio station at Chittagong and went on air to proclaim the independence of Bangladesh (nation of Bengalis). Meanwhile, Mujib was flown to a prison in West Pakistan.

04/01/1971

06/22/1971

ESCAPING TO INDIA
An estimated 10 million refugees fled East Pakistan in desperation, crossing the border into West Bengal, India. The influx of refugees placed a huge burden on the Indian government. Prime Minister Indira Gandhi appealed for international help and planned a military intervention to solve the crisis.

SHEIKH MUJIBUR RAHMAN
Popularly known as Sheikh Mujib, Rahman headed the Awami League that led the Bengali opposition to West Pakistan's ruling elite.

11/12/1970

FLOOD IN EAST PAKISTAN A devastating flood killed thousands in East Pakistan. Blaming the central government for failing to help the victims, the Awami League won nearly all the seats in East Pakistan in the national elections held the following month. The result gave Sheikh Mujib a clear majority in the regional assembly.

03/07/1971

MARTIAL LAW IMPOSED Unhappy at the election result, Pakistani President Yahya Khan postponed the formation of the National Assembly and imposed martial law in East Pakistan. In response, Mujib appealed to Bengalis to resist the government, stopping just short of calling for independence.

OPERATION SEARCHLIGHT

The Pakistani army's campaign to restore order degenerated into a rampage of terror and bloodshed. The military shelled Dhaka University, killing teachers and students. The dead were buried in mass graves. Dhaka's Hindu minority was singled out for the worst of the violence.

04/17/1971

THE FIGHT FOR FREEDOM Large numbers of Bengali soldiers defected from the Pakistan army to join the *Mukti Bahini*, an underground army of Bangladesh freedom fighters, in training camps along the Indian border. Leaders of the Awami League established an interim government in Calcutta, India.

> **The struggle** now is the struggle for **our emancipation**…
>
> **AWAMI LEAGUE LEADER SHEIKH MUJIB, SPEECH AT DHAKA RACECOURSE, MARCH 1, 1971**

12/14/1971

WAR BREAKS OUT As Indian troops massed on the East Pakistan border, Yahya Khan launched a preemptive airstrike into northwest India on December 3, but inflicted little damage. On December 6, the Indian government officially recognized Bangladesh. Eight days later, Indira Gandhi ordered nine army divisions to cross the border into East Pakistan.

12/16/1971

PAKISTAN SURRENDERS With air links to West Pakistan cut off and Dhaka blockaded from the sea, the Pakistan army surrendered, with 90,000 troops handing themselves over to Indian forces. A ceasefire was agreed the next day.

12/20/1971

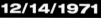

CELEBRATING FREEDOM Cheering crowds saluted the interim Bangladesh government on its return to Dhaka. Following Pakistan's defeat, Yahya Khan resigned as President. His successor, Zulfikar Ali Bhutto, immediately ordered Mujib's release.

01/12/1972

MUJIB RETURNS On his release, Sheikh Mujib traveled to London, where he addressed the world's media. From there he returned to Dhaka, to be greeted by euphoric crowds. On January 12, he formally took office as Prime Minister of the independent sovereign state of Bangladesh.

STAMP OF VICTORY This stamp, featuring a *Mukti Bahini* fighter, was issued in 1981 to commemorate the 10th anniversary of Bangladesh's independence.

Rule of Idi Amin

1971–1979

Idi Amin Dada, President of Uganda, was often treated as a buffoon by the international press. A former officer in the British colonial army in Africa, he took great pleasure in taunting Uganda's former colonial rulers, giving himself the titles of Conqueror of the British Empire and the uncrowned King of Scotland. However, the rule of this erratic and cruel leader was far from a joke; his regime was noted for gross human rights violations, ethnic violence, and political repression, and he was responsible for the deaths of more than 100,000 people.

09/07/1972

EXPULSION OF ASIANS
In a sudden and unexpected move, Amin announced that all Asians who were not Ugandan citizens must leave the country within 90 days. Around 60,000 second- and third-generation immigrants from India—holders of British passports—were affected. Forced to abandon their businesses and property, most fled to Britain, where they faced an uncertain future.

09/14/1972

FOREIGN RELATIONS
In another surprise move, Amin severed relations with Israel and sent a telegram to Kurt Waldheim, UN Secretary-General, and Israeli Prime Minister Golda Meir, praising Hitler's persecution of the Jews. As a result, the USA withdrew financial aid. Amin turned away from the West, seeking ties with the USSR, East Germany, and Libyan dictator Muammar Gaddafi.

07/10/1975

SUPPRESSING ALL OPPOSITION Amin was quick to quell any voice of dissent that rose against him. He imposed a death sentence on Denis Hills, a British subject living in Uganda, for describing him as a "village tyrant" in a book he was writing. Amin released Hills only when British Foreign Minister James Callaghan flew to Uganda to intercede on his behalf.

07/04/1976

ENTEBBE RAID
Tensions with the West peaked when Palestinian terrorists landed a hijacked plane full of Israeli hostages at Uganda's Entebbe Airport. Amin offered the terrorists supplies and the support of his armed forces. But despite his efforts, Israeli commandos freed the hostages in a daring rescue operation.

10/30/1978

INVASION FORCE
In October 1978 Amin launched an attack on neighboring Tanzania. President Nyerere responded by invading Uganda. The Tanzanian army, backed by the Uganda National Liberation Army (UNLA), captured the capital, Kampala, and Amin fled the country. He died in exile in 2003.

04/13/1979

NEW REGIME After Amin fled Uganda, leaving its economy in ruins, Yusufu Lule was sworn in as interim president amid much celebration. However, within a few months Milton Obote regained power.

01/25/1971

IN THE DRIVING SEAT

President Milton Obote was out of the country when General Idi Amin, fearing that Obote was about to put him on trial for misuse of army funds, grabbed power in a military coup and declared himself President. Amin promised a return to democracy and an end to political corruption. Many Ugandans initially welcomed his leadership after years of corrupt misgovernment under Obote.

02/01/1972

PUBLIC EXECUTION Amin unleashed a wave of killings as he purged the army of Obote loyalists. More than 6,000 people are thought to have died during his first year in power. Other victims of his oppression included religious leaders, judges, students, and homosexuals.

07/18/1974

KILLER AND CLOWN

Amin was notorious for extremes of behavior. He was capable of brutal sadism toward his enemies, using torture and massacre to further his political whims. At the same time, he was also known as an eccentric, granting himself a series of extravagant titles, and on one occasion, forcing four British businessmen to carry him on a throne to an official reception.

01/25/1977

VILLAIN OF AFRICA

Amin celebrated the start of his seventh year in power at Kampala. He kept all opposition at bay, ordering the killings of the Anglican Archbishop of Uganda, Janani Luwum, and two cabinet ministers, who dared to denounce his acts of violence.

I am **the hero** of **Africa**.

IDI AMIN, QUOTED IN *NEWSWEEK*, MARCH 12, 1973

The Troubles in Northern Ireland

1968–1998

Decades of tension in Northern Ireland erupted in 1968, sparking 30 years of violence. On one side were Catholic Republicans seeking to unite Northern Ireland with the Irish Republic. On the other were Protestant Unionists, who wished to remain in the United Kingdom.

10/05/1968

START OF THE TROUBLES Police in Derry used batons and water cannons to disperse a peaceful Catholic civil rights march. Irish nationalists responded with outrage, sparking three days of riots.

01/30/1972

BLOODY SUNDAY British paratroopers opened fire on a civil rights march in the Bogside, killing 13 and injuring 13 more. The victims were given last rites as they lay dying in the streets. An official tribunal said the soldiers had been shot at first, a finding that was overturned by a new inquiry in 2010.

03/24/1972

BRITISH DIRECT RULE In the aftermath of Bloody Sunday, support for the IRA increased, and protesters clashed more and more frequently with British troops. In response British Prime Minister Edward Heath suspended the Northern Ireland parliament and introduced direct rule from London. The death toll in 1972 was 496—the highest of the Troubles.

05/03/1981

IRA HUNGER STRIKES The British responded by locking up suspected militants at the infamous Maze Prison just outside Belfast. Many were held for years without trial, and were reported to have been harshly treated by prison guards. Several of the inmates, led by Bobby Sands, went on a hunger strike in protest.

> They **won't break me** because the **desire for freedom**… is in my heart.

LAST ENTRY IN BOBBY SANDS' PRISON DIARY, MARCH 17, 1981

11/15/1985

ANGLO-IRISH AGREEMENT In an effort to bring an end to the Troubles, Britain and the Republic of Ireland signed a deal that gave the Irish Republic a consultative role in Northern Ireland. The agreement was opposed by Protestant Unionists, who were not included in the discussions. They were furious that the Catholic Republic would have a say in Northern Irish affairs.

04/10/1998

PEACE DEAL REACHED Diplomatic efforts, encouraged by the USA, finally bore fruit. The Good Friday Agreement was signed by Northern Irish political parties, as well as the British and Irish governments. It received resounding popular support, and paved the way for an end to violence over the following years.

08/12/1969

BATTLE OF THE BOGSIDE Clashes between sectarian groups grew more frequent. During an annual Protestant parade through Derry, fighting broke out in the Bogside, a Catholic area of the city. Riots spread to Belfast, where entire streets were set ablaze. British troops were called in as the government attempted to quell the violence.

08/15/1969

NO-GO AREA The Catholic Bogside area declared itself Free Derry, and forcibly prevented the police and British forces from entering.

08/09/1971

SPREADING VIOLENCE The Irish Republican Army (IRA) had fought British rule for decades. They were opposed by the Ulster Freedom Fighters (UFF) and other Unionist groups. The police, the Royal Ulster Constabulary, were often accused of being as brutal as the terrorists, and secretly aiding the Unionists.

03/08/1973

BOMBING CAMPAIGN The IRA brought terror tactics to Britain. In 1973, hundreds were injured as a car bomb exploded outside the Old Bailey law courts in London. In 1974, another bomb killed 21 people in a Birmingham pub, and in 1984 Prime Minister Margaret Thatcher was targeted in an explosion at a Brighton hotel.

RALLY AGAINST INTERNMENT A poster by the Northern Ireland Civil Rights Association (NICRA) calls for an end to imprisonment without trial.

05/05/1981

DEATH OF BOBBY SANDS Bobby Sands died after 66 days without food, and more than 100,000 people lined the streets for his funeral. Nine more prisoners died before the strike was called off.

Massacre at the Olympics

1972

The Munich Summer Olympic Games were the first to be held in Germany since the Berlin Games of 1936, hosted during Hitler's Third Reich. Eager to emphasize the peaceful face of modern Germany, the organizers chose *Die Heiteren Spiele* ("the happy games") as their official motto. But happiness turned to tragedy when a group of Palestinian terrorists broke into the Olympic village and took 11 hostages from the Israeli team. The fate of the attackers and their hostages would scar the memory of the Games and horrify the world.

09/05/1972

TERRORISTS BREAK IN
At 4:30 am eight men wearing sweatsuits and carrying automatic rifles scaled the fence and headed for the Israeli quarters. The men belonged to Black September, a Palestinian paramilitary organization. Once inside, they rounded up the occupants of Apartments 1 and 2. Some of the powerfully built athletes fought back.

> " They've now said that there were **11 hostages**. Two were killed in their rooms yesterday morning, nine were killed at the airport tonight. They're **all gone**. "
>
> **ABC REPORTER JIM MCKAY, ANNOUNCING THE OFFICIAL CONFIRMATION OF THE MASSACRE, SEPTEMBER 1972**

09/05/1972

TRANSPORT OF TERRORISTS
As negotiation failed, the Palestinians demanded transportation to Cairo. The German police pretended to agree, but in reality they were preparing a trap. The terrorists were driven to a nearby airport, where they were told two helicopters would take them to their plane.

09/05/1972

REMAINS AT THE OLYMPIC VILLAGE
In the aftermath of the massacre, the Israelis counted their dead. Two team members had been shot dead in the apartment and nine were taken hostage—five coaches, two wrestlers, and two weightlifters. All were killed. Three surviving terrorists were taken captive.

09/06/1972

DEAD REMEMBERED
The Games were suspended for the following morning as 80,000 spectators and 3,000 athletes attended a memorial service in the Olympic stadium. Many criticized the Olympic committee's decision to let the Games continue the previous day despite the tragedy unfolding in the village.

08/26/1972

OPENING CEREMONY The Israeli team took part in the Parade of Nations during the opening ceremony in front of a huge crowd at the Olympic stadium. In the first week, American swimmer Mark Spitz made headlines by winning a record-breaking seven gold medals. All the signs were that this would be a great Olympics.

09/04/1972

LIGHT SECURITY After an evening at the theater, the Israeli team returned to their apartment building in a relatively isolated part of the Olympic village. The organizers had purposely kept security light to ensure a relaxed atmosphere, and only a chainlink fence surrounded the village.

09/05/1972

UNDER SIEGE German armed police responded swiftly by surrounding the building, even as the hostage-takers spelled out their demands. They wanted the release of 235 Palestinians held in Israeli prisons and of jailed German militants Andreas Baader and Ulrike Meinhof. The terrorists threw down the body of wrestling coach Moshe Weinberg to demonstrate their resolve.

09/05/1972

NEGOTIATIONS DRAG ON German officials kept up continuous communication with the terrorists in an attempt to negotiate the hostages' release. But the hostage-takers refused to back down, and Israel refused to free the 235 Palestinian prisoners.

09/05/1972

BUNGLED RESCUE German police had planned a dual ambush: one team would wait on the plane to capture gunmen coming in to inspect it, and a team of sharpshooters would shoot the hostage-takers in the helicopters. However, the terrorists spotted the trap. As police snipers opened fire, the Palestinians threw a grenade into one helicopter, killing four hostages, and shot dead all five hostages in the other helicopter. Five terrorists and a policeman were also killed.

09/07/1972

FUNERAL IN ISRAEL The bodies of the 11 murdered athletes were flown to Lod Airport in Israel, where a state funeral was held. The three surviving terrorists remained in jail until late October. They were released after Black September hijacked a Lufthansa jet and threatened to blow it up with all passengers on board.

MURDERED ATHLETES Photographs of the murdered athletes were circulated around the world. The violence of their final hours contrasted sharply with the Olympic message of peace and cooperation.

Chile in Turmoil

1970–1998

Chilean president Salvador Allende was the first Marxist to win a democratic election in South America. Despite initial popular support, his attempts to restructure Chile's economy proved disastrous and divisive. In 1973 he was overthrown in a right-wing coup led by General Augosto Pinochet, who installed himself as leader of a repressive military dictatorship that lasted almost two decades.

11/04/1970

MARXIST PRESIDENT
Veteran politician Salvador Allende was narrowly elected to the Chilean presidency in 1970, winning 36 percent of the vote. He quickly announced his intention to take Chile on a democratic road to socialism, a policy that alarmed the country's right-wing parties.

06/29/1973

TANKS ON THE STREETS By 1973 Chile faced an economic crisis with soaring inflation and widespread strikes. Seeing their chance, a group of army officers attempted a coup. Tanks opened fire on official buildings, but loyalist troops defeated the uprising. Allende remained president, but protests continued.

09/11/1973

ALLENDE OVERTHROWN General Pinochet, head of the army, had his own plans for power and had learned from his predecessor's mistakes. On September 11, troops surrounded the presidential palace. At noon, jet fighters attacked the palace with bombs and rockets.

09/11/1973

PINOCHET TAKES OVER General Pinochet lost no time. After being sworn in as the head of a four-man junta (military government), Pinochet declared that the coup had been necessary to save Chile from the yoke of Marxism. He ordered an immediate purge of Allende's supporters and other left-wingers. Democratic rule was indefinitely suspended.

> ## **Workers** of my country, I have **faith** in **Chile** and its **destiny**
>
> ALLENDE'S FINAL SPEECH, SEPTEMBER 11, 1973

09/11/1980

HARSH REGIME Pinochet ruled with an iron fist, abolishing political parties, trade unions, and freedom of speech. In 1980 he called the public to vote for a new constitution to increase his powers as president. Officials claimed that two-thirds of Chileans were in favour, but the vote was widely seen as rigged.

11/10/1971

REVOLUTIONARY GUEST The controversy deepened when Allende arranged a state visit from Fidel Castro, communist leader of Cuba. With Allende beside him, Castro visited copper mines and addressed vast rallies of workers. In Santiago, a group of right-wing women marched through the streets banging pots and pans in protest.

09/11/1973

ALLENDE BOWS OUT To the sound of explosions, Allende gave a farewell speech on live radio. He then ordered his aides to surrender and thanked them for their support. A few minutes later he killed himself with an AK-47 rifle, a gift from Fidel Castro. Firefighters carried his body from the still-smoking building.

09/15/1973

THOUSANDS TAKEN PRISONER In the days after the coup, Chile's National Stadium was used as a concentration camp for around 5,000 political detainees. Other detention centers sprang up around the country. Suspected dissidents were rounded up, and many were tortured and executed. Around 3,000 who "disappeared" remain unaccounted for to this day.

10/05/1988

POPULAR RESISTANCE In 1988, Pinochet ordered another vote to further extend his rule. This time, however, popular opposition was too strong, and he was defeated. He lost the subsequent presidential election but remained in command of the army, ensuring that the abuses committed by his regime were not investigated.

10/19/1998

PINOCHET ARRESTED It was 10 years before an attempt was made to call Pinochet to account. During a visit to a London hospital, he was arrested at the request of a Spanish judge who sought his extradition on charges of human rights abuse. Years of legal wrangling followed. Pinochet died in 2006 without standing trial.

Yom Kippur War
1973

On October 6, 1973 Egypt and Syria launched simultaneous attacks on Sinai and the Golan Heights, territories held by Israel since 1967. The day chosen for the attack was Yom Kippur (Day of Atonement), the holiest day of the Jewish year. Once again, Arab forces were ill-prepared to face the superior Israeli military, but this time the effects would be felt around the world.

ANWAR AL-SADAT

Virtually unknown before becoming President, Anwar al-Sadat succeeded Gamal Abdel Nasser in 1970. He was determined to restore Egyptian pride after the humiliating defeat in the Six-Day War in 1967.

10/06/1973

SYRIA ASSAULTS GOLAN HEIGHTS
Israeli soldiers on the Golan Heights faced unexpected sniper fire. As in Sinai, the attack here took the Israeli army by surprise; many soldiers were on leave for the Yom Kippur holiday. Syrian tanks rolled across the Purple Line (the 1967 ceasefire line) and advanced rapidly into Mount Hebron and the southern Golan Heights.

10/07/1973

INITIAL GAINS AT SINAI
The Egyptian attacking force consisted of 80,000 troops. They breached the Israeli defenses, a line of forts manned by a force of just 500 Israeli soldiers, and moved forward 15 miles (24 km) into the Sinai desert, where they dug themselves into trenches.

> **“**
> The **Palestine cause** is alive in the world today **because of oil**.
> **”**
>
> SAUDI OIL MINISTER
> SHEIKH AHMED ZAKI YAMANI, 1977

10/17/1973

AMERICAN MILITARY AID American-supplied Howitzer cannons helped the Israeli war effort against the Syrian army. Responding to Soviet military airlifts to Egypt and Syria, US President Richard Nixon authorized Operation Nickel Grass on October 12. This American action involved airlifting replacement tanks, artillery, and ammunition supplies in US military transport planes to Israel.

ISRAEL AND ITS NEIGHBORS

Since the Six-Day War, Israel had held the Sinai Peninsula, formerly Egyptian territory, and the Golan Heights, bordering Syria. Sadat and his allies planned a surprise attack to retake the disputed territories. They were supported with funds and material from at least nine of the region's Arab states.

- Israel 1949
- Area occupied by Israel after 1967 war
- Area occupied by Israel after 1973 war
- 1974: Demilitarized zone held by UN
- 1975: Demilitarized zone held by UN after 2nd Sinai Agreement
- Disputed frontier

10/06/1973

CROSSING THE CANAL

The Egyptian attack began with an intense aerial assault on Israeli positions in Sinai, on the east of the Suez Canal. By dusk advance troops had established five bridgeheads across the canal. Floating pontoon bridges were moved into place and a steady stream of tanks and trucks began driving across.

10/11/1973

ISRAELIS RETALIATE

Bolstered by reserve forces, the Israeli army counterattacked fiercely in the north. After four days of fighting, their forces had pushed the Syrian army back beyond the Purple Line and had advanced to within 35 miles (56 km) of Damascus, the Syrian capital. With the Golan Heights secure, the Israelis focused on Sinai.

10/17/1973

FIGHTING IN SINAI

The Israeli onslaught met with initial setbacks in Sinai, where the fighting slowed down before the Egyptian line was broken. One division crossed the Suez Canal south of Ismailia, where it advanced along the Suez–Cairo road to within 65 miles (104 km) of the Egyptian capital. Israeli soldiers captured thousands of Egyptian troops.

10/20/1973

OIL EMBARGO IMPOSED

Arab members of OPEC (Organization of Petroleum Exporting Countries) imposed an embargo on oil shipments to Europe and the USA in retaliation for the American military airlift. The price of oil rose by 130 percent by December. The embargo, which lasted until March 1974, sparked an economic recession.

FUEL RATION CARD

As oil supplies began to run out, Britain became one of many countries that imposed fuel rationing on car drivers.

10/24/1973

UN MEDIATES CEASEFIRE

A UN-brokered ceasefire came into effect as Israeli forces were on the point of destroying the Egyptian Third Army, cut off in Sinai. Israeli troops remained on the west side of the Suez Canal until the following January.

03/31/1974

EXCHANGE OF PRISONERS

Skirmishes continued on the Syrian border despite the ceasefire. US Secretary of State Henry Kissinger arranged for an exchange of Syrian and Israeli prisoners of war as part of a disengagement agreement. Israel agreed to withdraw to the Purple Line and a UN buffer zone was set up in the Golan Heights.

09/17/1978

CAMP DAVID ACCORDS

Months of intense diplomatic activity initiated by US President Jimmy Carter led to the historic signing of the Camp David Accords by Israel's President Menachem Begin and President Sadat of Egypt. Israel agreed to return Sinai to Egypt in return for Egypt's recognition of Israel as a nation.

SOVIET GRENADE

An RKG-3 anti-tank grenade of the type supplied to the Egyptian army by the USSR during the Yom Kippur War.

Watergate

1972–1974

When news broke of a bungled burglary in the Watergate office complex in the run-up to a Presidential election, few suspected that the story would become one of the greatest political scandals in US history. It led to the trial and conviction of a number of top White House officials, and the downfall of President Richard Nixon—the only American President ever to resign from office.

06/17/1972

BREAK-IN Police arrested five burglars as they broke into the Democratic Party headquarters at Watergate. Two days later *The Washington Post* revealed that the "burglers" had been planting bugs, and that one of them was James McCord, who worked for the committee to re-elect Richard Nixon.

11/07/1972

NIXON RE-ELECTED Despite the questions over Watergate, Nixon won a landslide victory in the presidential election, winning 49 out of 50 states. He celebrated the win with Vice President Spiro Agnew, who would be forced to resign for income tax evasion in October 1973.

05/17/1973

SENATE HEARING BEGINS Rumors of a White House cover-up would not go away, so the US Senate set up a committee to investigate. The hearings went on for a year, and were broadcast live on television from start to finish. They were watched by millions across the nation.

07/30/1974

TAPES RELEASED On the order of the Supreme Court, President Nixon finally gave up the tapes. In a key conversation recorded on June 23, 1972 he had asked for the FBI's investigation into the break-in to be stopped. This proved beyond doubt that he had played a leading role in the cover-up from the start.

08/08/1974

NIXON RESIGNS The President was confronted by furious crowds calling for him to be brought to trial. The incriminating tape had sealed his fate and on August 8 he resigned.

> " **Play it tough.** That's the way **they** play it and that's the way **we** are going to **play it**.

PRESIDENT NIXON, TAPED CONVERSATION, JUNE 23, 1972

06/19/1972

ON THE CASE
Washington Post reporters Carl Bernstein and Bob Woodward received a tip-off that senior White House staff had known about, and approved of, the break-in. Their source named himself "Deep Throat." He was later revealed to be high-ranking FBI official Mark Felt.

08/29/1972

WHITE HOUSE DENIAL Faced with such serious allegations, President Nixon announced that White House counsel John Dean had carried out a thorough investigation, and that no one in the White House or Nixon's Administration had been involved in the break-in. In reality, Dean had not conducted an investigation and was part of an attempt to cover up White House involvement.

06/25/1973

KEY WITNESS
John Dean, afraid that he might be prosecuted for his role in the conspiracy, agreed to work with the investigation. He electrified proceedings by stating that Nixon was involved in the cover-up and knew about payments used to buy the silence of the Watergate conspirators.

04/30/1974

TAPE TRANSCRIPTS
Nixon denied the allegations, but during the hearings it emerged that he had recorded meetings at the White House during which the cover-up was planned. The President fought hard, agreeing only to hand over edited transcripts of the tapes, numbering 1,200 pages.

08/09/1974

NEW PRESIDENT
Gerald Ford, who had become Vice President on Agnew's resignation, was sworn in as the 38th US President. Controversially, he granted Nixon a full and absolute pardon for all crimes "he committed or may have committed" in an effort to draw a line under the affair.

THE WHITE HOUSE
WASHINGTON

August 9, 1974

Dear Mr. Secretary:

I hereby resign the Office of President of the United States.

Sincerely,

Richard Nixon

The Honorable Henry A. Kissinger
The Secretary of State
Washington, D.C. 20520

LETTER OF RESIGNATION
Nixon followed constitutional law by writing to the Secretary of State to announce his resignation.

Division of Cyprus

1960–1974

A former British colony, Cyprus gained independence in 1960 following years of resistance to colonial rule. However, tensions between the island's Greek Cypriot majority and Turkish Cypriot minority continued to simmer. When the armed forces of mainland Greece and Turkey became involved, the island was threatened with war.

08/16/1960

CYPRUS GAINS INDEPENDENCE
Britain granted Cyprus independence in August 1960. The Republic of Cyprus was established under a set of complicated treaties, which failed to satisfy either the Greek or the Turkish communities. When President Archbishop Makarios III, a Greek Cypriot, proposed constitutional changes that were not acceptable to the Turks, they withdrew from the government and set up a rival administration.

03/26/1964

BRITISH INTERVENE
A Treaty of Guarantee had given Britain the right to intervene in Cyprus. As the situation worsened, British soldiers, backed by UN peacekeeping troops, stepped in and monitored activity along the Green Line. The volatile situation worsened as Greek Cypriots continued a campaign for enosis (union with Greece).

04/10/1964

TURKISH REFUGEES
Escalating violence led Turkish Cypriots to withdraw into secure enclaves. Many crowded into the Turkish quarter of Nicosia in tents and shacks, creating slumlike conditions. As some 20,000—about a fifth of their number—fled the worst areas of violence, Turkish settlements were looted and destroyed.

06/05/1964

TURKEY THREATENS INVASION On several occasions Turkey seemed close to military intervention. In June 1964, they once again threatened an invasion, launching air strikes on Cypriot ships. Only a warning from US President Lyndon B. Johnson to Turkish leader Ismet İnönü pursuaded them to withdraw.

> The Greek Cypriots will march on to **complete** the **final victory**.
>
> **CYPRIOT PRESIDENT ARCHBISHOP MAKARIOS, AUGUST 16, 1974**

12/21/1963

UNREST IN NICOSIA Communal violence erupted in Nicosia, Cyprus's capital, when a Greek Cypriot patrol killed two Turkish Cypriots on the edge of the Turkish quarter. As the news spread, fighting broke out along the line separating the Greek and Turkish quarters, known as the Green Line.

EOKA PISTOL This homemade weapon was used by the Greek Cypriot guerrilla group EOKA, first against British rule, then against Turkish Cypriots. Crudely designed, it was only effective at point-blank range.

05/10/1964

NATIONAL GUARD FORMED The House of Representatives, functioning now with only Greek Cypriot members, passed a bill forming a National Guard, and made all male Cypriots between 18 and 59 years eligible for military service. The National Guard absorbed militia groups into a single force, which served as a deterrent to a Turkish invasion.

04/21/1967

MILITARY POWER IN GREECE The situation further deteriorated when a military junta seized power in Greece and vowed to resolve the deadlock in Cyprus by force. Relations between the junta and President Makarios became increasingly strained after the latter decided enosis was no longer possible in the short term. Greece organized more pro-enosis Cypriot groups to subvert his government.

07/15/1974

GREECE-LED COUP The junta made several attempts on Makarios's life. On July 15, a bloody coup, supported by Greece's military regime, replaced Makarios with enosis activist and militia leader Nicos Sampson. Fierce fighting broke out between the supporters of Makarios and his detractors, but Makarios evaded capture and fled to Britain. Sampson proclaimed the establishment of The Hellenic Republic of Cyprus.

07/20/1974

TURKEY RETALIATES The coup prompted Turkey to send troops to northern Cyprus. The Greeks termed it an invasion, while the Turks claimed it was a peacekeeping operation. By the time a ceasefire was put in place three days later, Turkish troops had occupied the northern third of the island and 5,000 Greek Cypriots had fled their homes. The island was effectively partitioned.

UNEASY PEACE On August 13, 1974, following a peace deal, Cyprus was partitioned with the northern third inhabited by Turkish Cypriots and the southern two-thirds by Greek Cypriots.

Mediterranean Sea

TURKISH REPUBLIC OF NORTHERN CYPRUS

REPUBLIC OF CYPRUS

Dhekelia

Green Line (United Nations Buffer Zone)
United Kingdom Sovereign Base Area

Akrotiri

Carnation Revolution

1974–1976

When a bloodless army coup ended nearly 50 years of dictatorial rule in Portugal, rejoicing crowds threw carnations at the soldiers, who thrust them into the barrels of their guns. Euphoria soon gave way to months of political confusion and failed governments. The road to stable democracy would prove a rocky one for Portugal.

04/25/1974

04/26/1974

CARNATIONS, NOT BULLETS Civilian crowds flooded the streets in support of the rebels. They passed red carnations to the soldiers as a symbol of peaceful revolution. The coup was led by 140 army officers who had formed the Movement of the Armed Forces (MFA). Disillusioned with Portugal's decade-long colonial wars in Africa, they promised to restore peace, democracy, and freedom of speech.

01/05/1974

LEFT TURN Spinola was keen to maintain a moderate political stance, but after years of authoritarian right-wing rule, people wanted radical change. Veteran Marxist Alvaro Cunhal, who had spent more than 11 years in prison under Salazar, returned from exile to attend a political rally with Mário Soares, leader of the Socialist Party. More than 50 political parties, many on the far left, emerged at this time.

With the **revolution** of the 25th of April, Portugal recovered its **tradition** of **tolerance**...

PORTUGUESE PRESIDENT MÁRIO SOARES, IN A SPEECH GIVEN ON MARCH 17, 1989

05/25/1975

PORTUGAL VOTES There was a 90 percent turnout at the first free elections held in Portugal in 50 years. The elections were for a constituent assembly to rewrite the constitution. The Socialist Party secured 46 percent of the votes, but the far left fared badly.

06/01/1975

END OF COLONIAL RULE Portugal's long colonial wars finally dragged to a close as the new regime abruptly withdrew troops from its colonies in Africa and Indonesia. The newly independent nations celebrated their freedom, but the abrupt transition caused turbulence and, in some cases, civil war. Hundreds of thousands of colonists fled back home.

ARMY COUP Just after midnight on April 25, 1974, a Lisbon radio station broadcast a banned political song. This was the agreed signal for the army to move. Tanks rolled into Lisbon and by dawn the army had taken control of government offices. The only shots exchanged were outside PIDE (Portuguese security police) headquarters, where four people died. As news of the coup spread, excited crowds gathered in the center of Lisbon.

04/26/1974

SALAZAR'S SUPPORTERS ARRESTED The armed rebel forces moved swiftly to take over points of strategic importance across the country. Portugal's dictator, Antonio de Oliveira Salazar, and his successor, Marcelo Caetano, had used the hated PIDE police force to suppress civil liberties and political freedom. Their members and informants now found themselves at the sharp end of popular opinion, and many were arrested.

04/28/1974

FACING THE PRESS Opposed by the armed forces and the general populace, Caetano resigned. General Antonio Spinola was installed as head of an interim military government. He had fallen out of favour with the dictator's regime for advocating Portugal's withdrawal from Africa. He now addressed the world as the head of state.

05/01/1974

REVOLUTIONARY FERVOR More than 100,000 people marched through Lisbon to celebrate May Day and the release of hundreds of political prisoners, one of the first acts carried out by the military regime.

09/30/1974

SPINOLA RESIGNS By September Portugal was engulfed in a wave of strikes. A major section of the army remained under the control of radical left-wing officers. Alarmed by these moves, Spinola called for a demonstration by the "silent majority," but it failed to win support and Spinola resigned. In March 1975 he launched an unsuccessful coup and fled the country.

11/06/1975

RURAL TENSIONS Amid political instability, farmers launched a firebombing campaign in protest against the leftward turn taken by the revolution. As decolonization got under way, the mass return of destitute Portuguese citizens from the colonies added to the tensions of the so-called "hot summer."

05/25/1976

SOARES BECOMES PRIME MINISTER Held exactly two years after the Carnation Revolution, Portugal's first parliamentary elections resulted in victory for the Socialist Party and Mário Soares.

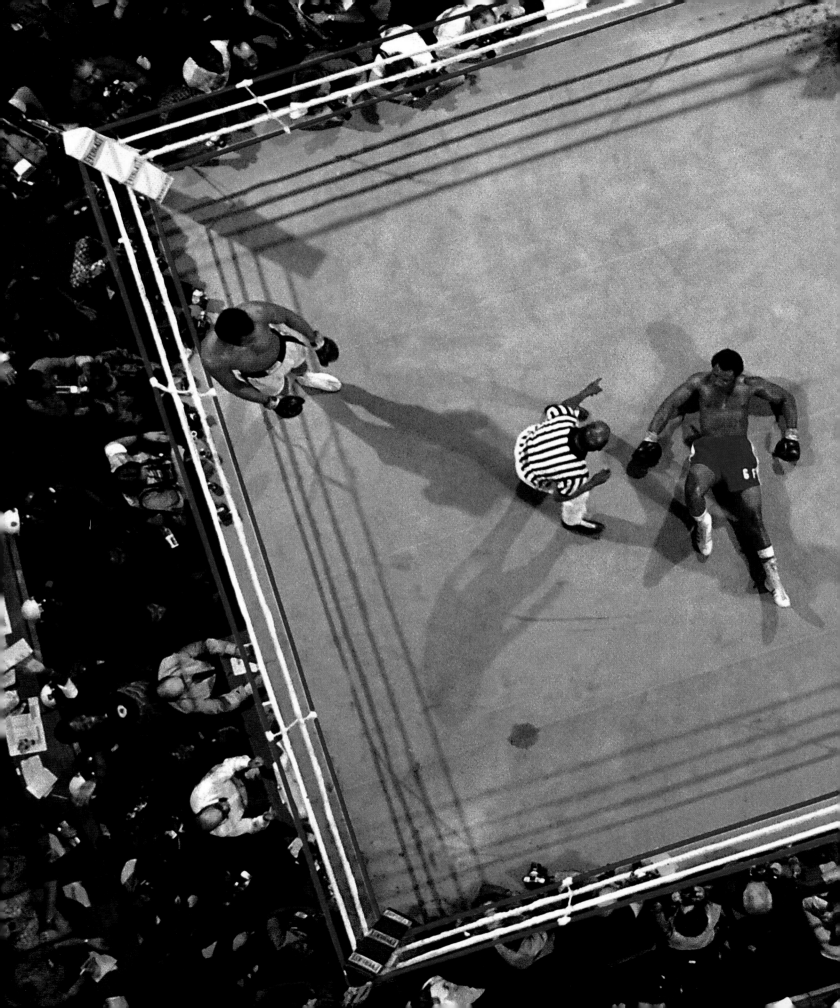

1974

Rumble in the Jungle

Providing a welcome distraction to the political turmoil in the US following the collapse of the Nixon presidency, the "Rumble in the Jungle" was set up by boxing promoter Don King. The event was staged in Kinshasa, Zaire, on October 30, 1974 after the country's president Mobutu Sese Seko agreed to sponsor the $5 million purse. The defending world heavyweight champion, George Foreman, was the overwhelming favorite, being younger and larger than his opponent, Muhammad Ali. A controversial figure, Ali had been suspended from boxing for three years from 1967 because of his refusal to comply with the US Army draft. Famed for his agile fighting style, Ali taunted Foreman in the buildup to the match claiming, "I'm so fast, man, I can run through a hurricane and don't get wet." However, things played out differently in the ring. Ali spent much of the fight on the ropes, allowing Foreman's formidable punches to land on his arms and sides in a tactic he later termed the "Rope-a-Dope." The effort of making the continual heavy punches took its toll on Foreman. By the seventh round, Ali began to dominate, and floored Foreman in the eighth. Against all odds, the older man had triumphed, and secured his status as a true sporting icon.

Lebanese Civil War

1975–1990

When the Palestine Liberation Army (PLO) was expelled from Jordan in 1970, it established a new base in Lebanon. It was welcomed by Muslims who believed the PLO would help in their struggle against the Phalange (a far-right Christian party). The smoldering hatred between these groups exploded into a civil war that included invasions, assassinations, and many atrocities on both sides.

05/20/1975

FACTIONS CLASH Violence erupted when Phalangist gunmen ambushed a bus full of Palestinians. They were seeking revenge for an earlier drive-by attack on Phalange leader Pierre Gemayel. Palestinian militia responded with rocket attacks on Phalange neighborhoods.

03/14/1978

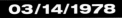

ISRAEL INVOLVED The Syrian presence failed to stop PLO guerrilla attacks on Israel and, after two years of uneasy peace, Israeli troops assaulted PLO positions in southern Lebanon. They occupied a 6-mile (10-km) wide zone along the border in an assault that cost the lives of 1,500 civilians.

08/12/1982

THE PLO WITHDRAW A multinational force including troops from the USA, France, and Italy arrived in Beirut to protect civilians and oversee the withdrawal of the PLO. The Palestinians had been persuaded to leave by US diplomat Philip Habib. More than 15,000 PLO guerrillas, led by Yasser Arafat, left Beirut and headed for Tunisia.

> **"** We can no longer stand any **foreign armed presence** on our land. **"**
>
> BASHIR GEMAYEL, LEBANESE PRESIDENT-ELECT, SEPTEMBER 1982

09/24/1982

PEACEKEEPERS RETURN After the Sabra-Shatila massacre, another force of US, French, and Italian troops was sent to Beirut to protect the populace. The US government pressed for the total withdrawal of all foreign troops, including those of Israel, Syria, and Iran, all of whom sought influence in Lebanon.

10/23/1983

TERRORIST ATTACKS International sympathy for Lebanese Muslims evaporated when Islamic militants detonated two bombs at the barracks of the peacekeepers. The attack caused the deaths of 241 US marines and 56 French paratroopers. The USA responded with outrage, and the entire peacekeeping force was withdrawn.

06/01/1976

SYRIAN TROOPS ENTER LEBANON As the violence dragged on, the President of Lebanon, Suleiman Franjieh, requested military aid from Syria to prevent the country from descending into anarchy. Fearing that PLO activities could spark war with Israel, the Syrians complied, sending a large army to impose a ceasefire.

03/19/1978

PEACEKEEPERS ARRIVE The United Nations ordered the Israelis to withdraw, but they refused. The UN responded by sending a task force to help restore government control. Israel grudgingly pulled out, handing the area over to its Christian allies.

06/06/1982

ISRAEL INVADES AGAIN Israeli forces were not absent for long. When the Israeli ambassador to the United Kingdom, Shlomo Argov, was shot and seriously wounded in London, Israel blamed the PLO for the attack. Three days later they attacked Lebanon once again, laying seige to the capital, Beirut.

09/16/1982

PALESTINIANS MASSACRED Once again peace was short-lived. Christian President-elect Bashir Gemayel was killed in a bomb blast. Phalangist militiamen, seeking revenge, turned on Palestinians in the Sabra and Shatila refugee camps. Hundreds died in a three-day massacre of unarmed refugees.

10/13/1990

CIVIL WAR IS OVER Fighting continued for several years, until Syria launched a major assault on the Lebanese government, destroying the Presidential Palace and army headquarters. Their presence greatly decreased violence between rival groups, effectively ending the civil war, but it would be 15 years before the Lebanese regained control of their country.

04/27/2005

CEDAR REVOLUTION Prime Minister Rafik Hariri, who had done much to rebuild the country, was assassinated. Many blamed his death on Syrian agents and, in the popular protests that followed, Syrian forces left Lebanon.

USA Withdraws from Vietnam

1968–1975

By 1968, despite a huge escalation of the USA's involvement in the Vietnam War, victory over the communists remained elusive. As the death toll continued to rise, public opinion in the West turned against the war, as its horrors were played out every night on their television screens.

03/03/1968

05/04/1970

KENT STATE SHOOTINGS Clashes erupted between anti-war protesters and police and military across the USA. In one incident, four students at Kent State University, Ohio, were shot dead by the National Guard. Protests against the war and for global peace became part of the counter-culture movement.

03/05/1971

01/27/1973

PEACE AT A PRICE
With protests at home and failure in the field, the US sued for peace, and the Paris Peace Accords were signed in 1973. Although Vietnamese soldiers on both sides continued fighting, US forces finally withdrew from the region and ended their eight-year bombing campaign.

03/10/1975

NORTH ADVANCES
The North Vietnamese Army opened Campaign 275, a lightning attack on the strategic Central Highlands of South Vietnam. This limited offensive defeated the main force of the South Vietnamese Army. The South's forces began a hasty retreat, which quickly became a rout across the country.

04/27/1975

THE FALL OF SAIGON
The North Vietnamese Army quickly marched on Saigon, the South Vietnamese capital, and soon surrounded the city. Three days later, on April 30, they took Saigon with little resistance. With the South Vietnamese government declared dissolved, the Vietnam War was finally over.

BATTLE OF HUE
Hue, in South Vietnam, was leveled in intense street-to-street fighting. Although a military victory for the USA, the huge loss of life made it a propaganda defeat, increasing calls for a US withdrawal.

03/16/1968

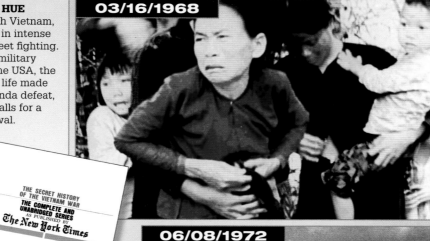

US TROOPS GUILTY OF WAR CRIMES
When a company of US marines entered the South Vietnamese hamlet of My Lai in pursuit of Viet Cong guerillas, they assumed the villagers to be communist supporters and launched an indiscriminate attack. More than 300 men, women, and children were killed, many of them unarmed. Survivors appeared on television, and the massacre prompted outrage around the world.

WAR-WEARY TROOPS
Harsh conditions and high casualty rates took their toll on US morale. Many soldiers were conscripts, plunged into conflict against their will. The leak of the Pentagon Papers, secret documents detailing the full extent of US involvement in the war, strengthened calls for withdrawal.

THE SECRET HISTORY OF THE VIETNAM WAR
THE COMPLETE AND UNABRIDGED SERIES
AS PUBLISHED BY
The New York Times

THE PENTAGON PAPERS

BASED ON INVESTIGATIVE REPORTING BY NEIL SHEEHAN
WRITTEN BY NEIL SHEEHAN, HEDRICK SMITH, E. W. KENWORTHY AND FOX BUTTERFIELD
WITH KEY DOCUMENTS AND 64 PAGES OF PHOTOGRAPHS

PENTAGON PAPERS
Leaked documents revealed that details of the war had been hidden from the US public.

06/08/1972

CIVILIAN CASUALTIES
The bombing campaign intensified, and in one air strike napalm was dropped on Trang Bang, in South Vietnam. The haunting image of nine-year-old Phan Thi Kim Phúc fleeing the blaze, having torn off her burning clothes, was shown around the world. Although badly burned, she survived.

04/29/1975

THE LAST AMERICANS ARE EVACUATED
The arrival of North Vietnamese troops in Saigon led to the hasty evacuation of the remaining US citizens. About 7,000 were taken by helicopter from the US Embassy roof.

> Vietnam was **lost in the living rooms** of America.
>
> **MARSHALL MCLUHAN, MAY 16, 1975**

Angolan Civil War

1975–2003

The Republic of Angola, a nation rich in diamonds and oil, was impoverished by years of civil war. A Portuguese colony, it became independent in 1975 after long years of violent struggle, raising the hopes of its people. However, within days, fighting broke out again, plunging the country into Africa's longest-running conflict.

11/11/1975

ANGOLA INDEPENDENT After years of blood-soaked colonialism, Portugal ceded independence to Angola. As statues of Portuguese leaders tumbled, it represented a victory for the Angolan independence movement. On Independence Day, the Popular Movement for the Liberation of Angola (MPLA) declared itself the ruling party, and Dr. Agostinho Neto, the new President.

09/10/1979

DOS SANTOS BECOMES PRESIDENT Following the death of President Neto, there was a relatively smooth transition to new leader José Eduardo dos Santos in 1979, but the violence between warring parties continued unabated. Each faction drew international support. The Soviet Union and Cuba supported the MPLA. The FNLA and UNITA were backed by the USA and South Africa.

12/22/1988

CUBAN TROOPS LEAVE ANGOLA Hopes for peace were raised when, after months of negotiation, Angola, Cuba, and South Africa reached an agreement ending foreign military presence. Both South Africa and Cuba pledged to withdraw their troops in Angola. However, this tripartite accord failed to resolve the internal conflict tearing the nation apart.

09/29/1992

UN MONITORS ELECTIONS An uneasy ceasefire between the government and UNITA led to an agreement to hold general elections. Dos Santos signed a peace accord with the leader of UNITA, Jonas Savimbi, to end the fighting. However, when the MPLA won the long-awaited election in 1992, Savimbi dragged Angola back into war.

09/14/1993

DISSENTERS CONTINUE FIGHTING The election was intended to end the war, but the violence grew worse. UNITA seized control of Huambo, Angola's second largest city, in a battle that cost 12,000 lives. By 1993 1,000 people were dying each day from deplorable living conditions and indiscriminate bombing.

05/31/1995

UN STEPS IN The UN agreed to send a peacekeeping force to Angola after the Lusaka Peace Treaty was signed by UNITA and the government. Their presence was dependent upon a public handshake between dos Santos and Savimbi. The UN forces hoped to oversee disarmament and the withdrawal of troops.

02/25/2002

JONAS SAVIMBI KILLED The peace process collapsed again, and yet again the nation descended into violence. Jonas Savimbi, once feted by the USA, became an international pariah. He was shot dead on February 25, 2002. UNITA quickly lost momentum, and a ceasefire was agreed on March 30.

PROSTHETIC LEG FOR LANDMINE VICTIM The civil war led to the proliferation of landmines across Angola. It is estimated that one in every 334 Angolans lost a limb to a landmine. Angola has the highest proportion of amputees in the world.

08/08/1976

FIGHTING BREAKS OUT The MPLA had two rivals: the National Front for the Liberation of Angola (FNLA) and the National Union for the Total Independence of Angola (UNITA). Within days of independence they were at war.

4FEV 61/76   **4FEV** 61/76

15 ANOS DE LUTA   ANTI-IMPERIALISTA

ANTI-IMPERIALIST POSTER This poster celebrates the historic moment Angola won independence from Portugal. The flags of the victorious MPLA party and the new independent Angola are held aloft.

05/30/1990

ECONOMY IN SHAMBLES Although rich in natural resources, including oil, diamonds, agriculture, and fisheries, the Angolan economy was left in tatters by the prolonged war. The government spent millions on weapons while its people starved. Agriculture was hit by the proliferation of landmines throughout the country. Trade activities ceased, education was ignored, and corruption and greed fed the ruling elite.

> Only **elections**… can provide a final solution… in the end, the **ballot** must decide, **not bullets**.
>
> **UNITA LEADER JONAS SAVIMBI, IN AN INTERVIEW, DECEMBER 1975**

01/12/2003

SHATTERED BY WAR By the end of the war, Angola was devastated. More than 4.5 million people were internally displaced and 500,000 killed. Around 450,000 Angolans fled the country and became refugees. In the aftermath, families began the agonizing task of trying to find their missing children.

Khmer Rouge

1970–1979

The Khmer Rouge was a communist guerrilla force formed to resist French colonial rule in Cambodia. Destabilized by war in neighboring Vietnam, Cambodia was in the throes of civil war in the 1970s. The Khmer Rouge, led by Pol Pot, seized control in 1975 and renamed the country Democratic Kampuchea. Their brief rule would become infamous as one of the most brutal regimes of the 20th century.

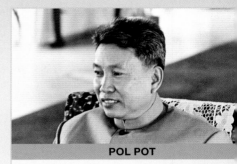

POL POT

Born Saloth Sar in 1925, Pol Pot became leader of the Kampuchean Communist Party (Khmer Rouge) after returning to Cambodia from studies in Paris.

09/05/1973

CIVIL WAR Pol Pot's guerrillas united with Sihanouk to fight Lon Nol, whose corrupt regime was kept in place only with US support. The war was marked by extreme brutality on both sides and casualties were high.

04/17/1975

KHMER ROUGE VICTORY When the USA withdrew from Vietnam, Lon Nol's regime collapsed. Khmer Rouge forces entered the capital, Phnom Penh. The people, mostly refugees from the civil war, joyously welcomed Pol Pot's troops as liberators, tragically unaware of the horrors that the new regime would unleash.

05/17/1975

RUTHLESS REPRESSION Thousands of Buddhist monks were stripped of their robes and forced into labor brigades. Private property was outlawed and schools were closed down. Anyone suspected of being middle class or an intellectual (which could mean simply wearing glasses) faced execution.

04/13/1979

VIETNAM INVADES Tensions grew with Vietnam, the traditional enemy of the Khmer people, despite the countries' shared communist beliefs. Following a border clash, a Vietnamese army invaded Cambodia. As their tanks entered Phnom Penh, the Khmer Rouge fled to mountains on the border with Thailand.

03/18/1970

US INTERVENES Cambodia's ruler Prince Sihanouk allowed North Vietnamese soldiers to operate from within Cambodia during the Vietnam War. He was ousted by army general Lon Nol in a US-backed coup. Shortly after, a joint US–South Vietnamese operation invaded Cambodia in an attempt to flush out Vietnamese communists. Thousands of civilians were killed in American bombing raids.

> To **destroy** you is **no loss**, to **preserve** you is **no gain**.
>
> A KHMER ROUGE SAYING REFERRING TO "SUBVERSIVE" ELEMENTS, 1975

04/20/1975

KILLING FIELDS Immediately, Pol Pot began to enforce his new regime. Phnom Penh's entire population of 2 million people was marched into the countryside at gunpoint and forced to work as rice farmers. Many had only minutes to prepare to leave. Thousands died during the mass exodus.

05/17/1975

YEAR ZERO The start of a new era—Year Zero—was proclaimed, and an eight-point program was announced to "purify" Cambodia from capitalism and foreign influences and to transform it into a rural, classless society as rapidly as possible. The identity of Pol Pot and the Khmer Rouge's leadership remained anonymous: it was simply known as Angkar (the organization).

05/06/1975

ANGKOR WAT CAPTURED Khmer Rouge soldiers occupied the iconic temple city of Angkor Wat, dating back to the early 12th century, halting restoration work. Many feared that these historical symbols would be destroyed, in a manner similar to the Cultural Revolution in China. However, the temples escaped relatively unscathed.

06/04/1978

TORTURE PRISON Tuol Sleng, a school in Phnom Penh, was converted into a prison. At any one time it held 1,000 prisoners, who were brutally tortured and murdered. Out of an estimated 17,000 prisoners incarcerated there, only 20 survived. Today, Tuol Sleng is a genocide museum. Photos of its victims, including many children, hang on its walls.

06/06/1979

KHMER ROUGE CONTINUES TO RESIST From his operating base in the mountains, Pol Pot regrouped his supporters to resist Cambodia's new Vietnam-backed government. He avoided capture but was never able to regain power. Pol Pot died in 1998, without having stood trial for his crimes.

10/15/1979

GRIM LEGACY The new government uncovered mass graves, grim evidence of the atrocities committed by the Khmer Rouge. Approximately one-fifth of the population died and tens of thousands were orphaned in the Pol Pot years. Landmines laid during the fighting continue to kill and maim, and will take 100 years to clear.

A CENTURY OF
Medicine

The 20th century witnessed phenomenal advances in medical care. Greater understanding led to breakthroughs in diagnosing and treating disease. Technology accounted for some of the greatest changes, with the emergence of robotic surgery, and the new field of genetic engineering had far-reaching implications for human health. By the end of the century, diseases that had killed millions throughout history were not only curable, but in some cases eradicated altogether.

1900–1915 The turn of the century was an exciting time for medicine. In 1901, Austrian biologist Karl Landsteiner discovered three different blood types: A, B, and O. Transfusion—donation of blood from one person to another—became much safer, because donor and recipient blood types could be matched. New vaccines greatly reduced the incidence of

BLOOD TYPE Karl Landsteiner's discovery of distinct blood types paved the way for safer blood transfusions, blood banks, and organ transplants.

formerly lethal diseases such as diphtheria, tetanus, and pertusis. At the same time, advances in the understanding of body chemistry made it possible to identify and treat diseases caused by vitamin deficiency and hormone imbalance.

20,000
The approximate number of genes that make up the human genome, discovered during the Human Genome Project.

1915–1950 Developing safe and reliable drugs was an ongoing challenge. German scientist Paul Ehrlich believed that a drug-borne "magic bullet" could kill the bacteria responsible for a disease without causing harm to the patient. He discovered Salvarsan, the first curative treatment for syphilis, but the drug had mixed

VACCINATION PROGRAM
Polio affected thousands of children, but in 1952 Jonas Salk and Albert Sabin developed a preventative vaccine.

success. In 1935, Gerhard Domagk proved that the sulfomide dye Protonsil stopped the multiplication of bacteria, allowing the body's own

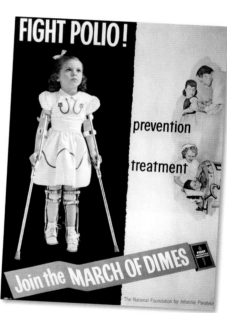

1910s
BLOOD TRANSFUSION KIT
Transfusion practice was greatly improved by the classification of blood types in 1901. Transfusions were regularly performed on World War I battlefields.

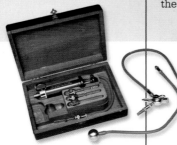

1920s
INSULIN SAMPLES Dr. Frederick Banting discovered a means to manufacture the hormone insulin, revolutionizing the treatment of diabetes. The condition would be widely treatable by the end of the century.

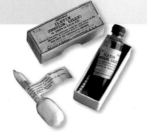

1930s
ELECTRON MICROSCOPE
Since the early 1930s, electron microscopes have transformed the field of cell biology, enabling scientists to see more detail than ever before.

1950s
DNA DOUBLE HELIX
DNA, the genetic material that defines every living thing, was discovered by Crick and Watson, opening a whole new understanding of the mechanism of life.

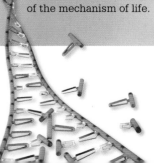

MECHANICAL HEART Developed in 1998, the Jarvik 2000 artificial heart can keep a patient alive long enough to receive a transplant.

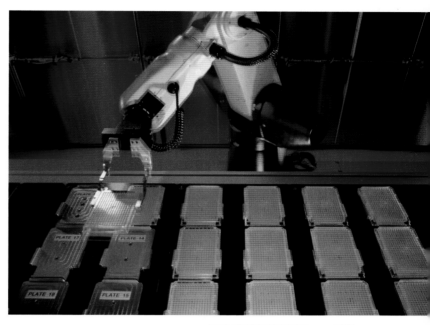

DNA SEQUENCING Human DNA was cloned in trays for analysis and sequencing during the Human Genome Project.

defenses to eliminate them. However, the real breakthrough came when Alexander Fleming discovered the first antibiotic, penicillin. By 1940, the drug had been isolated, and its bacteria-killing properties began to revolutionize the treatment of infection.

1950–1990 The first heart bypass was made possible in 1950 with the invention of the cardiac pacemaker, and in 1967 Dr. Christian Bernard performed the first heart transplant. His pioneering work paved the way for the transplant of lungs, kidneys, and liver in the following decades. When British scientists Frances Crick and James Watson published their discovery of the double-helix DNA structure in 1953, it led to the the development of gene therapy, instrumental in treating genetic illness. Diagnostics took a leap forward in 1975 with the introduction of the computerized axial tomography (CAT) scan, which produced images of the brain. Meanwhile, the development of increasingly sophisticated instruments in the later part of the century enabled less-invasive robotic and keyhole surgery to replace traditional methods. By the end of the century, greater understanding of viruses had helped eradicate smallpox, curtail polio, and treat malaria, but the virulence of AIDS, SARS, and certain strains of influenza posed new challenges for researchers.

1990– Toward the end of the century, the Human Genome Project mapped the human DNA sequence, enabling pioneering medical treatment based on individual genetic profiles. In 2010, doctors were able to sequence a patient's complete genome to reveal the genetic source of some diseases, a landmark in the advance of personalized medicine. Although diseases such as AIDS and cancer continued to defy treatment by the end of the century, new research promised great things for the future.

> ## **Advances in medicine**... have **saved** vastly **more lives** than have been lost in all the wars in history.
>
> **DR. CARL SAGAN, 1997**

1960s

ORAL CONTRACEPTIVES
Often known simply as "the pill," birth control transformed sexual relations in the West and gave women much greater freedom.

1970s

SMALLPOX CONQUERED
In 1966, the World Health Organization (WHO) announced a 10-year global smallpox eradication program. Smallpox was officially beaten in 1979.

1980s

AIDS PANDEMIC There is still no cure for Acquired Immune Deficiency Syndrome (AIDS), which emerged during the early 1980s. The red ribbon campaign has helped raise awareness and promote safer sex.

1990s

STEM CELL RESEARCH
By generating new cells to replace damaged and diseased tissue for organs in the body, stem cell therapy has revolutionized treatment for cancer and heart disease.

Soviet-Afghan War

1978–1988

On Christmas Eve 1979, the Soviet Union invaded Afghanistan. Their aim was to rescue a communist-backed government under threat by the growing number of Islamic rebels. The war that followed, and the rise of US-supported Mujahideen guerrilla fighters, would have consequences that neither side could foresee.

04/27/1978

COMMUNIST COUP
The Soviet Union made concerted efforts to become involved in Afghan society and politics. This led to the overthrow of President Daoud's nationalist regime in a communist coup known as the Saur Revolution. Many Afghans initially welcomed the change.

06/14/1979

AID FROM USSR A Soviet-Afghan Friendship Treaty, signed in December 1978, permitted economic aid and military assistance to Afghanistan if requested. The Soviets sent in a detachment of tanks to assist the government in fighting the growing insurgency.

07/03/1979

US EQUIPS RESISTANCE Afraid that the Soviets would turn Afghanistan into a puppet state, the USA helped finance, arm, and train the Mujahideen, anti-government forces. They covertly imported weapons in what proved to be one of the CIA's longest and most expensive operations.

09/14/1979

CHANGE OF LEADERSHIP In an intense power struggle, Prime Minister Amin deposed and killed President Taraki and took over as leader. The move outraged the Kremlin because they regarded Taraki as a close ally, and Amin as weak and unable to control the violence that was sweeping the country.

07/19/1980

BOYCOTT OF OLYMPICS
US President Jimmy Carter denounced the invasion as an act of Soviet imperialism. He announced that American athletes would boycott the 1980 Olympics in Moscow in protest, and persuaded 64 other nations to join the boycott. Behind the scenes, the USA was secretly increasing their support of anti-Soviet forces, hoping to draw the USSR into a long and costly guerrilla war.

03/28/1985

THE REFUGEE PROBLEM
The Soviets routinely attacked populated areas leading to widespread displacement of Afghans. Many fled to neighbouring Pakistan and Iran. More than 3 million fled to refugee camps in Pakistan alone. An estimated 6 million, more than a fifth of the population, left their homes between 1979 and 1992. Those who stayed behind faced brutal and unpredictable violence.

09/22/1986

04/30/1978

IN-FIGHTING BEGINS
The Communist Party was split into two factions: the Khalq and Parcham parties. Although they agreed to share power, President Mohammed Tureki, loyal to the Khalq party, began purging Parchamis. His policies also offended traditional Islamists. Rebellions broke out all over the country.

03/10/1979

AFGHAN RESISTANCE Afghanistan was spiraling into civil war. An Islamic resistance group declared a holy war against the godless communist regime, and Afghan soldiers mutinied and killed 100 Soviet citizens in Herat, western Afghanistan.

12/24/1979

USSR INVADES AFGHANISTAN The Soviets decided to invade under the guise of the friendship treaty. After seizing key positions in Kabul, hundreds of KGB agents dressed as Afghan soldiers attacked the presidential palace and assassinated Amin, installing deputy Babrak Kamal as President. Soviet troops then spread out across the country.

> We now have the **opportunity** of giving the **USSR** its **Vietnam War**.
>
> ZBIGNIEW BRZEZINSKI, US NATIONAL SECURITY ADVISOR, JANUARY 18, 1978

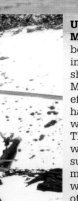

US SUPPLY STINGER MISSILES The Soviets believed that their stay in Afghanistan would be short-lived, but the Mujahideen were an effective guerrilla force, harrying the Russians with hit-and-run attacks. The USA supplied them with advanced weaponry such as the shoulder-mounted Stinger Missile, which shot down dozens of Soviet helicopters.

07/20/1988

SOVIETS BEGIN TO WITHDRAW
When Mikhail Gorbachev became Soviet leader, he had no intention of prolonging a war that was becoming unpopular at home. In May 1988, Pakistan, Afghanistan, the USA, and the USSR signed an agreement to withdraw troops. It left Afghanistan in chaos, paving the way for the radical Islamic Taliban movement to take power in the 1990s.

Iranian Revolution

1977–1979

Shah Reza Pahlavi ruled as emperor of Iran for nearly four decades before losing his grip on power. His key opponent, Ayatollah Khomeini, had been exiled but continued to call for an end to the Shah's reign. As support for Khomeini grew, revolution seemed inevitable.

SHAH OF IRAN

The Shah's attempts to modernize Iran along American lines alienated conservative Shi'ite Muslims. There was widespread distrust of his autocratic rule and extravagant lifestyle.

01/10/1977

PRO-KHOMEINI DEMONSTRATIONS
Opposition to the Shah centered around the Muslim cleric Ayatollah Khomeini, who had been exiled in 1963. The cleric promised economic and social reform and a return to traditional Islamic values.

02/04/1979

INTERIM REGIME
Political and social unrest reached a climax. Street battles raged between the pro-Khomeini faction and supporters of the imperial regime, as the two sides vied for authority. Khomeini refused to acknowledge Bakhtiar's government, and appointed Mehdi Bazargan as Prime Minister of Iran.

11/02/1979

REVOLUTION SUCCEEDS
On February 11, 1979 the jubilant revolutionaries celebrated their historic victory. Khomeini was swept into power and appointed Iran's political and religious leader for life. The country was declared an Islamic republic. Hundreds of the Shah's supporters were tried and executed, while others fled the country. The Westernization of Iran was reversed.

03/08/1979

WOMEN PROTEST Women lost the social gains they had made under the Shah and were forced to wear head coverings (hijab). Many organized a massive protest, but it was crushed by the regime.

01/01/1977

ANTI-SHAH PROTESTS Iranians took to the streets in a wave of angry protests against the Shah, who had become increasingly dictatorial. When security forces opened fire on demonstrators, it ended all dialogue between the protestors and the imperial regime. The Shah imposed martial law as the country descended into virtual civil war.

> You all have to **obey** the **Islamic Republic**. And if you don't, you all will **vanish**.
>
> AYATOLLAH KHOMEINI, SEPTEMBER 19, 1979

01/11/1979

WOMEN JOIN THE REVOLUTION Iranian women from all sectors of society took to the streets in support of Khomeini and added a significant impetus to the demonstrations. Under the Shah's regime, women had been granted greater liberty, but many conservative Islamic families felt that reforms had come at the cost of religious tradition.

01/16/1979

THE SHAH FLEES Popular opposition forced the Shah to flee the country. A million people took to the streets to cheer Khomeini and denounce the Shah, tearing down all statues of the deposed ruler.

01/17/1979

UNREST CONTINUES Before leaving Iran, the Shah appointed a new prime minister, Shahpur Bakhtiar, to run the country. However, Bakhtiar failed to stave off opposition. Fresh demonstrations broke out near Tehran, and unwilling to massacre fellow Iranians, army officers abandoned Bakhtiar's regime.

02/01/1979

KHOMEINI RETURNS In February Khomeini made a dramatic return to Iran, welcomed by millions of ecstatic supporters. They gathered at Tehran University to hear him speak, raising their fists as he outlined his vision of the future.

05/05/1979

REVOLUTIONARY GUARD In May Khomeini set up an army of "spiritual enforcers," known as the Revolutionary Guard, to enforce Islamic law and act as guardians of the revolution. They imprisoned opponents and tortured them in a regime as ruthless as that of the Shah.

CHANGE OF FLAG Following the revolution, the Iranian flag was changed. Its three colors, green, white, and red represent Islam, peace, and bravery.

Iranian Hostage Crisis

1979–1981

In 1979 Muslim cleric Ayatollah Khomeini became supreme leader of Iran. He introduced Sharia (a form of Islamic law) and urged his followers to turn against the West, especially the USA, which had supported the deposed Shah's regime. When US President Jimmy Carter agreed to let the Shah enter the USA for cancer treatment, Iranian anger at the Americans reached fever pitch.

11/09/1979

OPEN DEFIANCE On several occasions during the crisis, students burned American flags on top of the embassy wall. Khomeini supported their act, seen as an attack on American imperialism.

11/14/1979

CARTER IMPOSES ECONOMIC SANCTIONS Freeing the hostages became a top priority for US President Jimmy Carter. Military action was too risky. There was little he could do except halt Iranian oil imports, impose economic sanctions, and conduct intense diplomatic efforts behind the scenes in the hope of pressuring Iran.

11/18/1979

KHOMEINI'S RAY OF HOPE In mid-November hopes were raised when Khomeini ordered the release of 13 female and black hostages. However, it did little to alleviate the situation. Among other demands, Iran insisted on the Shah's return for trial in Tehran, but President Carter rejected these conditions.

04/24/1980

OPERATION EAGLE CLAW As America's frustration grew, President Carter ordered an ambitious rescue mission. However, it turned to disaster when a US helicopter and a military plane collided in the Iranian desert, killing eight American servicemen.

04/27/1980

DEAD SOLDIERS PARADED The charred remains of the rescue crew were taken to Tehran. Angry Iranians paraded the bodies through the streets, causing shock and anger in the USA. Secret operational documents relating to the mission were taken from the wreckage and broadcast to the world.

07/21/1980

RICHARD QUEEN RELEASED After 250 days of captivity, hostage Richard Queen was released on humanitarian grounds. He had already been moved to a hospital in Tehran because of an illness, later diagnosed as multiple sclerosis. While Queen received a hero's welcome at home, 52 hostages were still deprived of their freedom, despite the Shah's death on July 27, 1980.

01/20/1981

DIPLOMACY SUCCEEDS With help from Algerian intermediaries, and aided by the Shah's death, the crisis finally ended. Carter had worked tirelessly to bring the captives home, but lost his re-election campaign. As a final snub to Carter, the Iranians waited until after Ronald Reagan's inauguration as President to free the hostages.

11/04/1979

IRANIAN STUDENTS STORM EMBASSY

The new Islamic leader of Iran, Ayatollah Khomeini, called for an attack on American interests. When the USA offered medical treatment to the Shah, a group of outraged Iranian students stormed the US Embassy in Tehran, taking dozens of hostages.

11/04/1979

HOSTAGES PARADED

Six Americans managed to escape, but 66 were captured. Other non-US citizens were released by the hostage-takers. In a defiant gesture, the students paraded the blindfolded hostages in front of television cameras. They demanded the Shah be expelled from the USA and stand trial in Iran. It was a shocking sight for the American public.

> "You have **nothing** to complain about. The United States took **our whole country** hostage...
>
> **IRANIAN JAILER TO HOSTAGE BRUCE LAIGEN, NOVEMBER 1980**

WELCOME BACK TO FREEDOM

01/21/1981

HOSTAGES RETURN HOME

Following 444 days in captivity, the hostages finally arrived at a US Air Force base in West Germany. In return for their release, the USA agreed to unfreeze Iranian assets worth $8 billion, and give the hostage-takers immunity. The return of the hostages gave a huge boost to Reagan's presidency, but the incident strained the relationship between the USA and Iran.

Nicaraguan Revolution

1972–1990

The Somoza family had ruled Nicaragua as a military dictatorship since 1937, maintaining power through their control of the National Guard, and with the support of the USA. The Sandinista Liberation Front (FSLN)—named after revolutionary hero Augusto Sandino, who was assassinated on Somoza's orders in 1933—was founded by a group of Marxist students in 1961 to fight oppression. Although small in size, the FSLN was a thorn in the side of the Somoza regime, and its members were regularly arrested and imprisoned.

12/27/1974

GUERRILLA ATTACK The FSLN mounted an armed rebellion. Rebels stormed a party and kidnapped several guests, including members of the Somoza family. They secured a $1 million ransom and the release of 14 political prisoners. A series of guerrilla attacks against the regime followed.

01/02/1975

MILITARY CRACKDOWN Somoza responded by declaring martial law and ordering the National Guard to unleash a savage military crackdown on the rebels. Villages suspected of harboring Sandinista guerrillas were destroyed. Thousands of peasants disappeared, presumed killed. Sandinista founder Carlos Fonseca was among those who died.

07/19/1979

SANDINISTAS ENTER MANAGUA Crowds cheered the victorious Sandinista fighters as they took possession of Managua on July 19, 1979. The five-member Junta for National Reconstruction took power the next day.

08/22/1979

ORTEGA IN CHARGE The Junta, made up of Sandinistas and moderates, soon came to be dominated by charismatic revolutionary Daniel Ortega. The new government set in motion land reforms and nationalized property owned by Somoza and his cronies. Ortega was elected President of Nicaragua in 1984.

11/03/1986

IRAN-CONTRA AFFAIR Scandal rocked the USA when it emerged that the CIA had been funding the Contras, despite their links to drug-trafficking and human rights abuses. To make matters worse, the money had been earned from illegal sales of weapons to Iran. President Reagan was publicly embarrassed by the revelations.

ANASTASIO SOMOZA DEBAYLE

Nicknamed Tachito ("little Tacho") after his father Anastasio (Tacho) Somoza Garcia, he was the third and last member of his family to be President.

12/23/1972

EARTHQUAKE FUNDS EMBEZZLED More than 10,000 people died when a massive earthquake struck Managua, capital of Nicaragua, destroying most of the city and leaving thousands homeless. Millions of dollars of international aid flowed in—but most of it never reached the victims, going instead into government coffers. Somoza's blatant misuse of the funds drove up support for the Sandinista rebels.

01/10/1978

NATIONWIDE STRIKES
The assassination of Pedro Joaquín Chamorro, a long-time opponent of Somoza, sparked off mass protests calling for an end to the dictatorship. A group of prominent intellectuals, priests, and businessmen publicly stated their support for the rebels, and the USA broke off military aid to Somoza's regime.

07/17/1979

END OF THE ROAD FOR SOMOZA
City after city rose up in revolt. Heavy fighting broke out all over the country, and by the beginning of July 1979, Sandinista guerrillas controlled most of Nicaragua. Left with no choice, Somoza resigned and fled to the USA on July 17.

> **Every Nicaraguan** with dignity is a **Sandinista**...
>
> RADICAL PRIEST MIGUEL D'ESCOTO, IN AN INTERVIEW, JULY 2, 1979

08/23/1980

LITERACY CAMPAIGN
The government flooded the country with 95,000 volunteer "brigadistas"—students, teachers, housewives, and social workers—in a massive campaign to educate the population. Illiteracy rates were said to have fallen from more than 50 percent to 13 percent in the first two years.

07/06/1984

CONTRA REBELLION
The new government faced opposition from the Contras, a guerrilla army who opposed the Junta's left-wing politics. Fearful of communist influence in the region, US President Ronald Reagan authorized the CIA, the American intelligence agency, to covertly support the Contras.

SANDINISTA PROPAGANDA These leaflets were recovered by Contras during the war against the Junta and put on display as evidence of the Sandinista party's communist and pro-Cuban sympathies.

03/23/1988

END OF THE WAR
Under intense international pressure to find an end to the conflict, which had destroyed Nicaragua's economy, the Contras and FSLN agreed to negotiate. A peace agreement brokered in 1988 disbanded the Contras. In return, Ortega agreed to hold free elections.

04/25/1990

VICTORY FOR VIOLETA To the surprise of many, Violeta Chamorro, widow of Pedro Chamorro, was elected President. Once a member of the Junta, she had resigned in protest against Ortega's policies. Her election heralded an era of peace for the country.

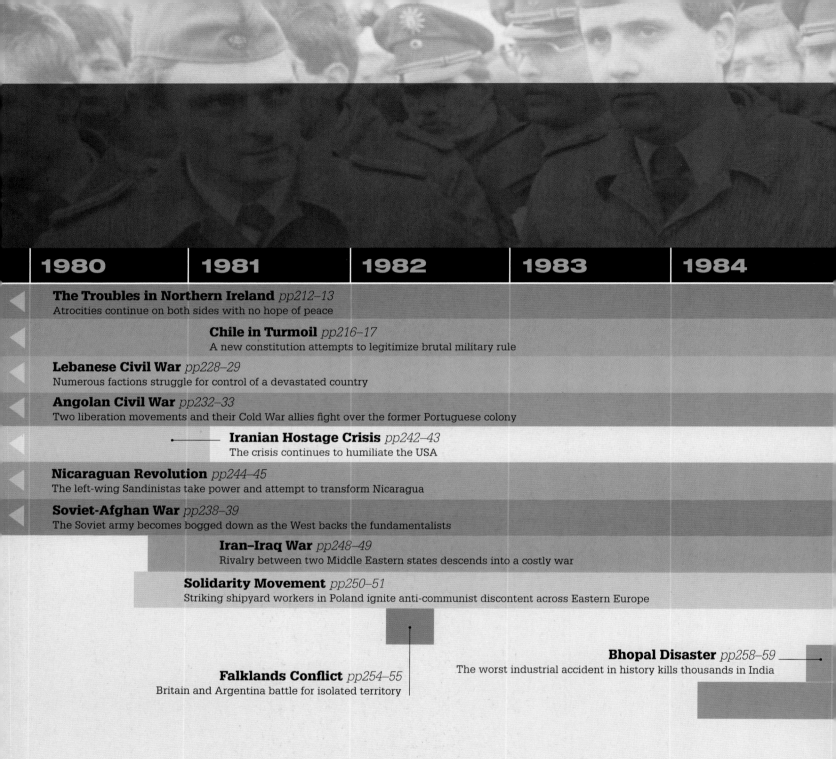

1980–89

1985 | 1986 | 1987 | 1988 | 1989

Ethiopian Famine *pp260–61*
Disaster hits the Horn of Africa

Glasnost Transforms the USSR *pp262–63*
A new leader seeks to rebuild the crumbling USSR

Chernobyl Disaster *pp264–65*
Nuclear disaster highlights a decrepit Soviet economy

Lockerbie Bombing
Hundreds are killed as a bomb explodes on a transatlantic flight

Fall of the Berlin Wall *pp270–71*
East Germany can no longer imprison its own people

Tiananmen Square *pp272–73*
Protests are brutally crushed in communist China

Iran–Iraq War

1980–1988

The neighboring countries of Iran and Iraq were bitter enemies and had fought repeatedly over their shared border for many years. When Iraq invaded Iran in 1980, what began as a swift incursion turned into one of the longest and bloodiest wars of the 20th century, claiming thousands of lives for minimal political gain.

INVASIONS

This map shows the key movements during the Iran–Iraq war. Following early Iraqi gains, both sides targeted each other's oilfields. In May 1982, an Iranian counterattack restored the pre-war border, and shifted the momentum of the conflict. Over the next two years, the Iranians gradually drove deeper into Iraqi territory.

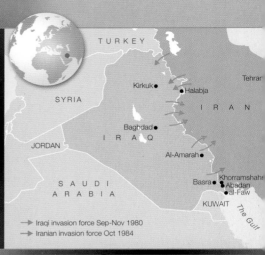

→ Iraqi invasion force Sep–Nov 1980
→ Iranian invasion force Oct 1984

09/27/1980

IRANIAN COUNTER ATTACKS

Iran mobilized to defend itself. The conflict escalated when its troops blockaded Iraqi ports. Iran declared its coastal waters to be war zones and launched attacks against two Iraqi air bases. Clashes broke out along the 720-mile (1,150-km) frontier and Khomeini urged Iraqis to overthrow their government.

05/12/1984

TANKER WAR
Iraq began attacking Iranian ships to undermine Iran's ability to fight at sea. Initially they targeted only vessels carrying military equipment, but by 1984 Iraq was using combat aircraft armed with Exocet missiles to take out tankers carrying oil.

02/09/1986

IRAN TAKES AL-FAW

Although the Iranians found it difficult hold captured Iraqi territory, in February 1986 they crossed the Shatt al-Arab waterway at the mouth of the Persian Gulf and captured the disused Iraqi oil port of al-Faw. They held the port for two years, despite Iraqi attempts to dislodge them.

> Whether it has been **declared** or not, **it is** in fact **war**.

IRAQI DEFENCE MINISTER ADNAN KHAIRALLAH,
JANUARY 1981

03/16/1988

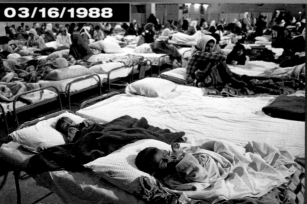

CIVILIAN TARGETS

When the local Kurds rebelled against Iraqi rule and supported the Iranian invasion in the north, Saddam's response was brutal. Chemical weapons were unleashed against the civilian populations of Kurdish towns. The worst hit was Halabja, where 5,000 people were killed. Another 7,000 suffered long-term illness or injury.

AYATOLLAH KHOMEINI

The spiritual leader of Iran, Khomeini felt that Hussein was the main obstacle to the advance of Islam in the region.

SADDAM HUSSEIN

Hussein, ruler of Iraq, felt threatened by the recent Islamic Revolution in Iran and believed the Khomeini regime wanted him gone.

09/22/1980

IRAQ INVADES IRAN In September 1980, Saddam Hussein ordered the invasion of Iran. He justified it on the basis of a territorial dispute over the Shatt al-Arab waterway that lies between the two states. He was convinced it would be a swift incursion.

03/10/1985

CHEMICAL WARFARE

Iraq was surprised by Iran's resilience. Their forces were faced with relentless attacks by mass waves of Iranian troops. To combat this, the Iraqis used chemical weapons such as the blister agent mustard gas, and the nerve gas, Tabun. The UN condemned the use of chemical weapons, which destroyed any international support for Iraq.

01/11/1986

NEUTRAL KUWAIT

During the war, Kuwait was officially neutral but openly sided with Iraq. Iranian attacks on tankers prompted Kuwait to ask the United States to register 11 Kuwaiti tankers as American ships so that they could be escorted through the Gulf by the US Navy. The Americans complied.

07/03/1988

JETLINER DOWNED A US warship, USS *Vincennes*, was on patrol in the Persian Gulf when the captain mistook an Iranian civilian jetliner for an attacking Iranian F14 fighter plane and launched a heat-seeking missile, killing all on board. Iran reacted with outrage. Most of the victims were pilgrims on their way to Mecca. Their funerals were marked by anti-US protests.

08/20/1988

CEASEFIRE AGREED After eight bloody years, the UN negotiated a ceasefire in Geneva, which both sides accepted. There were no winners. Half a million people had died and neither side had achieved its aims.

Solidarity Movement

1980–1989

By the 1980s economic recession and poor standards of living were causing widespread frustration in countries across communist Eastern Europe. The scene was set for popular rebellion against Soviet rule. The touchpaper was lit when shipyard workers in the Polish city of Gdansk went on strike. They went on to found Solidarity, a movement that rocked European communism to its core.

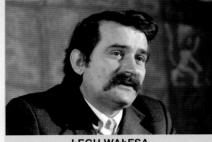

LECH WAŁĘSA

An electrician and political activist, Lech Wałęsa had been involved with promoting workers' rights for many years, and led many strikes.

09/17/1980

SOLIDARITY Wałęsa was hailed as the hero of the hour. Within days of the Gdansk Agreement, he led workers' representatives to form a national labour union. Solidarity was born and more than 10 million workers, intellectuals, and students hopeful for change bravely joined the union.

08/05/1981

RENEWED STRIKES With the country behind them, Solidarity transformed from a trade union into a revolutionary movement, using strikes to force changes in government policies. In August they organized a national strike which brought Poland to its knees.

PAX SOVIETICA

SOLIDARITY POSTER After martial law was imposed, posters such as this were printed in secret. It satirized Soviet propaganda and its endless promises of peace.

06/19/1983

THE POPE STEPS IN After Wałęsa was released from prison, Pope John Paul II visited Poland in a clear sign of endorsement for the union. He encouraged dialogue and urged Solidarity members to avoid inciting civil war. The Polish Catholic Church did a great deal to keep the flame of Solidarity alive.

07/21/1983

NORMALITY RESTORED Martial law was lifted in 1983. Even as people took to the streets to celebrate, there was a political stalemate. Solidarity could not threaten the communist regime, but the communist government had failed to destroy Solidarity or fix the economy.

08/14/1980

LENIN SHIPYARD PROTESTS The Lenin shipyards in Gdansk went on strike over poor wages. Lech Wałęsa galvanized the workers to stay at the yard and work with the wider populace to engineer a general strike in Poland. They drew up a list of demands including freedom of the press and the right to form independent trade unions.

08/31/1980

DEMANDS ACCEPTED The strikes brought Poland to a standstill. The communist government capitulated, signing an agreement ratifying many of the workers' demands. These changes became known as the Gdansk Agreement. Achieving the right to form labor unions independent of communist party control was unprecedented.

12/17/1982

MARTIAL LAW IS IMPOSED Fearing revolution, the government imposed martial law. Troops poured onto Poland's streets, the country's borders were sealed, and thousands of Solidarity members, including Wałęsa, were arrested. In some cases, tear gas was used to control the protestors.

> **"**
> He who puts out his hand to **stop the wheel of history** will have his **fingers crushed**.
>
> LECH WAŁĘSA, CBS INTERVIEW,
> NOVEMBER 15, 1989
> **"**

10/19/1984

PRIEST MURDERED In October Polish priest Jerzy Popiełuszko, a popular Solidarity activist, was kidnapped, beaten, and murdered by agents of the communist internal intelligence agency. His killing was a blunt message to the Church to stay out of politics. It sparked mass riots, even as prayer meetings were held to mourn his death.

06/04/1989

FIRST FREE ELECTION IN EASTERN EUROPE Polish Prime Minister General Wojciech Jaruzelski acceded to pressure from the West, from Solidarity, and the failing economy, and held democratic elections. Solidarity triumphed, and in 1990 Wałęsa became Poland's first post-communist president. His success inspired anti-communist movements across Europe.

1981

President Under Fire

Just 69 days into his first term as President of the United States, Ronald Reagan was targeted by an assassin. On March 30, 1981, as the President was leaving the Hilton Hotel in Washington, John Hinckley, Jr. opened fire. Reagan was swiftly bundled into his waiting car by a secret service agent. The shooting left police officer Thomas Delahanty (seen here in the foreground) and Press Secretary James Brady (behind) wounded. At first it seemed that Reagan had not been hit but he began to complain of chest pains and was taken to the hospital. One of the attacker's bullets had punctured his lung. Confusion reigned as conflicting reports poured in, but Reagan's reaction to the incident and reports of him laughing and joking from his hospital bed won the hearts of the American public. Reagan went on to serve two full terms as US President. His would-be assassin, John Hinckley, was found mentally unstable at trial.

Falklands Conflict

1982

The Falkland Islands in the South Atlantic Ocean had long been a source of friction between Britain and Argentina. With Argentina's economy in ruins, the increasingly unpopular military regime staged an audacious invasion of the British-held territory in an attempt to unite their country.

04/02/1982

STAKING A CLAIM The Argentine invasion took the British entirely by surprise. Some 600 troops made amphibious landings and assaulted the airport, the army barracks, and the home of the British governor. The next day, Argentine forces took control of the British territories of South Georgia and the South Sandwich Islands.

04/02/1982

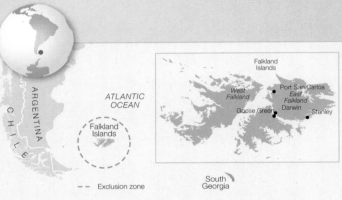

TOUGH TASK The main challenge for the British was the distance involved. Where the Argentines could rely on mainland airfields, British aircraft would have to be launched from carriers.

05/01/1982

BRITISH BOMBARD AIRPORT The focal point of the first British attack was Stanley Airport in the Falkland Islands. It was hit by a Vulcan bomber at dawn on May 1. Following this raid, Sea Harrier jets dropped cluster bombs on the airstrip to prevent Argentine jets from using it.

05/02/1982

BELGRANO SUNK In one of the most controversial incidents of the conflict, the nuclear-powered submarine HMS *Conqueror* sank the Argentine light cruiser *General Belgrano* with the loss of 323 lives. Images of survivors being rescued shocked the British public and strengthened the cause of antiwar campaigners.

04/05/1982

FIRST BRITISH SHIP ATTACKED The Argentines retaliated by attacking HMS *Sheffield*, killing 20 men and injuring 24. It was the first British warship to be attacked. The burned-out destroyer wallowed in the sea before capsizing and sinking on May 10. This put an end to any hopes of a diplomatic solution to the conflict.

05/14/1982

BRITISH TROOPS LAND Westland Sea Helicopters airlifted thousands of British troops from the aircraft carriers *Hermes* and *Invincible*. The first troops landed on the Falkland Islands on May 14.

EXOCET MISSILE The Falklands conflict introduced the modern guided missile to warfare, when the Argentines used Exocets to sink HMS *Sheffield*. The French-built anti-ship missile was designed to skim low over the waves and hit large warships with incredible force.

05/28/1982

ARGENTINES CAPTURED The first major land conflict took place around the villages of Darwin and Goose Green. The fierce battle lasted for a day and a night and resulted in 250 Argentine deaths. Although vastly outnumbered, the British troops took more than a thousand prisoners of war.

INITIAL BRITISH SURRENDER The small contingent of Royal Marines based on the islands put up some resistance but were hopelessly outnumbered. The Argentine Special Forces made the prisoners lie on their stomachs in the dirt—a humiliating image that was published all around the world within hours. Conflict was now inevitable.

04/05/1982

BRITAIN LAUNCHES OFFENSIVE In Britain, the invasion created a political crisis because the government was accused of neglecting the islands. The British government immediately cut off diplomatic ties with Argentina. It began to assemble a large naval taskforce of 30 warships, 6,000 troops, and auxiliary and transport vessels.

> ❝
> This is **British** territory. You're **not invited**…
> ❞
>
> SIR REX HUNT, BRITISH GOVERNOR OF FALKLAND ISLANDS, APRIL 2, 1982

06/14/1982

ARGENTINE SURRENDER Victory at Goose Green allowed British troops to march on Port Stanley, where they succeeded in taking the Argentine positions at Mount Kent and Mount Challenger. On June 14, Argentine Commander Mario Menendez signed a surrender document and his troops laid down their arms.

A CENTURY OF
Fashion

In a century of ever-changing fashion trends, hemlines rose, sank, and rose again. Increasing leisure time brought a demand for different kinds of sportswear. Radical changes in women's lives, and especially their move into the workplace, saw them increasingly opting for comfort and practicality over elaboration. At the beginning of the century, the aristocracy led the way in fashion. By the end, pop icons and movie stars were setting the trends.

1900–1920 Paris set the tone for style in the 1900s as French designers dominated the world of haute couture, creating exclusive hand-tailored outfits for wealthy and titled clients. Dresses were ornately decorated, and to achieve the fashionable S-bend silhouette of the day, women forced themselves into tightly laced corsets. The most influential couturier of the day was Paul Poiret. He introduced narrow, straighter shapes that allowed greater freedom of movement, though paradoxically the tight "hobble skirt,"

one of his innovations, reduced women to taking mincing, tiny steps. Another innovator was Venetian designer Mariano Fortuny, famous for his flowing shifts of finely pleated silk that clung to the body.

1920–1930 The age of the flapper in the 1920s brought radical change to the somber colors and outfits of World War I. Young women bobbed their hair and wore straight tunic shifts with skirts stopping well above the knee. Jazz was the rage and

CREATING CURVES
Edwardian (1901–1910) corsets thrust the bust forward and the hips back to create an S-bend figure and a tiny waist.

106

The number of haute couture fashion houses in Paris in 1946. The number had fallen to 18 by the year 2000.

Hollywood stars such as Louise Brooks became fashion icons. French tennis star Suzanne Lenglen shocked the staid English public by appearing in an above-the-calf tennis dress at Wimbledon.

1930–1950 The Depression years of the 1930s saw a return to more feminine styles: waists came back and hemlines dropped. Clothing was subject to strict rationing during World War II—Parisian designers were limited to 13 ft (4 m) of cloth for a coat and 3 ft (1 m) for a blouse. When, in February 1947, Paris

couturier Christian Dior launched the "New Look" dress, with a tiny waist and full skirt, his extravagant use of fabric

STYLE BIBLE 1929
American women were inspired to adopt the latest Parisian designs featured in *Vogue*, the most influential fashion magazine of the day, noted for its stylish covers.

1910s

PAUL POIRET
Many of Poiret's creations, including this 1914 dress, were inspired by Leon Bakst's designs for the Ballets Russes, which created a storm in Paris.

1920s

COCO CHANEL
While this flapper dress is a 1920s classic, many of Chanel's revolutionary designs, such as the collarless jacket and little black dress, are still popular today.

1930s

ELSA SCHIAPARELLI
Famous for sportswear, Schiaparelli introduced knitwear, such as this woolen suit, to fashion and designed the first wraparound dress.

1950s

BIKINI
Initially thought shocking, the bikini was popularized by French film star Brigitte Bardot, who was photographed in one on the beach at Cannes.

SPACE CHIC The futuristic white and metallic outfits of French designer André Courrèges, launched in 1964, immediately earned the name Space Age.

> The **fashion world** can truly be a jungle…It's a **fiercely competitive business**.

US DESIGNER CALVIN KLEIN, *PLAYBOY* INTERVIEW, MAY 1984

caused an outrage with protesters shouting "Mr. Dior, we abhor, skirts to the floor!"

1950–1970 Haute couture was in decline by the 1960s as designers concentrated on ready-to-wear lines. Paris now shared the fashion stage with New York, London, Milan, and Tokyo. Both Mary Quant and André Courrèges were credited with inventing the mini skirt, the decade's iconic garment. Pant suits and hot pants were

seen everywhere, although they were not always welcomed. By the end of the decade, the hippy look, with floor-length skirts, colorful psychedelic prints, and sheepskin coats, was becoming popular.

1970– Designers turned to trends set by rock stars and pop groups in the 1970s, such as platform shoes and sequins. In marked contrast to this were the studded leather jackets and spiked hair of punk fashion.

The 1980s saw a return to designer clothing with an emphasis on power dressing, epitomized by padded shoulders. Designers such as Ralph Lauren, Calvin Klein, and Versace dominated fashion. In the 1990s, a mixture of styles prevailed: Manolo Blahnik reintroduced stiletto heels but sneakers were also widely worn. Women chose clothes for casual smartness and comfort, with jeans the most ubiquitous item of all.

FASHION ROCKS British designer Vivienne Westwood created the punk fashions associated with the Sex Pistols rock band in the 1970s.

1960s

MARY QUANT
This minidress from 1967 was inspired by a soccer strip. Quant's innovative clothes appealed to the young generation of Swinging London.

1970s

YVES SAINT LAURENT
Famed for his haute couture and ready-to-wear lines, such as this gypsy-style outfit, Yves St. Laurent dominated Parisian fashion for more than 30 years.

1980s

CALVIN KLEIN
This Calvin Klein design has the boxy shoulders typical of '80s power dressing. By the 1980s the New York-based fashion empire had outlets all around the world.

1990s

VERSACE
The Italian fashion company catered for the luxury end of the international market and was famed for its glamorous evening wear.

Bhopal Disaster

1984

On December 3, 1984, poisonous gas leaked from a chemical factory in Bhopal, India. Thousands died within hours of the leak, and thousands more fell ill in the following months and years. As the awful tragedy unfolded, the Bhopal disaster became infamous as one of the worst industrial accidents in history.

12/02/1984

03/12/1984

EFFECTS OF GAS; HOSPITALS CROWDED Thousands crowded into Bhopal's Hamidia Hospital as poisonous gas seared their eyes and filled their mouths and lungs. The hospital was overwhelmed. A week later victims were still arriving at a rate of one a minute.

12/03/1984

PEOPLE ATTEMPT TO FLEE No one had been told what to do in the event of a gas leak. Advice from Union Carbide was to move upwind or stay indoors. However, thousands decided to flee the city clutching their few belongings, and chaos broke out as they tried to escape. Many were trampled underfoot.

> " We didn't know which way to run. "
>
> BHOPAL RESIDENT AHMED KHAN TO BBC
> JOURNALIST, DECEMBER 4, 1984

12/03/1984

LIVESTOCK POISONED Animals began to die. The bodies of thousands of dogs, cats, rats, and mice littered the streets. Farm animals, including goats, cows, and buffalo died from respiratory disorders, and the mass of carcasses had to be burned. Farmers lost their entire livelihoods as crops died, and soil and water were polluted.

12/05/1984

MASS CREMATIONS OF VICTIMS So many died so quickly that drastic measures had to be taken. At the Hindu cremation grounds many of the victims were burned on mass pyres. Mourners at the Muslim burial ground ran out of space for new burials, and were forced to dig up old graves to bury victims of the gas.

12/10/1984

UNION CARBIDE PLANT The American-owned Union Carbide factory was established in Bhopal in 1970 in response to India's increased demand for agricultural supplies. In 1979 the factory started producing large amounts of methyl isocyanate, an ingredient of pesticides. To reduce operating costs, safety measures and maintenance were drastically cut back.

12/03/1984

LEAK OF POISON GAS In the early hours of December 3, a safety system failed. Water leaked into a tank containing 40 tons of methyl isocyanate (MIC), and the reaction produced large amounts of toxic gas. The poisonous cloud floated across the sleeping city, where many lived in slums close to the plant. Panic spread through the night, and by morning the streets were choked with poison gas.

12/03/1984

UNION CARBIDE ARRIVES When word of the catastrophe reached Union Carbide in America, chairman Warren Anderson, together with a technical team, left for India. Upon arrival, Anderson was immediately arrested. He was urged by the Indian government to leave the country within 24 hours for his own safety.

12/04/1984

DEATH TOLL RISES At least 3,000 died in the first few days, and thousands more suffered terrible injuries. The final death toll may be as high as 25,000, with up to 500,000 survivors crippled by the poison.

CAMPAIGN FOR JUSTICE The Indian government passed the Bhopal Gas Leak Disaster Act, enabling them to act as legal representative of the victims. Lawyers immediately filed claims for $3.3 billion against Union Carbide. The legal battle would go on for years, while victims of the disaster struggled to rebuild their shattered lives.

12/03/1985

ONGOING ANGER One year after the leak, angry crowds marched through Bhopal to demand justice. It took until 1989 for a legal settlement to be agreed, and several more years for compensation to reach the victims. For relatives of the dead, and those living with the ongoing legacy of sickness and pollution, the compensation was too little, too late.

Ethiopian Famine

1984–1985

Since the fall of Emperor Haile Selassie's regime in 1974, Ethiopia had been at war with the northern province of Eritrea. One of the poorest nations in the world, Ethiopia was also stricken with drought. In 1984, facing the worst in a series of major famines, it looked to the West for help.

However, Western governments were reluctant to get involved, fearing that the military government of Mengistu Haile Mariam would divert the money to fund war. As they argued over what steps to take, the human cost of late intervention threatened the lives of millions.

10/23/1984

NEWS OF FAMINE
The wider public around the world remained unaware of the impending tragedy. In October Kenyan photojournalist Mohammed Amin and BBC reporter Michael Buerk broadcast an emotional account of the harsh conditions. Their images of famished children, reduced almost to skeletons, shocked the world and galvanized a huge international response. In just a few days, millions of dollars were donated in aid.

11/01/1984

03/25/1985

FUNDS DIVERTED TO FUEL THE WAR The Marxist regime had diverted almost half of its national budget to military spending in its war with the rebels. The international community condemned the Ethiopian government and accused it of spending aid money on weapons and supplies for the troops.

05/14/1985

THOUSANDS DISPLACED The government response to the famine was to uproot large numbers of peasants who lived in the affected areas in the north and resettle them in the south. About 600,000 people were moved, many forcibly, while thousands fled to refugee camps in neighboring Sudan.

03/06/1984

NO RAIN IN ETHIOPIA A record low rainfall was a major cause of the famine. The impact of drought was magnified by deforestation in the country and the depletion of soil by farmers who could not afford to let land lie fallow. Cattle suffered as they grew thinner and hungrier, and eventually died.

04/23/1984

HELP DELAYED Ethiopia appealed to the West for aid, but there were concerns that the money would be squandered. The West criticized Ethiopia for its socialist policies, suggesting the famine could have been averted. Aid agencies accused Western governments of not doing enough and, eventually, money was pledged.

FOOD SUPPLY The International Committee of the Red Cross sent sacks of food to Ethiopia. Such aid was the result of pressure tactics by aid agencies.

SIGNS OF RELIEF By November relief planes had started to arrive. More than 6 million people were threatened by famine, but aid was difficult to distribute. Attempts to airlift food and medical supplies were frustrated by bureaucracy and arguments broke out about the choice of airports. Getting aid to war-torn northern Ethiopia was risky. Airdropping supplies was challenging as turbulence kicked up the desert sand. Thousands swarmed to meet the first planes, sometimes fighting over food.

01/24/1985

THE WAR RAGES ON As Ethiopian feeding centers swelled with people desperate for food, their plight was compounded when the government stepped up its war with rebel movements in Eritrea and Tigray. The war over a 620-mile (1,000-km) border, containing a prized stretch of fertile land, drained Ethiopia of precious resources that could have been used to fight the effects of the drought. More than a million people died of starvation.

WEAPON OF WAR The AK-47 rifle was the chosen gun for Eritrean guerrillas against the Ethiopian regime. Cheap and reliable, it symbolized the proliferation of small arms in the country.

> " The closest thing to **hell on Earth**. "
>
> **WORKER AT THE KOREM AID CAMP**

07/13/1985

LIVE AID FOR AFRICA Irish musician Bob Geldof led a fund-raising crusade, culminating in the massive Live Aid concert. The world's most famous stars played at Wembley Stadium, London, and John F. Kennedy Stadium in Philadelphia. Two billion people watched, and money poured in, but the campaign had little long-term effect, and provoked debate about the best way to help the African people.

Glasnost Transforms the USSR

1985–1991

When Mikhail Gorbachev became leader of the Soviet Union, he inherited a stagnating economy, a disaffected populace exhausted by decades of Cold War, and a creaking political system based on tight government control. His response was to instigate radical reforms. Perestroika, or restructuring, promised to allow greater economic efficiency. Glasnost, or openness, permitted unprecedented freedom of the press and political expression. However, his proposals faced opposition from both diehard communists and pro-democracy campaigners, and implementing them would prove a huge challenge.

05/15/1988

RUSSIAN TROOPS LEAVE AFGHANISTAN The war in Afghanistan hindered Gorbachev's plans: it was expensive and hugely unpopular at home. In April 1988 Afghanistan and Pakistan signed an accord, with the USA and Soviet Union as guarantors. The accord allowed Soviet forces to withdraw without losing face. On May 15 the last troops began to leave.

12/03/1989

MALTA SUMMIT Shortly after the fall of the Berlin Wall in November 1989, Gorbachev met US President George H. W. Bush for a summit in Malta. The leaders declared that the Cold War was over. Gorbachev confirmed his commitment to transforming foreign relations, as economic strain forced the USSR to seek peace.

11/07/1990

PRO-DEMOCRACY PROTESTS Glasnost had made it possible for people to criticize the government. However, a mass demonstration in Moscow's Red Square during October Revolution celebrations embarrassed Gorbachev. Protestors demanded an end to communist rule, calling for multiparty elections, and denounced Vladimir Lenin, the architect and first head of the Soviet Union.

03/11/1985

GORBACHEV ELECTED GENERAL SECRETARY

A victorious Mikhail Gorbachev spoke to the nation following his election as general secretary of the Communist Party. His swift rise to power was seen as a sign of imminent change. He pledged to bring a new dynamism, particularly to the stagnant economy.

03/04/1986

NEW POLICIES ANNOUNCED
At the 27th Congress of the Communist Party, Gorbachev called for Glasnost, or openness in Soviet affairs. A few months later he announced Perestroika, a radical restructuring to allow greater economic freedoms. Both concepts were revolutionary.

08/23/1989

UNREST IN BALTICS

Calls for independence from the Soviet Union were increasing in the Baltic States. New political parties formed, and interethnic unrest escalated. An estimated 2 million residents formed a 373-mile (600-km) human chain stretching across Lithuania, Latvia, and Estonia to protest against the 50th anniversary of Soviet rule.

02/01/1990

VIOLENCE IN AZERBAIJAN

Civil unrest in Azerbaijan led to a Soviet crackdown, in which dozens were killed. Armenians had interpreted Glasnost as an opportunity to unite with Nagorno-Karabakh, a region within Azerbaijan demanding independence. Moscow declared emergency rule as it struggled to hold the Soviet Union together.

10/15/1990

INTERNATIONAL ACCLAIM

Despite problems at home, Gorbachev's increasing openness with the wider world led to international plaudits. He won the Nobel Peace Prize in 1990 and was feted by international leaders as a champion of democracy. However, in Moscow, which was hit by shortages of food and basic consumer goods, his celebrity status was regarded with more reserve.

06/12/1991

YELTSIN WINS ELECTION

Gorbachev's reforms were too progressive for some and not enough for others. His greatest critic was Boris Yeltsin, chairman of the Russian government, who insisted that communists should no longer dominate the government. In 1990 he stormed out of the Communist Party in a direct challenge to Gorbachev. Yeltsin was unanimously voted President of Russia in its first democratic elections in June 1991. This marked the beginning of the end of the Soviet regime.

> ## We **need democracy** just like **we need air** to breathe.
>
> **MIKHAIL GORBACHEV, JANUARY 27, 1987**

Chernobyl Disaster

1986

Nuclear power seemed a miracle of modern science, promising to repurpose the most dangerous technology of the Cold War to peaceful ends. The nuclear power complex at Chernobyl in the Soviet republic of Ukraine appeared to fulfill that promise—until an experimental safety procedure went badly wrong, resulting in the worst nuclear accident the world had ever seen.

04/26/1986

SAFETY TEST At 1:23 a.m., engineers ran a test of the emergency systems in Reactor 4. The test caused a power surge and the reactor exploded.

04/26/1986

CONTAINMENT MEASURES Firefighters had succeeded in putting out the smaller blazes, but were unable to reach the fire in the reactor core. Army helicopters were called in to dump sand, clay, lead, and boron into the reactor to smother the flames. They dropped more than 5,000 tons of material before the fire was extinguished, two weeks later.

04/27/1986

CIVILIAN DANGER As dangerously high levels of radiation were detected in the nearby city of Pripyat, some 53,000 residents were evacuated. They were told to pack for three days; most never returned.

> For the **first time** ever we have encountered in reality the **sinister power** of nuclear energy that has **escaped control**.
>
> SOVIET LEADER MIKHAIL GORBACHEV, IN A TELEVISION ADDRESS, MAY 15, 1986

06/01/1986

EUROPE TAKES PRECAUTIONS
As the fallout spread, European governments took action to prevent contaminated material from entering human food. Farmers were ordered to destroy crops and livestock. The areas worst affected were in the Soviet states of Ukraine, Belarus, and Russia, where the highest concentration of fallout was detected.

06/24/1986

CLEAN-UP OPERATION
As the immediate effects of the disaster came under control, the USSR faced a daunting task in dealing with the remains of Reactor 4. A plan was drawn up to build a vast steel and concrete sarcophagus to enclose the ruined reactor and its deadly contents, and prevent any further radioactive leakage.

11/30/1986

SARCOPHAGUS IS COMPLETED
Thousands of workers were employed in the construction project, which was hampered by the continuing danger of radiation poisoning. The sarcophagus was completed before the end of the year, but the vast cost put significant strain on the already struggling Soviet economy.

12/15/1986

ZONE OF ALIENATION
Radioactive fallout had rendered the area around the plant uninhabitable. More than 130,000 people were permanently evacuated, and all land within a 19-mile (30-km) radius was declared off-limits. Controversy still rages today over the long-term health effects of the disaster, with claims that cancer rates in the region have risen significantly.

04/26/1986

DOOMED HEROES The explosion started a fire in the center of the reactor. Firefighters rushed to the scene, many of them unaware that the site was dangerously radioactive.

INADEQUATE PROTECTION

Emergency workers had only basic safety gear, which did not protect them from the radiation.

04/26/1986

DAMAGE REVEALED

As morning broke, the full extent of the damage became apparent. The explosion had burst open the reactor vessel, exposing the radioactive elements inside to the air. Graphite control rods inside the reactor were still burning, and the smoke carried particles of radioactive dust into the atmosphere.

04/28/1986

FALLOUT SPREADS

Radioactive dust from the burning reactor—known as fallout—was carried by the wind across the USSR and into Western Europe. When radiation monitors in Sweden detected airborne contamination, Soviet leader Mikhail Gorbachev was forced to reveal the disaster to the USSR and the wider world.

Reykjavik

Oslo
Helsinki
Moscow
London
Warsaw
Chernobyl
Paris
Munich
Madrid
Rome
Istanbul
Athens
Ankara

KEY
Highly contaminated area
Broad range of radiation

05/11/1986

A TERRIBLE PRICE As the weeks passed, fire and rescue workers began to die of radiation sickness. The worst affected were those who had attended the initial blazes, receiving lethal doses of radiation. Many others suffered long-term effects.

02/29/1990

GHOST TOWN Pripyat was left to rot, inhabited only by a few thousand scientists and technicians who monitored the situation and maintained the sarcophagus. As the years passed, a few of the city's former residents returned illegally to their homes, but much of the city remains empty, a stark reminder of the disaster.

Revolution in the Philippines

1981–1986

President Ferdinand Marcos had ruled the Philippines for more than 20 years, much of which was under martial law. In 1986 he held a crooked election, and in just a few days was ousted by a people-power revolution which was marked, not by violence, but by sheer force of will.

06/16/1981

RULE OF THE DICTATOR
Marcos had a reputation for brutality. He suspended freedom of the press, suppressed popular protests, and ordered the arrest of opposition leaders. At a general election held in 1981, he was reelected as President, but opposition parties claimed that the election was fraudulent and boycotted the vote.

02/07/1986

MARCOS CLAIMS VICTORY Filipinos turned out to vote in significant numbers, but there was confusion about the result, leading to intense anger among the public. Amid accusations of fraud, Marcos declared himself the winner. The election was widely condemned.

02/08/1986

CITIZENS OPPOSE THE PRESIDENT
The day after the election, Filipinos tried to gain access to the ballot room in the Makati Municipal Building, Manila, shouting "Fraud" and "Marcos resign." Thirty computer workers also walked out from an election tabulation center, protesting the tampering of election results.

02/23/1986

02/25/1986

PEOPLE CHEER MARCOS' EXIT
On February 25 both Aquino and Marcos defiantly staged separate inaugurations, but Marcos had lost all credibility. Realizing the futility of his stand, he fled with his family and supporters to Hawaii. Outside Camp Crame, Filipinos greeted the news with wild cheering.

02/25/1986

SPOILS OF THE REGIME
Hundreds of Filipinos stormed into Malacanang Palace, home to the Marcos family, to view the opulence enjoyed by their former leader. One room housed the 3,400 pairs of shoes that belonged to First Lady Imelda Marcos. The President had reportedly stolen billions of dollars from his people.

08/21/1983

NINOY KILLED
Benigno Aquino, known by his nickname Ninoy, led the opposition to the Marcos regime while in exile in the USA. In 1983 the deteriorating economic situation in the Philippines persuaded him to return home. He was gunned down as he stepped off the plane at Manila Airport.

02/01/1986

OPPOSITION STRENGTHENS
Many believed that Marcos had ordered Ninoy's assassination. His death became a rallying point for the opposition. In the 1986 election, Ninoy's widow, Cory Aquino, challenged the Marcos government. Dismissed as a mere housewife by her critics, she became a potent symbol of opposition to the corrupt Marcos family.

14/02/1986

THE CHURCH GETS INVOLVED The Catholic Church was hugely influential in the Philippines. Led by Cardinal Jaime Sin, it condemned the elections as fraudulent and urged a non-violent struggle for justice. Even the most conservative elements of the Church eventually joined the anti-Marcos campaign.

02/22/1986

MARCOS SUPPORTERS SWITCH SIDES
On February 22, Juan Enrile, former Minister of Defense, and General Fidel Ramos, commander of the Philippine Paramilitary Constabulary, defected from the Marcos administration. They set up rebel headquarters in the military bases at Camp Aguinaldo and Camp Crame.

PROTESTS SWELL
Cardinal Sin made an appeal on the Catholic-run Radio Veritas for citizens to support the rebels. The response was overwhelming. Thousands took to the streets, carrying rosaries and flowers instead of weapons, and headed to Camp Crame to prevent military aircraft from landing. Ramos declared the event a "revolution of the people."

> **Enough** is enough, Mr. President. Your **time is up**!
>
> JUAN ENRILE, FORMER MINISTER OF DEFENSE, FEBRUARY 23, 1986

02/25/1986

A KICK IN THE FACE
The revolution was largely peaceful. The few shots fired were mainly in the air, and there were minimal reports of casualties or looting. The people demonstrated their contempt for the former leader by breaking into the presidential palace and destroying portraits and furniture. After the revolution, the palace was converted into a museum.

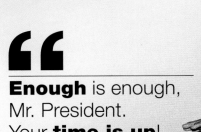

Space Shuttle Tragedy

On January 28, 1986, an audience of millions looked on in horror as the launch of Space Shuttle Challenger went tragically wrong. A mere 73 seconds after liftoff from the Kennedy Space Center, Florida, the shuttle was torn into pieces, killing all seven astronauts on board. The day had not started well: the scheduled launch had been delayed several times. Finally, at 11:38 a.m., the shuttle blasted off. It soon became clear that something was wrong as smoke puffed from one of the booster rockets. Less than a minute into the flight, flames burst from the rocket, causing a fuel tank to explode. President Ronald Reagan addressed the nation, paying homage to the lost crew. Among the astronauts was Christa McAuliffe, a teacher selected to give lessons from space. Investigations into the cause of the accident found that a critical O-ring seal had failed, allowing an escape of hot gas that caused the explosion. NASA would not launch another shuttle for nearly three years.

Fall of the Berlin Wall

1989

For decades Berlin stood at the epicenter of the Cold War, and the Berlin Wall, which divided communist East Berlin from the West, was an ugly symbol of the deep divisions between two ideologies. On one momentous night it was breached, uniting people who had been kept apart for a generation. As the wall tumbled, it heralded the end of communist rule in Europe.

05/01/1989

DISMANTLING THE IRON CURTAIN In May 1989 Hungarian Prime Minister Miklos Nemeth ordered guards to start dismantling the barbed wire fences along its border with Austria. East Germans began traveling to Hungary in order to get to the West via Austria. By September 13,000 East Germans had fled.

11/08/1989

PRESS CONFERENCE During a press conference Günter Schabowski, a Communist Party spokesman, announced that travel restrictions would be relaxed, allowing East German citizens across the Berlin Wall. His vague statement was taken as a promise that the era of division was over.

11/09/1989

CROWDS GATHER ON WALL The result of the announcement was dramatic. By nightfall, hundreds of thousands of Berliners, East and West, had begun converging on the wall. In the face of the swelling crowd, East German border guards let them pass.

11/10/1989

THE WALL COMES DOWN To the cheers of onlookers, East German army units abandoned their guard towers and, assisted by soldiers from West Berlin, began to dismantle sections of the wall to create more crossing points. Within 48 hours, more than 3 million people had crossed the border.

12/03/1989

GORBACHEV MEETS BUSH With Soviet influence in Europe on the wane, the Cold War officially came to an end. US President George H. W. Bush met Soviet leader Mikhail Gorbachev for a historic summit on board a Soviet ship at Malta's Marsaxlokk Harbor. The conflict had spanned four decades, and at times had threatened to engulf the world in violence.

11/09/1990

ONE YEAR LATER A year after the wall was breached, Berliners gathered in their thousands to celebrate the momentous event. On October 3 the process of reunification between East and West Germany had been formally concluded, marking the birth of a new Europe.

11/04/1989

MASS RALLY More than a million people attended a pro-democracy rally in East Berlin's central square, under the motto "for our country." This tide of popular rebellion was the culmination of years of opposition to the division of Berlin. Communist rule in East Germany was already tottering as the USSR faced economic ruin.

11/09/1989

THE BORDER OPENS When the checkpoints finally opened, just before midnight, crowds poured through from East Berlin. West Berliners on the other side welcomed them with joyful hugs and bottles of champagne. Friends and family members who had been separated for decades were finally reunited.

11/12/1989

PEOPLE ATTACK WALL Ecstatic crowds joined in the demolition work, hacking large chunks out of the 28-mile (45-km) barrier. As the weeks passed Berliners arrived with pickaxes and sledgehammers to dismantle the wall piece by piece.

FRAGMENT OF THE BERLIN WALL Many Berliners chipped off chunks of wall to keep as souvenirs. Hundreds of pieces were donated to institutions around the world as symbols of peace and freedom.

Tiananmen Square

1989

The spring of 1989 witnessed the largest pro-democracy demonstration in the history of China's communist regime. The protests began among university students in Beijing, but soon spread across the nation. They ended on June 4, with a dramatic crackdown by soldiers from the People's Liberation Army.

04/15/1989

LEADING REFORMIST DIES When outspoken politician Hu Yaobang died, his supporters, mostly university students, began to gather in Tiananmen Square in Beijing. It was an opportunity not just to mourn but also to express dissatisfaction with the slow pace of reform. The protests spread nationwide.

04/26/1989

DENG DENOUNCES PROTEST Officials of the Beijing People's Government were outraged at the students' conduct. Deeply alarmed at the growing unrest, communist leader Deng Xiaoping ordered a crackdown on the demonstrators. Troops were brought into Beijing and ordered to suppress the protests.

05/13/1989

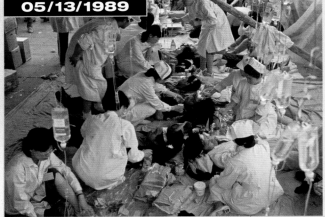

HUNGER STRIKE When their demands for reform were ignored, the protesters launched a hunger strike, which grew rapidly from 800 students to 3,000. Sympathetic citizens surged onto the streets and the movement gained increasing support from society, including Buddhist monks and important intellectuals. The Chinese Red Cross sent in a large team to provide medical assistance to the students.

05/15/1989

GORBACHEV VISITS CHINA It was a tense time. Soviet leader Mikhail Gorbachev was due to arrive for the first Sino-Soviet summit in 30 years, but the student movement threatened further unrest. The embarrassed government found itself constantly rearranging plans to avoid interruption by protesters and had to cancel a greeting ceremony in Tiananmen Square.

05/19/1989

ZHAO ZIYANG ATTEMPTS A COMPROMISE Party General Secretary Zhao Ziyang advocated negotiation with the students. A reformist, he attempted to seize the moment, and possibly power, by visiting the students and making an impassioned plea for compromise. It was his last public appearance. He was soon removed from office.

05/20/1989

06/05/1989

OPEN DEFIANCE In the midst of the violence, one man became an icon of peaceful resistance, blocking a column of tanks by standing in their path. The photograph became a defining image of the protests, but such acts were powerless to prevent the army's advance. Troops opened fire and cleared the Square.

> ❝ The **biggest display of defiance** in the 40-year history of **Communist China**.
>
> *WASHINGTON POST,* **JUNE 1989** ❞

GODDESS OF DEMOCRACY Students built a statue and dubbed it the "Goddess of Democracy" after the Statue of Liberty in the USA. It became a defining image of the protests.

04/18/1989

WAVE OF UNREST The demonstrations across the country called for greater freedom and democracy, and an end to corruption. Thousands of students traveled to Tiananmen Square despite being warned that they risked severe punishment.

MARTIAL LAW IMPOSED Deng decided that martial law was the only way to disperse the students. He sent troops into the city center, but citizens rushed from their homes to block their way. Many lay down on the street in front of the tanks, and thousands of protesters paraded through the city. The troops pulled back to the outskirts of Beijing on May 23.

06/04/1989

PROTESTERS AND POLICE CLASH In June the troops received orders to reclaim Tiananmen Square at any cost. Heavily armed tanks moved toward the center of the city from several directions, and soldiers opened fire on people who tried to prevent their advance. Roadblocks were set up in the surrounding suburbs and pitched street battles took place between civilians and the army. The conflict escalated, with many killed or wounded.

06/09/1989

PICKING UP THE PIECES The capital was in a state of shock at the scale of the violence. Hundreds had died and thousands were injured. The army claimed a great victory against the unarmed student protesters. Deng appeared in public and made a speech praising the heroic efforts of the military officers.

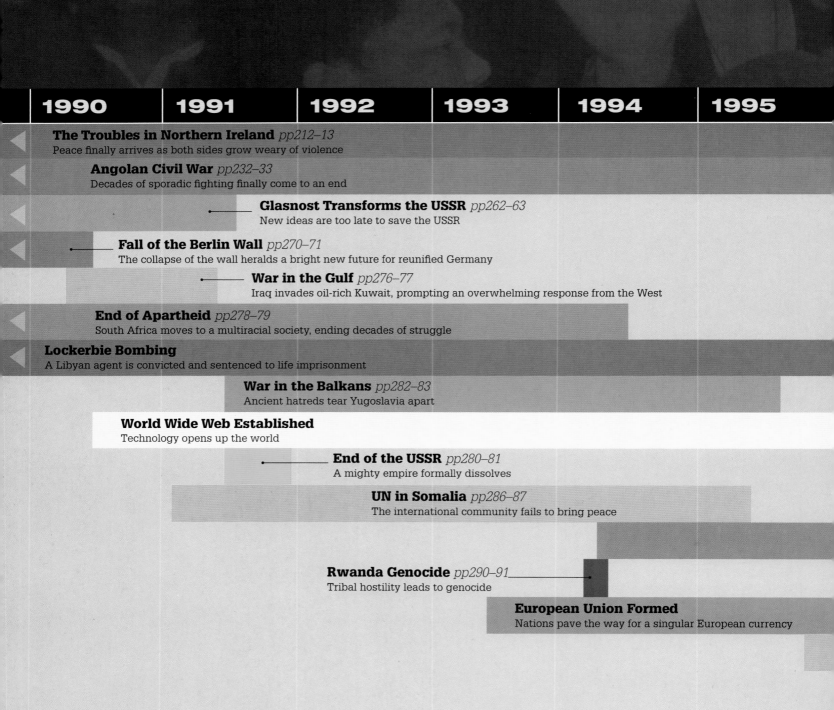

1990	**1991**	**1992**	**1993**	**1994**	**1995**

The Troubles in Northern Ireland *pp212–13*
Peace finally arrives as both sides grow weary of violence

Angolan Civil War *pp232–33*
Decades of sporadic fighting finally come to an end

Glasnost Transforms the USSR *pp262–63*
New ideas are too late to save the USSR

Fall of the Berlin Wall *pp270–71*
The collapse of the wall heralds a bright new future for reunified Germany

War in the Gulf *pp276–77*
Iraq invades oil-rich Kuwait, prompting an overwhelming response from the West

End of Apartheid *pp278–79*
South Africa moves to a multiracial society, ending decades of struggle

Lockerbie Bombing
A Libyan agent is convicted and sentenced to life imprisonment

War in the Balkans *pp282–83*
Ancient hatreds tear Yugoslavia apart

World Wide Web Established
Technology opens up the world

End of the USSR *pp280–81*
A mighty empire formally dissolves

UN in Somalia *pp286–87*
The international community fails to bring peace

Rwanda Genocide *pp290–91*
Tribal hostility leads to genocide

European Union Formed
Nations pave the way for a singular European currency

1990-

1996 1997 1998 1999 2000 2010

The Chechen Crisis *pp288–89*
Russia attempts to impose its will in Chechnya with bloody consequences

Clinton Impeached *pp294–95*
A US President is put on trial for only the second time in history

Kosovo War
NATO air strikes fail to avert a humanitarian crisis

9/11 and the War on Terror *pp298–99*
Attacks on the World Trade Center change the world

Global Economic Crisis *pp300–01*
The West faces up to its debts as a recession hits

Arab Spring *pp302–03*
Uprisings take place across the Arab world

War in the Gulf

1990–1991

Iraq's leader Saddam Hussein had barely emerged from a costly war with Iran before he threatened to invade Kuwait. It was an act of political desperation, and he gambled that the West would not intervene. His actions, however, unleashed a massive military response by the international community.

IRAQ AND KUWAIT

Kuwait, a small Gulf nation, had some of the world's richest oil reserves. However, positioned to the south of Iraq and east of Saudi Arabia, its location made it vulnerable to attack. There had been repeated spats with Iraq over oil production and the debt owed by Iraq for financial assistance given during its war with Iran in the 1980s.

08/18/1990

FOREIGN HOSTAGES
Saddam Hussein responded by capturing more than 800 foreign nationals and placing them in key locations in Kuwait, using them as human shields to deter a coalition attack. Five-year-old Stuart Lockwood was made to pose with Saddam during a televised propaganda stunt.

06/12/1990

FLEEING REFUGEES
As the tension mounted, Saddam released the captive foreign nationals but refused to withdraw his troops. Kuwaitis fled in the thousands across the desert to Jordan, in dusty cars and trucks stuffed with belongings. The refugees reported food shortages and brutal treatment by Iraqi soldiers.

01/18/1991

ISRAEL ATTACKED
Iraq launched a series of scud missile attacks on the cities of Haifa and Tel Aviv in Israel. By drawing Israel into the conflict, Saddam hoped to split the coalition and win the backing of Arab countries who would come to Iraq's aid. Israel, at the urging of the US, refrained from retaliating amid fears that the conflict would spread across the Middle East.

02/01/1991

IRAQIS TORCH OIL WELLS As Iraqi troops were pushed back to the borders of Kuwait, they set fire to more than 600 oil wells and released vast amounts of crude oil into the Persian Gulf. It was a grim reminder to the West of their reliance on oil from the Middle East.

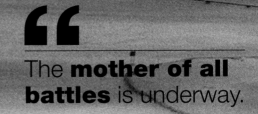

02/25/1991

HIGHWAY OF DEATH The Iraqi army was crushed, and its troops began a headlong retreat. The main highway out of Kuwait was packed with fleeing vehicles laden with plunder from Kuwait City. Thousands of Iraqi soldiers were killed and wounded as the road was attacked from the air.

> ## "The **mother of all battles** is underway.
>
> **SADDAM HUSSEIN, JANUARY 17, 1991**

08/02/1990

IRAQ INVADES KUWAIT
Saddam Hussein believed that Kuwait was flooding the market with low-priced oil, causing Iraq to lose profit on its own oil. After repeated threats, Iraq invaded its oil-rich neighbor with an army of 10,000 troops and hundreds of tanks. After two days of combat, most of Kuwait was overrun.

08/08/1990

OPERATION DESERT SHIELD The United Nations immediately demanded the withdrawal of Iraqi troops and issued a trade embargo. The USA formed a coalition of 34 nations, and a huge logistical operation began as allied forces massed in Saudi Arabia.

01/17/1991

FIRST RAID IN BAGHDAD The UN told Iraq it must voluntarily withdraw from Kuwait by January 15, 1991. When Iraq ignored the deadline, the coalition began Operation Desert Storm with a massive air offensive against Iraqi strategic positions. Baghdad's skyline lit up with anti-aircraft tracer fire during the attack, but the city suffered heavy damage.

02/13/1991

TRAGIC ACCIDENT When coalition forces targeted the Al-Firdos air-raid shelter in west Baghdad with two laser-guided precision bombs, they believed the bunker held military and political leaders. Instead, the missiles killed more than 300 civilians. The USA accused Iraq of using ordinary citizens as human shields. However, despite this incident, there were relatively few civilian casualties.

02/24/1991

GROUND OPERATION Coalition troops entered Kuwait in overwhelming force. They were issued gas masks, anticipating the use of chemical weapons by Iraq. The offensive was swift and well organized, and within 48 hours more than 25,000 Iraqi troops and 270 tanks had been captured.

02/27/1991

LIBERATION OF KUWAIT
On February 27, Saddam ordered his army to withdraw from Kuwait. The following day Kuwait City was liberated after 208 days of Iraqi occupation, and on file US President, George H.W. Bush, announced a ceasefire. Saddam's brutal aggression had been defeated by concerted global action.

End of Apartheid

1960–1994

The apartheid system governed every aspect of life in South Africa. Black and mixed-race people were denied even basic rights. Opposition to the regime, headed by black rights groups such as the African National Congress (ANC), became one of the defining campaigns in the struggle for racial equality.

03/01/1960

BRUTAL OPPRESSION Police opened fire on anti-apartheid protesters in Sharpeville. The ANC and other groups responded with violence and, in 1964, ANC leaders, including Nelson Mandela, were imprisoned.

10/09/1978

BOTHA REFORMS After the resignation of John Vorster, P.W. Botha became Prime Minister. He told white colleagues to adapt and proposed that "coloreds and Indians" should have representatives in parliament. The reforms infuriated right-wing extremists, and angered black South Africans, who were excluded.

07/01/1984

DESMOND TUTU WINS NOBEL PRIZE Tireless anti-apartheid campaigner Desmond Tutu was awarded the Nobel Peace Prize in 1984 for speaking out against the regime. It sent a powerful message to Botha's government that the international community opposed apartheid and supported the struggle against racism.

09/20/1989

DE KLERK BECOMES PRESIDENT When F. W. de Klerk became President of South Africa he called for a new, nonracist society, without apartheid divisions. He lifted the ban on protest marches, and ended many of the restrictions of apartheid, including segregated beaches, parks, and lavatories.

10/15/1989

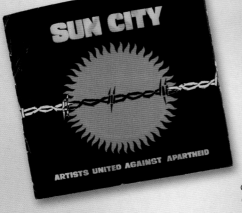

SUN CITY SINGLE This single by anti-apartheid campaigners supported a cultural boycott of South Africa.

02/04/1990

GLOBAL SUPPORT FOR MANDELA The anti-apartheid campaign spread around the world, with rallies supporting Mandela taking place from New York to Stockholm. South Africa had been subject to economic, cultural, and academic boycotts, and banned from participating in sporting events. Protesters greeted the reforms with joy.

05/04/1990

DE KLERK AND MANDELA MEET De Klerk and Mandela, now leader of the ANC, began negotiations to dismantle the apartheid regime. The talks took place against a background of political violence. On May 4, 1990, they agreed a plan to tackle violence and establish stability. Their famous handshake marked a new beginning for South African politics.

04/27/1994

FIRST MULTIRACIAL ELECTIONS On April 27, 1994, millions of South Africans, both black and white, waited patiently to vote in the first multiracial elections held in South Africa since apartheid.

06/16/1976

RIOTING IN SOWETO
On June 16, 1976, a march by 10,000 students, protesting against the use of Afrikaans as the main teaching language in schools, ended in bloodshed. Angry youths in Soweto threw stones and used cars as roadblocks, and police responded with heavy weaponry. It was the worst violence seen in the country for 16 years.

09/12/1977

STEPHEN BIKO KILLED The death of anti-apartheid activist Stephen Biko in police custody caused immediate controversy and international outrage. His funeral was attended by 15,000 mourners.

WALTER SISULU RELEASED
An even bolder move by de Klerk was the release of political prisoners, including African National Congress (ANC) leaders who had been imprisoned with Nelson Mandela in the Rivonia Trial of 1964. Walter Sisulu, former Secretary-General of the ANC, was greeted with jubilation at a rally to welcome him home.

02/02/1990

VIOLENCE IN PIETERMARITZBURG On February 2, 1990, de Klerk lifted the ban on the ANC and other political parties. Violence erupted in Pietermaritzburg as the Inkatha Freedom Party and ANC activists struggled over political power.

02/11/1990

MANDELA IS RELEASED
The release of leading ANC activist Nelson Mandela, after 27 years in captivity, marked the official end of apartheid. His walk to freedom was watched by millions around the world and celebrated by ecstatic crowds.

> During my lifetime I have **dedicated myself** to this **struggle** of the **African people**.
>
> **NELSON MANDELA, ON HIS RELEASE FROM PRISON, FEBRUARY 11, 1990**

05/10/1994

PRESIDENT MANDELA

Nelson Mandela became South Africa's first black president, ending more than 300 years of white rule. He urged a policy of truth and reconciliation to heal the old divisions and unite white and black South Africans.

End of the USSR

1991

The Soviet Union was on the brink of economic collapse. Its leader, Mikhail Gorbachev, fought to implement reform, but was resisted by both hard-line communists who wanted to preserve the old ways, and radical reformists calling for faster changes. The Union was dying a lingering death, but its dramatic end, in 1991, stunned the world.

MIKHAIL GORBACHEV
As leader of the Communist Party and the Soviet Union, Mikhail Gorbachev attempted to radically reform the USSR.

BORIS YELTSIN
Boris Yeltsin, President of Russia, was a rival and fierce critic of Gorbachev, saying his reforms did not go far enough.

08/19/1991

GATHERING MOMENTUM
Ordinary citizens, some still clutching their shopping, rushed to the Russian Parliament to protect the building from attack. Years of liberal reform had lessened the menace of the old regime and people felt more confident in protesting. TV crews broadcast the rebellion, encouraging others to join in.

08/19/1991

DEFINING MOMENT
Boris Yeltsin chose this moment to clamber on board a tank and deliver a rousing speech urging the troops not to fire on their own people. He denounced the coup, declaring it an act of terror. His speech was broadcast across the world, and came to symbolize popular resistance to a hardline communist elite determined to return Russia to the days of party dictatorship.

08/20/1991

PEOPLE BUILD BARRICADES An attack on the parliament building seemed imminent. Despite repeated warnings that more tanks were on their way, thousands of people worked through the night to build defenses, constructing barricades and forming human chains.

08/22/1991

08/24/1991

TRIUMPHANT Yeltsin knew he had to act swiftly. He united with the leaders of Belarus and Ukraine to declare the end of the USSR. By the end of December, 10 of the 15 member states had declared their independence, and Gorbachev had resigned. The Soviet Union, once a vast superpower, was no more.

08/19/1991

MILITARY MIGHT

Soviet citizens woke up to news reports that Gorbachev had been taken ill. In fact, he had been imprisoned by hardline communists attempting a military coup. Tanks rolled through the streets of Moscow and TV channels read out decrees from the coup leaders declaring a state of emergency. Their aim was to undo Gorbachev's democratic reforms.

> I decided, **whatever** order was given, I **wouldn't** shoot.

MAJOR SERGEY YEVDOKIMOV, TANK COMMANDER, AUGUST 19, 1991

08/20/1991

PROPAGANDA

The coup had stalled. Without the support of the military, the plotters could not take power. They also began to lose their control over the media. While their outlets claimed that Gorbachev was unwell and that the rebels represented the official government, the truth started to emerge.

THE COUP IS DEFEATED

Faced with massive popular resistance, and with the eyes of the world upon them, the hardliners backed down. Yeltsin, leader of the resistance, was the man of the moment. He now had the support he needed to push for an end to communist rule. Backed by jubilant crowds, he suspended the Communist Party in Russia.

08/23/1991

GORBACHEV HUMILIATED

Gorbachev had been politically destroyed by the revolt. When he returned to parliament in Moscow, Yeltsin insisted he read out the names of those who had plotted against him. The attempt by communist hard-liners to turn the clock back pushed popular opinion in favor of the breakup of the USSR.

THE NEW RUSSIA

The USSR broke up into 15 separate countries, which agreed to co-operate loosely as the Commonwealth of Independent States (CIS). They tried to coordinate policy on a range of economic issues, including trade and energy supplies, but the CIS failed to fulfill the hopes for greater post-Soviet collaboration.

LITHUANIA
ESTONIA
LATVIA
BELARUS
UKRAINE
MOLDOVA
Black Sea
GEORGIA
ARMENIA
AZERBAIJAN
TURKMENISTAN
Caspian Sea
Aral Sea
Kara Sea
RUSSIAN FEDERATION
KAZAKHSTAN
UZBEKISTAN
KYRGYZSTAN
TAJIKISTAN

KEY
☐ Russian Federation
☐ Former USSR

War in the Balkans

1991–1995

With the fall of communism, Yugoslavia began to fall apart. The old state was formed of an uneasy alliance of ethnic and religious groups, which now sought independence. The Serbs were the largest group, and their leader, Slobodan Milošević, wanted the country to remain unified at any cost. As his supporters cracked down on independence movements, the scene was set for bloody civil war.

SLOBODAN MILOŠEVIĆ

The Serbs had played a leading role in the running of Yugoslavia, and their president, Slobodan Milošević, sought to maintain their dominance as the old socialist republic fragmented.

04/06/1992

UNREST SPREADS
When Bosnia, a region with a significant Christian Serb minority, declared independence, Milošević's forces struck again. They began a horrific campaign of targeted violence against Croats and Muslims in the region, laying siege to the capital, Sarajevo. Local forces struggled to protect civilians.

08/14/1992

ETHNIC CLEANSING Milošević's troops attempted to wipe out those they considered non-Serbian. Men were imprisoned in camps, while women were routinely raped so that they would produce Serbian offspring. UN peacekeeping forces in Bosnia proved powerless to intervene.

04/18/1993

MILLIONS DISPLACED Radovan Karadžić, political leader of the Serbs in Bosnia, endorsed the expulsion of more than a million Croats and Muslims from Bosnia. The UN attempted to set up safe havens, but atrocities continued.

02/19/1994

CEASEFIRE IMPOSED
Demands for international intervention came to a head when the shelling of a marketplace in Sarajevo resulted in the deaths of 68 civilians. The USA issued an ultimatum through NATO insisting on the withdrawal of Serb forces. A ceasefire was declared, enforced by NATO tanks.

08/08/1995

CROATIAN SERBS FLEE
The Croatian army struck back against the Serbs, attacking the Serb-held city of Krajina in Croatia. More than 200,000 Croatian Serbs were forced to flee their homes in the worst refugee crisis of the war, and the Croatian army was accused of its own campaign of ethnic cleansing.

08/30/1995

NATO STRIKES In a dramatic bid to end the violence, NATO launched a series of airstrikes against the Serbian military in Bosnia. Although the attacks were controversial, they put Milošević under pressure to negotiate.

12/14/1995

PEACE IS AGREED
Milošević joined Croatian and Bosnian representatives in Paris to sign the Dayton Agreement, bringing the conflict to an end. Despite the emphasis on peace, there was growing evidence of a campaign of rape and murder of civilians by Serb forces. Several Serbian leaders, including Milošević, would be charged with crimes against humanity.

08/25/1991

SIEGE OF VUKOVAR When Croatia proclaimed independence in July 1991, the largely Serbian Yugoslav Army, assisted by Serbian paramilitary groups, overwhelmed the city of Vukovar in eastern Croatia. An estimated 1,700 Croats were massacred.

07/01/1995

MASSACRE IN SREBRENICA
It was the calm before the storm. In 1995 Bosnian Serbs unleashed a hurricane of violence against Muslims in Srebrenica in eastern Bosnia. In the worst mass murder in Europe since World War II, 8,000 Bosnian Muslims were separated from their families and slaughtered.

YUGOSLAV-SERB ARMY CAP
The red star on this military cap of the federal Yugoslav army was once a symbol of resistance against fascism.

> Our time... has shown us that man's capacity for **evil** knows **no limits**.
>
> **UN GENERAL SECRETARY KOFI ANNAN, COMMENTING ON ETHNIC CLEANSING, 1997**

09/18/1997

MASS GRAVES
The extent of Serbian brutality began to become apparent with the grim discovery of mass graves outside Srebrenica. Karadžić, Milošević, and several prominent Serbian military commanders fled into hiding as proof of their crimes emerged. The hunt to bring them to justice would go on for years.

New countries

NEW STATES As the conflict subsided, the former Yugoslavia had split into six separate states. Further violence would follow: almost 1 million people were displaced, and NATO launched further airstrikes against the Serbian military, as the region of Kosovo sought autonomy in 1998–1999. The quest for peace in the region would take years.

1995

Aftermath of a Massacre

The war in Bosnia saw some of the worst atrocities in Europe since the end of World War II. Serbian military and paramilitary groups, determined to rid the country of Muslims and Croats, herded captives into concentration camps. Men were starved to death, or simply shot. Women were raped repeatedly, in an attempt to ensure that they produced Serbian offspring. In the town of Srebrenica, more than 8,000 people, mostly men and boys, were murdered and their bodies buried in mass graves. This picture shows some of the 20,000 survivors forced to march through hostile territory in a desperate search for safety. The atrocity was all the more shocking because the United Nations had declared Srebrenica a safe zone: 400 UN soldiers failed to prevent the Serbs from occupying the town. It was a shameful moment for the UN, and paved the way for more aggressive military interventions by the international community in following years.

UN in Somalia

1991–1995

Civil war had devastated Somalia, reducing it to a country run by heavily armed bandits. As drought and famine added to the misery, the United Nations intervened to help end the crisis. Their presence, however, escalated into one of the most ill-considered humanitarian missions ever carried out.

01/10/1991

HUMANITARIAN CRISIS
When Somalia's leader Siad Barre was overthrown in January 1991, the country imploded. Bitter clan rivalries led to civil war and fighting spread across the country, destroying agriculture and inflicting famine. An estimated 300,000 people died of starvation that year.

12/04/1992

UN TROOPS IN SOMALIA UN efforts failed to halt the violence and displacement of the Somali people. American President George H. W. Bush proposed that US troops lead an international UN force to end the crisis. Troops from 14 UN countries landed in Somalia in December 1992.

12/12/1992

FOOD DISTRIBUTION
US forces, leading a United Task Force, faced a tense and rapidly changing situation. Their principal aim was to secure the distribution of food and protect supplies from bandits. Within months food supplies flowed, gangs were suppressed, and seeds and livestock were distributed.

06/17/1993

AIDID SWAYS ANTI-UN SENTIMENTS
Capturing Aidid became a priority, but he was elusive. UN attacks on his strongholds only bolstered his position. He remained defiant, speaking out against UN intervention and presenting himself as a victim of aggression. In the USA he was regarded as an outlaw, but in Somalia he was becoming a folk hero.

08/08/1993

TASK FORCE DEPLOYED The killing of US soldiers during fighting in Somalia convinced Clinton that the UN needed more firepower. He deployed Task Force Ranger, an assault force which included a helicopter unit, to the capital Mogadishu. Their mission was to arrest Aidid.

05/05/1995

UN PULLS OUT President Clinton decided to withdraw US troops from Somalia, although his diplomats remained. The search for Aidid was abandoned; instead, the UN sought negotiations with the warlord. They admitted defeat in May 1995, and the civil war continued. The UN mission was regarded as a tragic failure.

> **"** The **UN** should learn to **say no**. **"**
>
> **US PRESIDENT BILL CLINTON QUOTED IN *THE ECONOMIST*, JUNE 2003**

12/03/1992

UN RELIEF EFFORT
A ceasefire agreement in 1992 allowed a UN monitoring mission into Somalia to oversee the provision of humanitarian aid. However, the UN convoys were hijacked, food was looted and exchanged for weapons, and aid workers were attacked. About 3 million people faced starvation, while 2 million fled.

UN BERET The bright blue beret is the distinctive symbol of UN peacekeeping forces, marking them out as protectors and mediators rather than combatants. In Somalia, however, they became increasingly embroiled in the local conflict.

05/04/1993

US TROOPS LEAVE MOGADISHU Newly elected US President Bill Clinton wanted to scale down the American military presence in Somalia. As American troops began to pull out, the UN opted for an expanded mission that aimed to rebuild Somalia, restore law and order, and install a new government.

06/10/1993

UN FORCES LAUNCH OFFENSIVE With the US presence vastly reduced, fighting resumed between Somali warlords. On June 5, 1993, 24 UN soldiers from Pakistan were killed while inspecting a Somali weapons storage site. Somalia's chief warlord, Farrah Aidid, was believed to be responsible and UN troops attacked targets associated with him.

10/03/1993

BATTLE OF MOGADISHU Task Force Ranger's attack on the Olympic Hotel in Mogadishu, in search of Aidid, resulted in a drawn-out battle in which two Black Hawk helicopters were shot down. Bodies of US soldiers killed in the battle were dragged through the streets, causing shock and anger in the USA.

The Chechen Crisis

1991–2006

The region of Chechnya had been under Russian control for more than 200 years. With the collapse of the Soviet Union, the Chechen people sought to realize a long-held dream of independence. But the Russians had other ideas, and their determination to maintain control in the province at any cost sparked a bitter campaign of war and terrorism.

DISPUTED REGION 1,100 miles (1,700 km) south of Moscow, Chechnya had long resisted Russian rule. In the chaos surrounding the break up of the USSR in 1991, a Soviet officer, Dzhokhar Dudayev, declared the region independent.

06/19/1995

CHECHENS TAKE HOSTAGES Chechen rebels led by Shamil Basayev entered the Russian region of Stavropol Kray and took 1,500 people hostage in a hospital in Budennovsk. More than a hundred were killed in a botched assault by Russian troops trying to free the hostages, but the Chechens escaped.

07/23/1997

MASKHADOV'S REIGN Russian forces eventually withdrew in 1997. Their campaign had been brutal, and an estimated 60,000–100,000 people were thought to have died in the war. Aslan Maskhadov, a Chechen military leader, was elected as the President, but Chechnya was in chaos and he struggled to control deep unrest.

02/13/2000

RUSSIANS DESTROY GROZNY Russian bombers launched a savage attack on Grozny, laying siege to the city in what they described as a counter-terrorism operation. Much of the city was razed, leaving thousands homeless.

10/23/2002

MOSCOW THEATER SIEGE Violence continued unabated. Chechen separatists took 700 people captive at a Moscow theater. The rebels, strapped with explosives, demanded that Russian troops withdraw from Chechnya. When Russian forces stormed the venue, 129 hostages and 41 Chechen guerrillas were killed.

11/27/2005

12/07/1994

RUSSIAN TROOPS ENTER CHECHNYA In 1994 civil war broke out between Dudayev's supporters and disaffected Chechens, who were backed by Russia. Boris Yeltsin, the Russian President, called a state of emergency, and ordered the military to prepare for action. In December Russian troops entered Chechnya, under orders to end its bid for independence and arrest Dudayev.

12/10/1994

CHECHENS RESIST Russian troops faced fierce resistance as they made their way through Chechnya to Grozny, the capital city. They had underestimated the guerrilla tactics used by Chechen rebels. It took them almost three weeks to reach the city. Grozny was destroyed and casualties on both sides were high. The rebels were forced to withdraw, and Russia installed a government of "national revival."

05/01/1998

MARTIAL LAW IMPOSED Chechnya once again descended into lawlessness when violence broke out between pro- and anti-Maskhadov factions. On May 1, 1998 Russia's presidential representative in Chechnya, Valentin Vlasov, was kidnapped, spurring Maskhadov to impose martial law.

09/09/1999

BOMBING IN RUSSIA In September 1999 more than 200 people were killed in bomb attacks in several Russian cities. Russia blamed the Chechens, but the Chechens believed it was a pretext for starting another war. Russia declared that the Chechen rebels were terrorists and threatened to eliminate them.

09/01/2004

BESLAN SIEGE Worse was to come, as the Chechen separatists showed an alarming ruthlessness and willingness to die for their cause. In 2004 they attacked a school in the city of Beslan in the Russian province of North Ossetia-Alania, taking more than 1,200 hostages—many of them children. More than 300 died in a ferocious firefight as Russian troops attempted a rescue. Shocking images of dead and wounded children appeared in the media.

RUSSIA-BACKED ELECTIONS Amid tight security, Chechnya held parliamentary elections in a bid to show that it was becoming more stable. Separatists were not allowed to take part. United Russia, the party favored by Russia, took the majority vote and Ramzan Kadyrov became Prime Minister. Russian President Vladimir Putin praised the result and vowed to rebuild Grozny.

10/07/2006

CRITICS SILENCED Anna Politkovskaya, a fierce critic of the Kremlin and one of the few Russian journalists who dared to write about the war in Chechnya, was shot dead. She had campaigned against ongoing war crimes and human rights abuses by Russian forces in the province. Her death symbolized Russia's tightening of press freedom, and the continuing struggle for an end to violence in Chechnya.

> **No one** has a **moral right** to tell us to talk to **child killers**.
>
> RUSSIAN PRESIDENT VLADIMIR PUTIN, ON CALLS TO NEGOTIATE WITH CHECHEN SEPARATISTS, SEPTEMBER 2004

Rwanda Genocide

1994

Rwanda, a tiny country in Central Africa, had witnessed decades of unrest between the majority Hutu and the minority Tutsi tribes. With the economy in tatters, Rwandan President Juvénal Habyarimana, a Hutu, lost popularity, and opposition to the regime escalated. His murder in 1994 sparked off an orgy of ethnic cleansing that descended into genocide.

04/06/1994

THE PRESIDENT IS SHOT DOWN A plane carrying President Habyarimana was shot down over Kigali, Rwanda's capital, killing all 10 passengers. No group claimed responsibility. Hutus blamed the Tutsi rebels of the Rwandan Patriotic Front (RPF), claiming they had plotted to overthrow the President.

04/07/1994

MILITIA MOBILIZED The carnage intensified after the Rwandan Army promoted an unofficial Hutu youth militia called the *Interahamwe*, meaning "those who act together." Members of the militia roamed the countryside, killing as they went.

04/09/1994

FOREIGNERS EVACUATED The situation deteriorated as the RPF mobilized a response to the Hutu aggression, prompting an evacuation of foreign nationals. UN personnel helped Americans and Europeans leave Rwanda.

04/21/1994

UN PULLS OUT Following the murder of 10 Belgian soldiers, the UN cut its force in Rwanda from 2,500 to 500. Despite reports from the International Red Cross that more than 100,000 Rwandans had been killed, the remaining peacekeeping troops were not authorized to intervene, and watched helplessly.

04/07/1994

VICTORY FOR RPF The RPF, led by rebel leader Paul Kagame, was a well-organized and disciplined guerrilla group. It quickly overran government forces in Kigali and the southern town of Butare. The RPF leadership announced its intention of forming a new government, forcing more Hutus to flee.

07/06/1994

CHILD SOLDIERS Children, some as young as nine, were used as soldiers and became a common feature of the war. They were well trained and indoctrinated at special camps. It is thought that as many as 5,000 children were involved in the fighting, many of them recruited by the RPF.

07/21/1994

PEACE COMES TOO LATE With the RPF in control of most of the country, a ceasefire was agreed. The civil war was declared over on July 18, and a government of national unity was formed. For thousands who had fled the country, the news of peace came too late. Dysentery and cholera struck the refugee camps. An estimated 12,000 died and were buried in mass graves.

04/07/1994

MASSACRE OF TUTSIS
The killings began the day after the President's death. Government-backed Hutu death squads began murdering Tutsis. Hutus who had proposed negotiating with the Tutsis were also killed. The violence soon spread through the country, with Hutus intent on wiping out the Tutsi community. The machete was the weapon of choice, inflicting horrific wounds on the victims.

04/30/1994

THOUSANDS DISPLACED More tragedy followed as some 2 million refugees fled to Zaire, Tanzania, Burundi, and Uganda. Many were Hutus rather than Tutsis, trying to escape from the RPF, which made rapid progress against the Rwandan army. Thousands faced humanitarian crisis in vast refugee camps.

05/11/1994

AID TO CAMPS With refugees pouring into relief centers in Goma, Zaire, resources in the city were soon overwhelmed. The suffering was unrelenting, as poor sanitation spread disease. The Red Cross and other aid agencies worked tirelessly to provide food and medical assistance, but with as many as 300,000 people in a single camp, the situation rapidly deteriorated.

> **Rwanda** is clinically **dead** as a nation.

WOLE SOYINKA, NIGERIAN NOBEL LAUREATE, QUOTED IN *LOS ANGELES TIMES*, MAY 11, 1994

01/12/1998

HORRORS OF THE WAR
An estimated 800,000—more than a tenth of Rwanda's population—were killed in the 100-day carnage. In the aftermath of the conflict, memorial sites sprang up at the scenes of the worst atrocities. Skulls of victims lie on shelves at a genocide memorial in Ntarama Church, near Kigali, where 5,000 lost their lives in a horrific attack.

A CENTURY OF

Technology

New advances in technology throughout the 20th century brought seismic change to our social, political, and economic lives. In fact, it is estimated that more inventions have been devised since 1900 than in the rest of human history.

A whirlwind of new advances brought humanity from a largely rural existence to a "global village" of mass connectivity. As the 21st century took shape, there seemed no limit to what technology could achieve—for those who could afford it.

1900–1920 When electricity became widely available for domestic use, it brought modern technology right into the home. Electric heat and light replaced gas and candles, and devices such the vacuum cleaner, designed in 1902, transformed housework. In the kitchen, the problem of preserving food was solved by the invention of the refrigerator. Housework would never be the same again. The first plastics also began to appear in home appliances.

$1,565

The cost of a basic unit of the first IBM PC, which included the main system, a keyboard, and a color screen.

1920–1950 With the invention of the thermionic valve, or vacuum tube, radar, radio, and television were born, ushering in the broadcast age. News traveled around the world in hours rather than weeks. Music suddenly became available anywhere at any time. Television created whole new genres of entertainment and spread them to millions of viewers.

WASHING MACHINE
This device, from 1929, uses an electric motor to churn clothes in a drum. Machines of this kind greatly reduced the drudgery of housework.

Valve technology also powered the first electronic computers, such as Pennsylvania University's ENIAC (Electronic Numerical Integrator and Computer), which was built in 1945. However, it would be some years before computers made their mark.

FIRST COMPUTER Numerous technicians worked on the ENIAC, the world's first fully electronic computer. Its 18,000 tubes and cabinets occupied an entire room.

1950–1980 New technology developed during World War II drove the advances of the 1950s and 1960s. The power of the

---

1900s

VACUUM CLEANER
Early self-contained electric vacuum cleaners promised to make cleaning much easier, but their weight and bulk limited their use.

1910s

INCANDESCENT LIGHT
Although lightbulbs had been available since the late 19th century, they only entered widespread use in the 1910s as new models became more reliable and longer lasting.

1920s

RADIO Kick-starting the mass-media age, radio brought music, news, and chat into the lives of ordinary citizens. The first commercial public radio station was established in the USA in the 1920s.

1930s

TELEVISION The first television images in the 1920s were fuzzy and dim. However, by the 1930s, the introduction of cathode ray tubes allowed for much clearer broadcasts.

atomic bomb was harnessed to build the first nuclear power plant in 1951, at Arco, Idaho, in the USA. The rocket weapons used by Germany during the war became the basis of the Space Age, and in 1957 the Soviet's Sputnik I became the first artificial satellite. Computers finally came into their own as valves were superseded by transistors—tiny sandwiches of silicon crystal that could be used to build microchips. At a stroke, technology shifted scale from mass to micro, bringing incredible advances from color television to credit cards, robots, and instamatic cameras.

DESERT WINDMILLS The first wind farm was built in the USA in the 1980s, part of the search for new sources of energy less damaging to the environment.

PERSONAL COMPUTERS In the 1980s and 1990s computers became more accessible, moving into schools and homes. Pioneers such as Bill Gates became some of the world's richest people.

1980–1990 Microchip technology made computers smaller, cheaper, and more powerful than ever. In 1981 IBM presented the first personal computer (PC), and Apple launched the Macintosh in 1984. The rapid advance of computers transformed almost every aspect of human life, from work and learning to shopping and socializing. Satellites provided communication links that could span the Earth, and played a pivotal role in the development of global telecommunications. Pictures from space also offered new insight into humanity's impact on our planet, prompting campaigns to prevent damage to the ozone layer and slow the cutting of rain forests.

1990–present In 1991, the launch of the World Wide Web, a global system of interconnected computer networks, brought the

digital revolution. It became possible to share ideas and information around the world at the touch of a button. Mobile phones kept the world connected even on the move, and the invention of smart phones made the internet a mobile resource. With new advances arriving every year, digital technology seemed set to usher the world into an exciting future, promising everyone an equal voice.

> **"**
> … sufficiently **advanced technology** is **indistinguishable** from **magic**.
> SCIENCE-FICTION AUTHOR ARTHUR C. CLARKE, *PROFILES OF THE FUTURE*, 1961 **"**

1950s

TAPE RECORDER Using plastic-covered magnetic tape, the reel-to-reel tape recorder was widely available by the 1950s, leading to audio cassettes and portable cassette players.

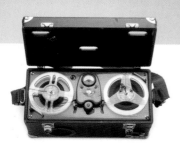

1960s

POLAROID CAMERA By the mid 1960s Polaroid's instant camera was cheap and accessible. The new color film inside the camera could be developed in under a minute.

1980s

CORDLESS PHONE Greater frequency range meant that cordless phones became a must-have accessory. However, interference and static in the early days required users to stand still while talking.

2000s

IPAD Tablet computers with touch screens, such as Apple's iPad, symbolize a lifestyle based on portable, connected technology.

Clinton Impeached

1995–1999

US President Bill Clinton had been dogged for years by rumors of sexual indiscretion. When reports emerged of an affair with a White House intern—and that he had lied about the affair under oath—he faced political ruin. Pursued by prosecutor Kenneth Starr, he became only the second US President to be impeached, or threatened with legal removal from office, by the House of Representatives.

11/15/1995

SECRET TAPES Monica Lewinsky, a White House intern, began an affair with President Clinton in 1995. Over the next 18 months, Lewinsky shared details of the affair with a coworker, Linda Tripp, who secretly recorded the conversations. Clinton was at the time being sued for sexual harassment by a former employee in Arkansas, Paula Jones.

01/22/1998

KENNETH STARR TAKES UP THE CASE

During the Paula Jones sexual harassment case, Lewinsky and Clinton denied, under oath, having a relationship. Independent Counsel Kenneth Starr, who had been sent the taped conversations between Lewinsky and Tripp, wanted to accuse the President of perjury.

01/26/1998

AFFAIR DENIED

When the media finally reported the alleged Clinton–Lewinsky sexual liaison, it made front-page news across America. With his wife Hillary by his side, Clinton called a press conference where he angrily denied having an affair. His words would come to haunt him over the following months.

EVIDENCE IN A DRESS

The FBI tested a dress belonging to Lewinsky, allegedly stained with semen during a sexual encounter with the President. DNA testing revealed that the source of the stain was, indeed, Clinton. The news caused a sensation.

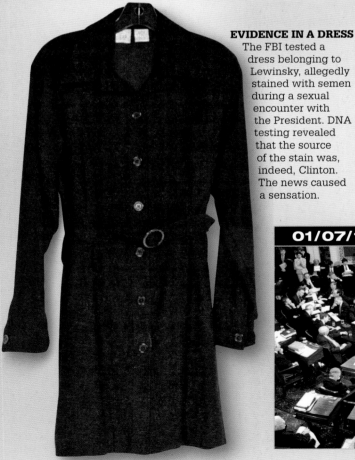

03/12/1998

TRIPP GIVES TAPES TO GRAND JURY The Grand Jury decided they had enough evidence to investigate Clinton for lying under oath about his affair with Lewinsky. One of the key witnesses was Linda Tripp. During the trial, she was labeled the most hated woman in America for betraying her friend's trust and confidence.

08/17/1998

CLINTON TESTIFIES In August Clinton testified before the Grand Jury, where he disclosed that he did indeed have "inappropriate intimate contact" with Monica Lewinsky, but he was adamant that he had not perjured himself during the Paula Jones case. He lashed out at Starr and insisted that he was entitled to a private life.

01/07/1999

IMPEACHMENT TRIAL BEGINS In the course of the hearings, 13 Republican prosecutors presented their case to oust Clinton from office. The Democrats accused them of making it a political trial. In response, Republicans focused on arguments to justify their pursuit of the President and denied that they were engaged in a political vendetta. Clinton did not attend the trial.

10/23/1996

AFFIR COMES TO LIGHT When photographers caught Lewinsky and Clinton hugging each other at a fundraiser, it seemed to strengthen the rumor of an affair between the two. However, the media decided not to publish the story until the evidence was confirmed.

09/09/1998

STARR'S REPORT MADE PUBLIC When Starr released his report on the case, it contained 11 possible grounds for impeachment—a process where public officials could be removed from office for misconduct. Congress voted to make the report public. It was published in full by the press and posted on the internet, where millions read the explicit details.

12/19/1998

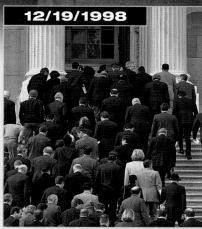

CLINTON IMPEACHED Democrats staged a walkout to protest the impeachment, but they failed to stop proceedings. The impeachment enquiry continued, focusing on two key charges: lying under oath and attempting to obstruct justice by persuading others to lie. Clinton went on trial in the Senate.

02/01/1999

LEWINSKY BEFORE THE SENATE Despite objections from Democrats, the prosecutors called Lewinsky and questioned her for two hours during a video-taped deposition.

02/12/1999

CLINTON ACQUITTED The Senate needed a two-thirds majority of votes to convict the President, but they failed to win even a bare majority. Rejecting the charge of perjury, 45 Democrats and 10 Republicans voted "not guilty." On the charge of obstruction of justice, the Senate was split fifty-fifty. Clinton was acquitted.

> **"** I **did not have** sexual relations with **that woman**... These allegations **are false**. **"**
>
> **US PRESIDENT BILL CLINTON, JANUARY 26, 1998**

1999

Party of the Millennium

Spectacular fireworks heralded the dawn of a new millennium as more than 20 tons of explosives were blasted into the night sky above the Sydney Harbor Bridge and Opera House at midnight on January 1, 2000. Celebrations took place all over the world. Parties ranged from the simple blowing of conch shells and the ringing of church bells to vast beach parties and public gatherings. Fears of a technological meltdown known as the "Millennium Bug"—which some had suggested would cause computers to fail and jets to drop out of the sky as the date clicked over to the year 2000—proved to be exaggerated. World leaders spoke of facing the future with confidence, optimism, and a spirit of international collaboration. In the new millennium global challenges, such as the threat of terrorism and environmental disaster, would be met with global cooperation.

9/11 and the War on Terror

2001–2011

In 2001, terrorist attacks on the United States of America by Islamic fundamentalists stunned the entire world. The USA and its allies invaded Afghanistan in an attempt to bring the perpetrators to justice. Further attacks followed, as the War on Terror spread to become a global conflict.

OSAMA BIN LADEN

The leader of al-Qaeda, a militant Islamic organization, Osama Bin Laden was the mastermind behind many terrorist attacks.

09/20/2001

BUSH DECLARES WAR ON TERROR The world was in shock. President George W. Bush promised retaliation. Intelligence services had linked the atrocities with al-Qaeda, and Bush told the US to prepare for war. He was offered the full support of British Prime Minister Tony Blair and the North Atlantic Treaty Organization (NATO).

12/10/2001

ATTACKING AFGHANISTAN
The US launched an offensive in Afghanistan, the training ground for al-Qaeda. The Taliban, a powerful Islamic militant regime, refused to hand over Bin Laden. American warplanes bombed Taliban targets and bases reportedly belonging to the al-Qaeda network.

01/11/2002

GUANTANAMO BAY OPENS The US imprisoned around 600 men and took them to a camp at a US naval base in Guantanamo Bay, Cuba. Controversially held without trial, they were interrogated about their suspected involvement in terrorist networks.

10/13/2002

BALI BOMBINGS The terrorist attacks continued. Two bombs exploded in a busy tourist district on the Indonesian island of Bali, killing 202 people. A group linked to al-Qaeda claimed responsibility.

03/01/2003

9/11 MASTERMIND CAPTURED Khalid Sheikh Mohammed, captured by Pakistani security officials working with the CIA, was thought to be one of al-Qaeda's most senior leaders, and the man behind 9/11. His arrest was regarded as the most significant since the beginning of the War on Terror.

03/11/2004

MADRID TRAIN BOMBINGS Bombs exploded on four trains in Madrid, killing 191 people and injuring nearly 2,000 more. It soon became clear that an al-Qaeda-influenced cell was to blame. Those terrorists who were captured received symbolic jail sentences of more than 39,000 years.

09/11/2001

9/11 ATTACKS On September 11, 2001 Islamic extremists launched a series of devastating terrorist attacks against American targets. Two airliners hit the World Trade Center in New York City, another struck the Pentagon in Washington, DC, and a fourth crashed in Pennsylvania. Almost 3,000 people were killed.

9/11 FIREMAN'S HELMET
343 fire fighters and paramedics lost their lives in the attack on the World Trade Center in New York. The site became known as Ground Zero.

04/09/2003

INVASION OF IRAQ
The US Congress voted to authorize President Bush to use force against Iraq and its President, Saddam Hussein, arguing Iraq had weapons of mass destruction that posed a threat to global security. The US-led invasion crushed the Iraqi army. Saddam was captured and killed, but bloody civil war followed in Iraq.

> **"**
> If killing those who **kill our sons** is terrorism, then let history be witness that **we are terrorists**.
>
> OSAMA BIN LADEN,
> OCTOBER 2001
> **"**

07/07/2005

ATTACKS IN LONDON
Less than four years after 9/11, Islamic extremists attacked targets in central London. Suicide bombers detonated bombs on three underground trains and a double-decker bus in retaliation for Britain's involvement in Iraq and Afghanistan. 56 people were killed and more than 700 wounded.

05/01/2011

BIN LADEN KILLED US President Obama ordered an attack on a compound in Abbottabad, Pakistan. As the President and his team waited, news came in that Bin Laden was dead. The first phase of the War on Terror was over, but al-Qaeda supporters remain active.

Global Economic Crisis

2007–

The the new millennium brought ominous signs of worldwide recession. Unconventional mortgage products and a steep rise in consumer credit had increased debt around the world. When bad news from a French investment bank, BNP Paribas, triggered a sharp rise in the cost of credit, the financial world began to realize how serious the situation was.

02/08/2007

HOUSE CRISIS Banks had for year offered mortgages to "sub-prime" customers who could not afford to repay them. When the bubble burs the US housing market crashed.

09/04/2007

RUN ON THE BANK The crisis began to spread. British bank Northern Rock was granted emergency financial support from the Bank of England, but panic ensued among borrowers. Depositors lined to withdraw money in a run on the bank that only ended when the government guaranteed that savings were safe.

09/07/2008

US GOVERNMENT BAILOUT In a bleak year for stock market investors, several "Black Monday" events saw global bank shares plummet dramatically. The giant US mortgage lenders Fannie Mae and Freddie Mac were bailed out by the government on the advice of the US Treasury Secretary Hank Paulson.

09/15/2008

LEHMAN BROTHERS FAILS Staggered by the mortgage crisis and by gross overvaluation of its assets, gigantic Wall Street bank Lehman Brothers went bankrupt. Its collapse stunned the world, prompting Western governments to inject billions into their own banks in an attempt to stop the crisis from spreading.

11/14/2008

G-20 GROUP SUMMIT The leaders of the G-20 group of the world's major economies met for the first time in the USA to head off a global financial meltdown. Hosted by President George W. Bush, they presented a united front in finding a solution that would calm the jittery markets and boost business confidence.

01/16/2009

RIOTS IN LITHUANIA The crisis spilled into the economies of central and eastern Europe. In Lithuania, the economy sank into a deep recession, sparking anger among its citizens. In early 2009, about 7,000 protesters gathered in front of Lithuania's Parliament, in Vilnius, and violent clashes with police ensued.

01/28/2009

CONTROVERSIAL BAILOUT The German Chancellor, Angela Merkel, initiated a $50-billion economic rescue package for financial institutions in Europe, in the hope of jump-starting economic growth. The move angered many who felt the money would have been better used for education and childcare.

08/09/2007

CREDIT MARKETS FREEZE

The crisis deepened when French bank BNP Paribas stopped investors taking money out of two of its funds, a sign that banks were refusing to deal with one another. Reality dawned that bankers had gambled on trillions of dollars worth of risky investments that had substantially dropped in value. Instead of lending cash, banks started to hoard.

EURO CRISIS

The Euro came under severe threat as the weaker economies in the European monetary union struggled to overcome the debt crisis.

> ## The **economic times**… are arguably the **worst**… in 60 years.
>
> **ALISTAIR DARLING, UK CHANCELLOR OF THE EXCHEQUER, AUGUST 30, 2008**

11/28/2008

ICELAND IN TURMOIL

The G-20 leaders were unable to stop the rot. Three major banks collapsed in Iceland, sinking the country into severe recession. The government resigned and crowds protested in front of the Parliament in Reykjavik. The crisis had begun to bring down not just banks, but whole countries.

05/05/2010

RIOTING SPREADS

Unemployment soared in countries across the Western world. As governments struggled with debt, protesters marched against cuts to public services. One of the worst affected countries was Greece, where debt had left the economy in ruins. Three people were killed during rioting in Athens.

07/21/2011

EURO DEBT CRISIS Greece, Portugal, Spain, Ireland, and Italy came under pressure to lower enormous sovereign debts and cut budget deficits. After weeks of negotiations, Greece was offered a bailout by both its European partners and the International Monetary Fund (IMF) to help it avoid a default. Amid concerns about the survival of the Euro, a rescue plan was devised as Ireland and Portugal also sought a bailout. Hundreds of billions were given out in a series of deals, but the Eurozone remained fragile.

Arab Spring

2011–

A few months at the beginning of 2011 transformed the face of North Africa and the Middle East. An extraordinary series of uprisings spread from country to country, as popular resistance overturned a series of decades-old authoritarian regimes.

THE COUNTRIES OF THE ARAB SPRING The protests began in Tunisia and quickly spread throughout the Middle East and North Africa, affecting 17 countries.

01/28/2011

ACTIVISM IN EGYPT In Egypt, thousands of protesters took to the streets despite the use of lethal violence by government forces. After 18 days of protests, President Hosni Mubarak was forced to resign, and was arrested for ordering the killing of demonstrators.

02/14/2011

PROTESTS IN BAHRAIN Anti-government protesters in Bahrain attempted their own rebellion, but were suppressed with brutal force by the police and army.

02/15/2011

CIVIL WAR IN LIBYA Libyan dictator Colonel Muammar Gaddafi attempted to repress dissidents with a similar program of violence, sparking a civil war. His opponents, the National Transitional Council, declared themselves the legal government of Libya and requested international aid in overthrowing Gaddafi.

10/20/2011

LIBERATION IN LIBYA As civilian casualties mounted in Libya, the UN authorized military action to protect noncombatants from attack by Gaddafi's army. The National Transitional Council took control of major cities, and Gaddafi was captured and killed in his home town of Sirte. Thousands of Libyans waving the new flag of Libya filled Tripoli's Martyrs' Square to celebrate the liberation of the nation.

01/05/2011

TUNISIAN CLASHES
Mohamed Bouazizi, a Tunisian street vendor, set himself on fire in protest against the brutality of the country's police. His story spread, and as he lay dying in a hospital, he was visited by President Zine el Abidine. Protesters throughout Tunisia demanded democracy, clashing violently with police. On January 14, el Abidine and his family fled the country. The Arab Spring had begun.

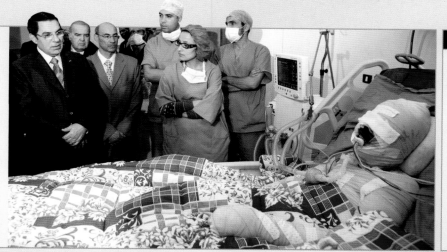

01/16/2011

RIOTING IN ALGERIA
Civil disorder spread from Tunisia to Algeria, where people rioted over a lack of jobs and high food prices. In the capital, Algiers, thousands of citizens defied government warnings not to rally, and called for democratic reforms and the removal of President Abdelaziz Bouteflika. Bank employees and hospital staff led strikes, demanding better pay and benefits.

02/18/2011

OTHER UPRISINGS
Further uprisings took place in Yemen, Jordan, Morocco, Lebanon, Oman and Saudi Arabia, but were met with brutal violence by state security forces. Some regimes were forced to implement modest constitutional reforms, and the Yemeni government of Ali Saleh collapsed in 2012.

03/16/2011

SYRIANS RISE UP
Some of the worst violence against civilians was seen in Syria. President Bashar Assad promised reform, but failed to deliver. As protests escalated, the Syrian army began a crackdown, killing thousands of civilians by shelling rebel towns and cities. Protests nevertheless continued.

10/23/2011

TUNISIANS GO TO THE POLLS Following the departure of el Abidine, Tunisia held its first democratic elections. The winners were Ennahda, a moderate Islamic party, who vowed to prove that Islam and democracy were compatible, promising to be a model for a new Arab world.

01/05/2012

UNCERTAIN FUTURE A year after the first protests, the outcome remained unclear. Governments in Tunisia and Libya had fallen, but Egypt remained under army rule despite the departure of Mubarak. The leaders of Iraq, Sudan, and Yemen promised democratic reform, but dissent rumbled on. In Syria, Assad's regime continued its brutal suppression of protesters. As religious and sectarian divisions began to widen, the outcome for the region remained uncertain.

Our **freedom** is not up for **negotiation**.

MOHAMED ELBARADEI,
EGYPTIAN RESISTANCE LEADER,
FEBRUARY 2, 2011

2011

Libyan Civil War

Rebel fighters celebrated a victory over troops loyal to Libyan dictator Muammar Gaddafi. Fighting began in February 2011 with protests in the city of Benghazi, amid calls for more freedom and an end to political corruption. Loyalist forces attacked Benghazi in March, prompting the rebels to call for aid from the international community. The UN passed a resolution enabling member states to take measures to prevent attacks on civilians. A multinational coalition provided logistical assistance to the rebels, and enforced a no-fly zone and naval blockade. The international community recognized the National Transitional Council as the legal representative of Libya but Gaddafi refused to relinquish power. Hostilities continued into October, when he was captured and killed by rebels. The end of the war was declared on October 23, 2011. There was much celebration, but tensions between tribes loyal to Gaddafi and local militias continued.

Timeline

Key events in the USA and around the world, from 1900 to the present day.

1900–1909

" Unthinking respect for **authority** is the greatest **enemy of truth**. "

ALBERT EINSTEIN, LETTER TO JOST WINTELER, 1901

1900

January 24	The Boers defeat Britain at the Battle of Spion Kop
September 8	The Galveston Hurricane kills more than 6,000 in Texas
December 7	Max Planck's discoveries give rise to quantum physics

1901

January 22	Queen Victoria dies aged 81 at Osborne House, Isle of White
September 7	The Boxer Rebellion in China ends in defeat for the Boxers
September 14	US President William McKinley dies eight days after being shot
December 12	Marconi sends the first trans-Atlantic wireless radio signal

1902

May 8	Mount Pelée volcano on Martinique erupts, killing 30,000
May 31	The Boer War ends with the Treaty of Vereeniging

1903

June 16	The Ford Motor Company is founded in Detroit, Michigan, by Henry Ford
November 17	The Bolshevik Party is founded by Vladimir Lenin
December 17	The Wright Brothers make the first powered flight at Kitty Hawk, North Carolina

1904

January 12	The Herero Rebellion against German rule in Southwest Africa begins
April 8	The Entente Cordiale is signed between Britain and France

1905

January 22	Bloody Sunday in St. Petersburg ignites the Russian Revolution of 1905
May 27–28	Japan defeats the Russian navy at the Battle of Tsushima

June 30	Albert Einstein publishes his Special Theory of Relativity
July 11	The Niagara Movement for civil rights first meets in Ontario

1906

February 10	The launch of HMS *Dreadnought* initiates Anglo-German naval rivalry
April 18	An earthquake devastates San Francisco, California
July 12	The Dreyfus Affair in France spurs debate about anti-Semitism in the Establishment

1907

July 25	Japan establishes a protectorate over Korea
August 31	The Anglo-Russian Entente is signed in St. Petersburg
November 16	Oklahoma becomes the 46th state of the USA

1908

June 30	The Tunguska Event: a comet or an asteroid hits the Earth and cause devastation in Siberia
July 26	The Federal Bureau of Investigation (FBI) is created as the Bureau of Investigation
October 6	Austria-Hungary annexes Bosnia and Herzegovina

1909

February 21	The National Association for the Advancement of Colored People is founded in New York
April 6	American Robert Peary claims to have reached the North Pole

1910–1919

" While the **state exists**, there can be **no freedom**. When there is **freedom**, there will be **no state**. "

VLADIMIR LENIN, *THE STATE AND REVOLUTION*, 1917

1910

May 20	Women march in New York at the first large suffragist parade
May 31	The Union of South Africa is established as a dominion of the British Empire

1911

May 31	The fall of dictator Porfirio Díaz sparks the Mexican Revolution
December 14	Norwegian explorer Roald Amundsen becomes the first person to reach the South Pole

1912

January 1	The Republic of China is established by Sun Yat-Sen
January 6	New Mexico becomes the 47th state of the USA
February 14	Arizona becomes the 48th state of the USA
April 14	RMS *Titanic* sinks on its first voyage across the Atlantic

1913

February 22	Mexican President Francisco Madero is assassinated
May 29	Igor Stravinsky's *The Rite of Spring* ballet premieres in Paris
December 23	The Federal Reserve is created

1914

June 28	Austrian Archduke Franz Ferdinand is assassinated in Sarajevo, Bosnia, precipitating events that lead to World War I
August 1	Germany declares war on Russia
August 3	Germany goes to war with Russia's ally, France
August 4	Germany invades Belgium and Britain declares war in response
August 15	The Panama Canal opens
November 4	Britain and France declare war on the Ottoman Empire

1915

April 24	Ottoman forces begin a massacre of Armenians
April 25	The Allies attack Ottoman forces in Gallipoli
May 7	RMS *Lusitania* is sunk by a German submarine
May 24	Italy enters World War I on the Allied side

1916

March	Albert Einstein publishes his General Theory of Relativity
April 24	In the Easter Rising, Irish republicans fight British rule

1917

April 6	The USA declares war on Germany
November 2	The Balfour Declaration supports the creation of a Jewish homeland in Palestine
November 7	The Russian Revolution sees the Bolsheviks take power

1918

January 8	President Wilson's Fourteen Points articulate US war aims
March 4	Spanish Flu, which kills tens of millions worldwide, is reported
July 17	Czar Nicholas II and his family are executed by the Bolsheviks
November 11	Germany agrees an armistice

1919

January 21	Irish republicans declare independence from Britain
June 28	The Treaty of Versailles officially ends World War I
October 2	Eight Chicago Sox baseball team members conspire to throw the World Series

1920–1929

" Democracy is beautiful in theory. In practice it **is a fallacy. "**

BENITO MUSSOLINI, *THE NEW YORK TIMES*, 1928

1920

August 18	The Nineteenth Amendment gives the vote to US women
November 2	KDKA, in Pittsburgh, becomes the first commercially licensed radio station in the world

1921

March 18	The Peace of Riga ends war between Poland and Russia
May 19	The Emergency Quota Act sets US immigration limits

1922

October 28	Benito Mussolini and his fascist Blackshirts take power in Italy
November 26	The tomb of Tutankhamun is discovered by Howard Carter
December 6	The Irish Free State officially comes into existence
December 30	The Union of Soviet Socialist Republics (USSR) is formed from Russia and its allies

1923

May 24	The Irish Civil War ends
September 1	Tokyo is destroyed by the Great Kanto earthquake
October 29	The Ottoman Empire is officially replaced by the Republic of Turkey

1924

September	The Dawes Plan reduces German war reparations
November 23	Edwin Hubble announces the existence of numerous galaxies

1925

July 18	Adolf Hitler publishes his political ideas in *Mein Kampf*
July 21	In Tennessee, John Scopes is convicted for teaching evolution

1926

March 16	American physicist Robert Goddard launches the world's first liquid-fueled rocket
November 15	NBC makes its first official radio broadcast

1927

February 23	Werner Heisenberg announces his uncertainty principle of quantum mechanics
May 21	Charles Lindbergh makes the first non-stop solo flight across the Atlantic Ocean

1928

September 3	Biologist Alexander Fleming accidentally discovers penicillin
November 18	Walt Disney's Mickey Mouse first appears in an animation

1929

May 16	The first Academy Awards are presented in Hollywood
October 29	The Wall Street Crash sees stock market prices collapse

1930–1939

" Let me assert my belief that the **only thing** we have **to fear is fear** itself. **"**

PRESIDENT FRANKLIN D. ROOSEVELT, MARCH 4, 1933

1930

February 18	Clyde Tombaugh confirms the existence of Pluto, which is considered a planet until 2006
March 12	Mahatma Gandhi begins his Salt March against British India
July 30	Uruguay win soccer's first World Cup in Montevideo

1931

May 1	The Empire State Building, in New York City, is completed
September 18	The Mukden Incident sees Japan invade Manchuria
December 31	The British Commonwealth of Nations is created

1932

April 14	John Cockcroft and Ernest Walton split an atom's nucleus
June 15	The Chaco War breaks out between Bolivia and Paraguay
July 28	The Bonus Army demands its army bonuses in Washington

1933

January 30	Adolf Hitler becomes chancellor of Germany
March 4	Franklin D. Roosevelt is inaugurated as US president

1934

May 9	The Great Plains sees one of the Dust Bowl's worst storms
October 16	Chinese Communists begin the Long March to escape their Nationalist rivals

1935

August 14	The Social Security Act creates the US social security system
October 3	Italy invades Abyssinia (modern Ethiopia)

1936

March 7	German forces reoccupy the demilitarized Rhineland
July 17	The Spanish Civil War begins
November 2	The BBC launches the world's first regular television broadcasting service
December 11	King Edward VIII abdicates to marry US divorcee Mrs. Simpson

1937

May 6	The *Hindenburg* airship is destroyed in New Jersey
May 25	Pablo Picasso's *Guernica* is first exhibited in Paris
May 27	The Golden Gate Bridge is opened in San Francisco
July 7	The Marco Polo Bridge Incident leads to Japan invading China

1938

March 12	Germany annexes Austria in the *Anschluss* ("link-up")
September 29	Germany takes the Sudetenland from Czechoslovakia after the Munich Agreement

1939

March 15	Germany occupies the remaining Czech lands
August 23	Germany and the USSR agree a non-aggression pact
September 1	Germany invades Poland
September 3	Britain and France declare war on Germany, beginning World War II

1940–1949

❝ We shall go on **to the end**… we shall **defend our island**… we shall **never surrender**. **❞**

WINSTON CHURCHILL, SPEECH TO THE BRITISH
PARLIAMENT, JUNE 4, 1940

1940

May 10	Winston Churchill becomes British Prime Minister
June 10	Italy declares war on Britain and France
June 21	France surrenders to Germany
September 16	The USA introduces selective peacetime conscription
October 31	The Battle of Britain ends with an RAF victory

1941

March 11	Lend-Lease allows the USA to help supply Britain's war effort
June 22	Germany invades the USSR
August 14	The USA and Britain sign the Atlantic Charter on war aims
December 7	Japan attacks Pearl Harbor, bringing the USA into the war

1942

January 20	The Nazis begin planning the Holocaust at Wannsee, Berlin
June 4	The Battle of Midway gives the USA the initiative in the Pacific
November 11	The Battle of El Alamein is a major Allied victory in Africa

1943

February 2	The USSR defeats Germany at the Battle of Stalingrad
July 5	Germany's defeat by the USSR at the Battle of Kursk turns the tide of war in the East
October 13	Italy declares war on Germany

1944

June 6	The Allies land in Normandy, France, on D-Day
July 22	The post-war global financial system is agreed at the Bretton Woods Conference
December 16	US and German forces engage in the Battle of the Bulge

1945

February 11	The post-war map of Europe is agreed at the Yalta Conference
April 12	President Franklin D. Roosevelt dies of a brain hemorrhage
May 8	Germany surrenders, bringing the war in Europe to an end
June 26	The United Nations charter is signed in San Francisco
August 6	The first atomic bomb is dropped on Hiroshima, Japan
September 2	Japan officially surrenders, bringing World War II to an end

1946

February 14	ENIAC, the first general-purpose electronic computer, is announced in Pennsylvania
March 5	Winston Churchill makes his "Iron Curtain" Cold War speech
July 4	The Philippines officially gains independence from the USA
October 16	Senior Nazis are hanged at Nuremberg for war crimes and crimes against humanity

1947

February 12	Christian Dior revolutionizes fashion with his "New Look"
June 5	The US Marshall Plan helps rebuild war-devastated Europe
July 8	The Roswell UFO incident in New Mexico is made public
August 14	India and Pakistan gain independence from Britain

1948

January 30	Mahatma Gandhi is shot dead
May 14	Israel is established, leading to the first Arab-Israeli War

1949

April 18	Eire becomes the Republic of Ireland
May 12	The Berlin Blockade is lifted
August 24	The North Atlantic Treaty Organization (NATO) is formed
August 29	The USSR tests a atomic bomb
October 1	The People's Republic of China is proclaimed
October 16	The Greek Civil War ends

1950–1959

❝ History does not entrust **the care of freedom** to the weak or to the timid. **❞**

PRESIDENT DWIGHT D. EISENHOWER,
INAUGURAL ADDRESS, JANUARY 20, 1953

1950

June 25	The Korean War begins
July 7	Apartheid legislation is introduced into South Africa
October 7	China invades Tibet

1951

April 11	President Truman fires General MacArthur from the Korean War
September 8	The Treaty of San Francisco formalizes peace with Japan

1952

May 2	The world's first passenger jet airline service is inaugurated by a BOAC De Havilland Comet
November 1	The USA tests the first thermonuclear weapon

1953

February 28	Francis Crick and James Watson discover the structure of DNA
May 29	Edmund Hillary and Tensing Norgay conquer Mount Everest
June 19	Julius and Ethel Rosenberg are executed for atomic espionage
July 27	The Korean War ends with an armistice signed at Panmunjom

1954

May 7	France is defeated in Indo-China
October 31	The Algerian War of Independence begins
December 2	Communist witch-hunts in the USA end with the censure of Joseph McCarthy

1955

May 14	The Warsaw Pact alliance of Communist states is formed
December 1	Rosa Parks refuses to give up her bus seat, giving impetus to the Civil Rights Movement

1956

June 29	The US Federal Highway Act enables the interstate system
October 26	The USSR invades Hungary to crush anti-communist revolution
October 31	Britain and France attack Egypt's Suez Canal zone

1957

March 25	The European Economic Community (EEC) is created
June 10	The oral contraceptive pill is approved for use
October 4	The USSR launches *Sputnik 1*, the first artificial satellite

1958

July 29	The National Aeronautics and Space Administration (NASA) is established

1959

January 3	Alaska becomes the 49th state of the USA
January 6	Fidel Castro ousts Fulgencio Batista to take control of Cuba
August 21	Hawaii becomes the 50th state of the USA

1960–1969

❝ Every Communist must grasp the truth: **political power** grows out of the **barrel of a gun**. **❞**

MAO ZEDONG, *THE LITTLE RED BOOK*, 1964

1960

March 21	In South Africa, 69 anti-Apartheid protesters are killed at Sharpeville
May 1	A US U-2 spy plane is shot down over the USSR

1961

April 12	Soviet Yuri Gagarin becomes the first human in space
April 17	The Bay of Pigs invasion of Cuba fails to topple Castro
May 5	Alan Shepard, in *Freedom 7*, is the first American in space
August 13	Construction of the Berlin Wall begins

1962

May 31	Nazi war criminal Adolf Eichmann, organizer of the Holocaust, is executed in Israel
July 3	France grants independence to Algeria after eight years of war
October 5	In Britain, The Beatles release "Love Me Do," their first single
October 14	The Cuban Missile Crisis begins, threatening nuclear war

1963

August 28	Martin Luther King, Jr. delivers his "I Have a Dream" speech
November 22	US President John F. Kennedy is assassinated in Dallas, Texas

1964

June 12	Nelson Mandela is imprisoned for life in South Africa
July 2	The Civil Rights Act abolishes racial segregation in the USA
August 7	The Gulf of Tonkin Resolution sees greater US involvement in the Vietnam War

1965

February 21	Civil Rights activist Malcolm X is assassinated in New York
August 6	The Voting Rights Act ends practices that disenfranchize African Americans

1966

May 16	The Cultural Revolution begins in China

1967

April 21	A coup in Greece establishes a military dictatorship
June 5	The Six-Day War sees Israel defeat Egypt, Jordan, and Syria
December 3	The world's first human heart transplant is performed in Cape Town, South Africa

1968

January 30	In Vietnam, North Vietnamese forces launch the Tet Offensive
April 4	Martin Luther King, Jr. is assassinated in Memphis
May 2	Student protests and civil disobedience paralyze France
August 20	The USSR launches an invasion of Czechoslovakia

1969

June 28	New York's Stonewall Riots begin the gay rights movement
July 20	Neil Armstrong becomes the first human on the Moon
August 14	British troops are deployed on the streets of Northern Ireland

1970–1979

❝ Don't listen to those who speak of **democracy**. They all are **against Islam**. **❞**

AYATOLLAH RUHOLLAH KHOMEINI, SPEECH TO STUDENTS IN QOM, IRAN, MARCH 13, 1979

1970

January 15	The Nigerian Civil War ends in defeat for the Republic of Biafra
May 4	The National Guard shoot dead four unarmed protesters at Kent State University, Ohio
November 13	The Bhola Cyclone kills hundreds of thousands in East Pakistan (now Bangladesh)

1971

March 26	East Pakistan declares its independence from Pakistan
August 15	The Bretton Woods post-war financial system ends

1972

February 21	President Richard Nixon makes a historic trip to China
June 17	A Washington break-in begins the Watergate scandal
September 5	Arab terrorists murder Israeli athletes at the Olympic Games

1973

January 27	The Paris Peace Accords see the USA begin a withdrawal from the Vietnam War
September 11	General Augusto Pinochet seizes power in Chile
October 6	The Yom Kippur War begins; Israel defeats Egypt and Syria
October 16	Arab producers cut oil output and increase its price, leading to economic crisis in the West

1974

April 25	The Carnation Revolution begins in Portugal
July 20	Turkey invades Cyprus
August 8	Following the Watergate scandal, President Richard Nixon resigns

1975

April 4	Microsoft is founded by Bill Gates in Alburquerque, New Mexico
April 13	The Lebanese Civil War begins

April 30 — The Vietnam War ends with the fall of Saigon

1976

April 1 — Apple is formed by Steve Jobs and Steve Wozniak in California

June 16 — In South Africa, 176 students are killed in the Soweto Uprising

July 20 — The *Viking 1* spacecraft lands on the surface of Mars

July 28 — The largest earthquake of the century kills hundreds of thousands in Tangshan, China

1977

March 27 — In the worst aviation accident of the century, 583 are killed at Tenerife airport, Canary Islands

October 26 — Smallpox is eradicated, with the last case diagnosed in Somalia

1978

July 25 — The world's first test-tube baby is born through *in vitro fertilization* in England

September 17 — The Camp David Accords see Israel and Egypt agree a peace

October 16 — John Paul II becomes the first non-Italian Pope for 455 years

1979

January 7 — Cambodia's genocidal Khmer Rouge regime is overthrown

February 11 — The Shah of Iran is overthrown by followers of Ayatollah Ruhollah Khomeini

July 17 — Nicaragua's Anastasio Somoza Debayle is overthrown by the Sandinista Liberation Front

November 4 — Iranian hostage crisis sees 63 held at the US embassy, Tehran

December 27 — The USSR invades Afghanistan

1980–1989

❝ Soviet **people** want **full-blooded** and unconditional **democracy**. ❞

MIKHAIL GORBACHEV, SPEECH, JULY 1988

1980

April 18 — Black-majority Zimbabwe gains independence from Britain

August 7 — Shipyard strikes ignite anti-communist feeling in Poland

September 22 — The eight-year-long Iran–Iraq War begins

December 8 — Former Beatle John Lennon is murdered in New York

1981

January 20 — The Iran Hostage Crisis ends after 444 days when 52 US citizens are released

March 30 — John Hinckley narrowly fails to kill newly inaugurated President Ronald Reagan

April 12 — *Columbia*, the first space shuttle, is launched

June 5 — AIDS is first reported by the US Center for Disease Control

1982

April 2 — The Falklands conflict between Britain and Argentina begins

June 6 — Israel invades southern Lebanon

August 17 — The first compact discs become available to the public

1983

June 13 — The *Pioneer 10* space probe is the first man-made object to officially leave the Solar System

July 15 — The Nintendo Entertainment System is released in Japan

1984

January 24 — The first Apple Macintosh personal computer is launched

July 28 — The Summer Olympic Games open in Los Angeles

October 23 — News of the Ethiopian Famine first reaches the West

October 31 — Indian Prime Minister Indira Gandhi is assassinated

December 3 — Thousands are killed in Bhopal, India, after gas leaks from a Union Carbide pesticide plant

1985

March 11 — Reformist Mikhail Gorbachev becomes leader of the USSR

May 16 — A hole in the ozone layer is discovered over Antarctica

July 13 — The Live Aid concerts raise money for famine relief

November 20 — The Windows operating system is released by Microsoft

1986

January 28 — The space shuttle *Challenger* disintegrates after takeoff

February 25 — Philippine president Ferdinand Marcos is overthrown

April 26 — The Chernobyl nuclear disaster takes place in the USSR

November 3 — The Iran-Contra weapons-for-hostages affair is made public

1987

October 19 — Black Monday sees huge stock market falls across the world

December 8 — The USA and USSR agree the Intermediate-Range Nuclear Forces Treaty in Washington

December 8 — The First Intifada uprising in the Palestine Territories begins

1988

November 2 — The Morris worm becomes the Internet's first computer worm

December 21 — Libyan agents blow up Flight Pan Am 103 over Lockerbie, Scotland, killing 270 people

1989

March 24 — The *Exxon Valdez* oil spill in Alaska leads to a massive environmental disaster

June 4 — The Tiananmen Square Protest in Beijing is brutally crushed

November 9 — The fall of the Berlin Wall symbolizes the end of Europe's communist regimes

1990–1999

❝ Our march to **freedom is irreversible**. We must not allow fear to stand in our way. ❞

NELSON MANDELA, ON HIS RELEASE FROM PRISON, FEBRUARY 11, 1990

1990

February 11 — Nelson Mandela is released from prison after 27 years

August 2 — Iraq invades Kuwait, beginning the Gulf War

October 3 — East and West Germany are reunified as a single nation

December 25 — The World Wide Web is founded by Tim Berners-Lee

1991

January 26 — The Somali Civil War begins

June 25 — Croatia and Slovenia leave Yugoslavia, sparking civil war

December 26 — The USSR formally dissolves, ending the Cold War

1992

January 16 — Civil war in El Salvador officially ends after 12 years

April 29	The South Central Riots break out in Los Angeles

1993

April 19	The 51-day siege by the FBI of the Branch Davidian sect in Waco, Texas, ends violently
October 4	The Russian Constitutional Crisis ends in victory for President Boris Yeltsin
November 1	The European Union (EU) comes into force as a result of the 1992 Maastricht Treaty

1994

January 17	The Northridge Earthquake kills 57 people in Los Angeles
April 7	The Rwandan Genocide begins, killing about 800,000
May 10	Nelson Mandela becomes President of South Africa
December 11	The First Chechen War begins

1995

January 1	The World Trade Organization is created
April 18	US terrorists kill 168 in the Oklahoma City bombing
November 4	Israeli Prime Minister Yitzhak Rabin is assassinated
December 14	The Dayton Agreement ends the Bosnian War in Yugoslavia

1996

July 5	Dolly the Sheep is the first successfully cloned mammal
July 19	The Summer Olympic Games open in Atlanta, Georgia

1997

July 1	The British hand sovereignty over Hong Kong back to China
December 11	The Kyoto Protocol on climate change is adopted by the UN

1998

April 11	The Good Friday Agreement on the future of Northern Ireland within the UK is signed
August 2	The Second Congo War begins; by the time it ends in 2003 it has killed more people than any other war since 1945
September 4	Google is founded in Menlo Park, California

1999

February 12	President Bill Clinton is acquitted by the Senate after being impeached for perjury
March 24	NATO launches air attacks against the Federal Republic of Yugoslavia in the Kosovo War
August 26	A Second Chechen War breaks out in the Caucasus

2000–2011

ff Making **mistakes** in centuries past would have consequences we could overcome. We **don't have that luxury** any more. **"**

AL GORE, ENVIRONMENTAL ACTIVIST, 2006

2000

January 11	An amnesty ends the nine-year Algerian Civil War
June 26	A rough draft of the Human Genome Project is announced
September 27	The Second Intifada uprising in Palestine begins
November 2	The International Space Station enters operation

2001

September 11	America is rocked by terrorist attacks on the World Trade Center and other targets
October 7	US forces invade Afghanistan to destroy the Taliban regime

2002

January 1	Twelve European countries adopt the Euro single currency
April 4	A ceasefire brings to an end the 27-year Angolan Civil War
August 26	The Earth Summit on sustainable development opens

2003

February 9	A guerilla war in Darfur, western Sudan, begins
March 19	The Iraq War begins as a US-led coalition invades Iraq to overthrow Saddam Hussein

2004

March 11	Terrorist attacks on four trains in Madrid kill 191 people
May 1	The European Union grows as 10 more countries join
December 26	The Indian Ocean Tsunami kills hundreds of thousands

2005

April 19	Benedict XVI succeeds John Paul II as Pope
July 7	Terrorist attacks at rush-hour in London kill 52 people
August 29	Hurricane Katrina brings devastation to New Orleans

2006

July 12	The 2006 Lebanon War begins with an Israeli invasion
August 24	Pluto is demoted from planet to dwarf planet
December 30	Saddam Hussein is executed by the Iraqi Special Tribunal

2007

January 4	Nancy Pelosi becomes the first woman Speaker of the House of Representatives
July 7	The Live Earth environmental awareness concerts are held

2008

July 31	The presence of water on Mars is confirmed by NASA
August 7	Russia and Georgia go to war over separatist South Ossetia
September 15	Wall Street investment bank Lehman Brothers goes bankrupt, triggering the Global Financial Crisis

2009

January 20	Barack Obama becomes the first African-American President of the USA
January 24	The first of the conservative Tea Party protests is an anti-tax campaign in New York
May 18	The Sri Lankan Civil War ends after 26 years with the defeat of the Tamil Tiger separatists

2010

January 4	The 2,717-ft (828-m) high Burj Khalifa, Dubai, is opened as the world's tallest building
January 12	An earthquake in Haiti kills hundreds of thousands

2011

January 14	The Arab Spring sees the fall of the Tunisian government
March 11	A huge earthquake and tsunami hits eastern Japan
May 1	Al-Qaeda leader Osama Bin Laden is killed by US forces
October 23	The Libyan Civil War sees victory for forces opposed to Colonel Muammar Gaddafi
December 18	The last US combat troops are withdrawn from Iraq

INDEX

Page numbers in bold indicate the main treatment of a topic.